Technical & Fundamental Analysis for Beginners

Take $1k to $10k Using Charting and Stock Trends of the
Financial Market + Grow Your Investment Portfolio Like A Pro
Using Financial Statements and Ratios of Any Business

A.Z Penn

A.Z Penn

Technical & Fundamental Analysis for Beginners

TABLE OF CONTENTS

<u>Technical Analysis for Beginners</u>

Fundamental Analysis for Beginners

Technical Analysis for Beginners

Take $1k to $10k Using Charting and Stock Trends of the Financial Markets with Zero Trading Experience Required

A.Z Penn

HOW TO GET THE MOST OUT OF THIS BOOK

To help you along your trading journey, for this book in particular, I've created a free bonus companion masterclass which includes video analysis of real life stock examples to expand on some of the key topics discussed in this book. I also provide additional resources that will help you get the best possible result.

I highly recommend you sign up now to get the most out of this book. You can do that by visiting the link or scanning the QR code below:

www.az-penn.com

Free bonus #1: **Charting Simplified Masterclass ($67 value)**

In this 5 part video masterclass you'll be discovering various simple and easy to use strategies on making profitable trades. By showing you real life stock examples of a few charting indicators - you will be able to determine whether a stock is worth trading or not.

Free bonus #2: **The Technical Trader Cheatsheet ($12 value)**

In this cheatsheet you will be learning the 9 secret lessons that the greatest technical traders taught me. Believe me, when I started out, I thought I had everything set up to make a million on the stock market; but I was definitely in for a surprise.

Free bonus #3: **Colored Images - Technical Analysis for Beginners**

To keep our books at a reasonable price for you, we print in black & white. But here are all the images in full color.

All of these bonuses are 100% free, with no strings attached. You don't need to provide any personal details except your email address.

To get your bonuses, go to the link or QR code:

www.az-penn.com

Introduction

A lot of people will tell you that "stock trading won't make you money". But you should take a good look at who's saying that. Are they all richer than you? I doubt it. Have they tried trading the markets? Probably not. Do they want you to put your money into a pension scheme, a jatropha farm, an investment fund, a laundrette, or a film financing package instead? I bet quite a few of them do, so they have a vested interest in telling you that trading doesn't pay.

And they're wrong. Stock trading *can* make money if you are disciplined and work hard. That can help you become financially independent. By making intelligent trades, starting small, you can build your portfolio over time and create a platform for even greater future success.

But you need the right tools. You need to be able to take your own decisions, sometimes doing the opposite of the crowd, sometimes taking advantage of the way the money is flowing. And to do that, you need to understand the markets, and how to spot market trends and key change indicators. One of the best ways to do this is by using technical analysis (charts).

A chart simply represents the prices at which shares are being bought and sold. But this gives you a way of analyzing how investors are behaving - if you like, a chart is a kind of shorthand behavioral analysis of the market. As you know from your experience of people at work or at home, if you know how people usually behave, you can usually guess what they're going to do next.

Mum *always* responds to your feeling under the weather by making you your favorite comfort food. So you know, next time you have a headache, that's what she'll do. Stock market behavior is a bit more complex than that, but the essentials are the same; most investors tend to behave in relatively predictable ways. Charts are a way of analyzing that behavior.

If you've already been trading without being able to interpret the information that charts are giving you, or without knowing about these techniques at all, you may have had a very disappointing experience. You may have lost money. You may even be ready to give up.

Or you may have to depend on other traders. You might be using a particular newsletter or subscription service, like Tim Alerts or Superman Trades, or a trading coach. But if you are still following someone else's lead, you're not really independent, mentally or financially. And of course, these services come at a cost, sometimes quite a high cost.

Or you may just be annoyed when you hear other people talking about how "Tesla's just forming a death cross" or "Apple went through a key resistance level today". You have some kind of an idea about what they mean, but you don't really know exactly how it works or how the theory behind it stacks up, and you want to.

I've been there - having someone tell me that the Golden Cross meant I should be buying a share, and wondering what on earth the Golden Cross was and why I should take any notice of it, and being annoyed that I didn't know, and feeling a bit of an idiot. (And I've also been, if not broke, pretty close to the edge. Just so you know.)

That's why I wrote this book. It puts all the information you need about technical analysis - using charts to predict share price movements - in one place, and it puts it in a logical order so that you can take the easy path rather than the steep route up the learning curve.

The going can get tough. Retracement percentages, Bollinger bands, MACDs, oscillation ranges - the language isn't exactly user-friendly. So the book is divided into bite-sized sections that are easy to get through. If you come across any difficult words, there's a whole glossary section at the end. If you need to read a chapter a couple of times to take it all in, that's fine. That will give you a good grounding in the basic concepts before you take on the next chapter.

And there will be a little quiz at the end of each chapter (answers on page 256) so that you can see whether you've taken the concepts well on board, or whether you might benefit from re-reading the chapter or looking at some real-life charts to see if you can trace the patterns.

This book will take you from complete beginner to knowledge of the most advanced charting techniques. Only experience of using them, though, will make you a true master of trading, so I've included plenty of real-world examples for you to practice on. As you start applying the principles to the market in real-time, you'll see how they work, and you'll gain in confidence.

I hope, thanks to this book, that you'll be able to avoid learning the hard way - that's the way I did it. I thought having qualifications in accounting & finance was enough to make money trading - it wasn't. I made mistakes because I didn't know the basics of charting; I messed up because I didn't recognize some of the traps that the stock market lays for investors (that's why there's a whole chapter on avoiding the traps); I made mistakes because I didn't have enough confidence to trust the signals that the charts were showing me.

They say you learn from your mistakes. I certainly did! And what I learned was to go back and make sure I really understood technical analysis, how it works, why it works, and how to use it to make good trades and quickly get out of loss-making positions.

If you've bought this book, you've just made your first step on the way to successful stock trading. I won't lie, it's not going to be easy. It will be tough to learn everything you need to know. There will be days when things go wrong. But if you persevere, you'll develop your expertise, you'll become more confident, and you'll find that soon, it's making a difference to your trading.

If it makes a difference to your trading, it will also make a difference to your life. You'll be making extra money - whether that's to get yourself on a solid financial footing, or to afford a few luxuries. And you'll have a skill that you can be proud of.

And now, let's get started.

1

Chapter 1: What is Technical Analysis?

Technical Analysis is a way of looking at securities price data and using it to predict the probable future performance of that security. Let's say 'security' because you could use it for the stock market, to trade individual shares, or to trade a market ETF. But you could also use it for futures on commodities, for bonds, or currencies, or even for cryptocurrencies. (However, in this book, I'm going to talk mainly about the stock market, because that's the market I know best, and it's probably the best place to get started.)

Securities price data can be made into different kinds of charts - graphically representing the movement of prices. That's a representation of market behavior - that is, what the thousands of people involved in the stock market, from managers of huge pension funds to market traders and retail investors, have been thinking and doing. We know that people behave in certain ways, and that affects the supply and demand of stock.

Statistically, for instance, most people who invested in a stock at $52, if it falls, will hold onto it. They want their $52 back again. So if the stock does get back to that level, they'll sell it. (It's actually dumb investor behavior, but it's very common behavior.) Technical analysis relies on that predictability to analyze common patterns and suggest how they may play out in the future.

While technical analysis could involve running algorithms for a trading program, usually it's approached by drawing and analyzing charts, and that's what I'm going to teach you in this book.

What Technical Analysis Isn't

Technical Analysis isn't a substitute for having a brain and using it. It is not a 100% guaranteed method of spotting profitable situations. It is a *probability* indicator. It will tell you that a stock is *likely* to go up, and may even suggest how much. It will warn you that the market might be topping out, but it will not deliver a certainty that it will do so.

Technical Analysis (let's just abbreviate that to TA as we continue) also doesn't look at what a stock actually does. It will give you the same answer whether you're looking at Coca-Cola shares, Barclays Bank, the Dow Jones Industrial Index, the Brent oil price or a South Korean government bond. It takes no account of credit quality, news, earnings, valuation or any other 'real world' data - all of which can be called 'fundamental analysis' and is a completely different universe.

Technical and Fundamental Analysis are two different schools. However, they're not mutually exclusive. For instance, if you are risk-averse, you might decide you will only trade large shares, do not have excessive debt, and are in mature markets. Some fundamental investors use TA to try to find the best entry point for their stocks, and to spot potential problems arising.

If you're a technical trader, you also do need to be aware of the news affecting any security you're trading. But for the most part, using a TA approach, you don't need to have a view on whether Intel has fallen too far behind the semiconductor market to reverse its market share decline, or whether KFC really does cook the best Popcorn Chicken Nuggets in the world. You'll get a chart signal and you'll trade the shares and that's all you need to know.

Why You Need to Learn Technical Analysis

When I started, I had a good friend who was a little further along the road than me, and occasionally Saj would give me a tip. Sometimes I did pretty well out of his tips. That gave me a false sense of confidence.

Then one day he gave me a tip that looked great. It was a classic chart pattern, that should have been a great breakout. I bought. And I thought it was great, it was the start of an uptrend that would keep going.

Well, I just didn't know quite enough. It did do well. The stock broke out of the trading range and started going up - just what it was supposed to do.

It wasn't Saj's fault. He was away on some training week in Manchester and probably wasn't checking the market all that often, and I was pretty busy that week - we both had day jobs, after all - and for whatever reason, we just didn't connect. But there was a warning signal that the breakout wasn't going to last. This won't mean anything to you right now, but the price hit a resistance level and failed to break through, then it retested it and failed again. That's a classic warning - your fun is over, time to close the trade.

When I looked at the stock market the next morning, half my profits had disappeared already. I couldn't get hold of Saj, I didn't know what to do, and I watched like a rabbit in headlights as the stock kept going down. In the end, I panicked and dumped the stock - and I'm glad I did, because it kept going down. I was lucky; I managed to get out with a small profit. It could have been much worse.

The moral of that story is that following someone else is not going to get you the returns you want. You have to do the work yourself. That's why you shouldn't buy someone else's stock chart newsletter, follow a blogger, or follow tips in the press. Following a guru, even a good one, and an honest one (as some aren't), is never safe. You need to do the work yourself and understand what you're doing.

The Origins of Technical Analysis

TA isn't new. In Japan, traders in the rice market back in the eighteenth century developed their own way of graphically representing the price movement in the market. That gave us what we now call candlestick charts. And they are still being used today, because they show human behavior based on the sentiments of greed, fear, caution or opportunism, and while a lot has changed in a few centuries, basic human behavior hasn't changed at all.

In 19th century America, Charles Dow (yes, that *is* the same Dow as in 'Dow Jones' - he was a co -founder of the Wall Street Journal, too) worked on a theory of price movement and developed various ways of using this to predict future prices. His ideas were further developed in the 1920s to 1940s culminating in the 1948 publication of Edwards & Magee's *Technical Analysis of Stock Trends*, the founding text of the discipline.

In a pre-computer world, technical analysts drew their own charts every day. I'm not old enough to remember that world, thank goodness, but a friend of my father's told me that when he started working in the London Stock Exchange back in the 1980s, one of the partners of the firm still spent the first half an hour of the day putting the latest prices into his chart book and making a note of any patterns that suggested a trade. The chart book was almost as big as his desk - there was just room left for his yard-long ruler, his black, red, blue and green pencils and an old-fashioned wind-it-up pencil sharpener.

Then came the days of very expensive computer graphics services, and now of course you can get immensely powerful charting software if you just pick the right broker. The great days of free charting sites unfortunately are over, except for very basic price charts - your best bet for good free stuff is Bigcharts.com - but there are a few good sites like Stockcharts.com which charge modest monthly fees (and, most importantly, give you a free trial).

TA has kept developing over the years. In the 1980s, western traders discovered candlestick charts, for instance, and a more recent import from Japan has been Ichimoku. I can't help thinking that Ichimoku 'cloud' charting arriving at the same time as cloud computing is more than just a coincidence!

Emphases also change with time. For instance, in some decades it's been trendedness that was the main focus of technical analysts, while at other times it's been breakouts and other discontinuous behavior. However, TA has never been out of fashion.

Just to add, if you're serious about Technical Analysis, you'll want to find some good sources of charts. I like finviz.com, which lets you ask for 'good channels' or 'rising wedges' (particular chart patterns) as well as for stocks by ticker; Stockcharts.com, which has a premium level offering extended facilities; and Bigcharts.com. But many brokers also have good packages - I hear good things about TD Ameritrade's thinkorswim platform, for instance.

We've shown charts from quite a few sources in this book so that you can get used to seeing the way you'll get the information presented on the screen.

The Pros and Cons of Technical Analysis

TA isn't for everyone, and nor is trading. There are many 'buy and hold' investors who aren't fans of TA and trading. They follow gurus like Peter Lynch and Warren Buffett, who say 'buy great companies at a good price' and just hold on for the ride. (In fact, if they used TA, they might be able to buy their shares more cheaply in the first place.) And TA indeed has its pros and cons.

Let's take a look at some of the pros first...

- You do not need a deep understanding of what the companies do, or how their products compare to their rivals'.
- You don't need to be able to read a balance sheet or spend ages poring through annual reports and note 24 to the accounts, section iii.

- If you are a very visual person, charting is really going to suit you because it summarises stock market behavior in a very visual way which you'll find easy to understand.

- Many TA patterns have a high probability (e.g., 70% chance of being right). That beats monkeys throwing darts at the share price pages of the Financial Times, right?

- TA is more suited to short-term trading than fundamental analysis. Fundamental analysis is more suited to a longer-term approach.

- Research shows that if you bought the stock market, over time you'd make a return of about 8% a year by just buying and holding. But if you traded in and out of the market using TA to buy at or near lows, and sell at or near highs, and got 70% of your trades right, then you could double that return.

- If you trade actively using TA, using a good trading discipline, you could increase your initial stake significantly in a short time. Let's face it, it's much easier to become a millionaire at an 8% a year return if you already have $500,000 to invest!

Some of the cons?

- Because TA looks so easy, you can con yourself that you know how to do it without really having understood the principles. It's very easy to *think* you see a pattern that's not actually there. That's why you need to paper trade before you put real money in the market.

- Because TA misses out on all the fundamental information, you might be buying trash. Buying the bounce could be a bad trade if the company goes bust before you can exit! And 'real world' news events could trash a good trade.

- Some TA indicators have a built-in lag. So you may get into a trade a little bit late or out a bit too late.

- TA doesn't work for securities that are illiquid and don't trade frequently. If you think about it, infrequent trading doesn't give you a big enough statistical sample of traders and investors for the signals to be valid.

- 'Buy and hold' actually isn't a bad way for investors who have a busy (and profitable) day job and want somewhere to make a return by investing their surplus funds for the long term without having to do a lot of work. If you don't have the time to devote to doing analysis and trading, and have a good day job, TA might add a little to your returns, but trading is not for you.

Don't forget, fundamental and technical analysis are not mutually exclusive. Some traders who usually trade on gut feel and instinct - and do very well at it - still use TA to refine their thoughts on exactly when to enter and exit a trade.

And also don't forget that whenever we're talking about TA, we're talking about *probabilities* and not certainties. There is no 100% certainty in trading, except that if you make money... you'll have to pay tax on it. (Yeah. Tough!)

A Little Bit of Philosophy

You may have heard of 'random walk' and the 'efficient market theory'. The first says that price changes are random. The second says that at any point in time, the market knows everything that can possibly be known about a stock, so the price reflects that. Both these academic theories would make TA impossible. However, as one City trader once said to me, "That's why those guys are academics and I'm a trader - and I'm the one making all the money!"

In fact, even random events are subject to statistical norms. For instance, if you toss a coin 100 times, you may not be able to predict any single coin toss, but unless someone's cheating, you'll end up with results somewhere between 48 heads and 52 tails and the reverse, even if not exactly 50/50. TA looks at statistical norms and anomalies. And if you introduce humans and a certain load of facts into the bargain, stock markets are never going to be completely random, if only because human emotions are involved.

At the same time, Efficient Market Theory seems to be disproved just about every time there's a profit warning from a big company. Everything that's known might be known - but people will take different views of it. With TA, we're not looking at everything known about the stock, but about how different people are acting on that knowledge.

Let's go a little bit further. The existing price charts are part of the existing knowledge in the market about that stock. So are price patterns like trendlines and breakouts. And yet... trading breakouts still works the majority of the time! Indeed, some writers think that because people use trendlines, target levels and breakouts, many of these prophecies are self-fulfilling.

So it's in my interest to write this book, because the more of you are using these tried and tested TA techniques, the better they're going to work!

Anyway, that was a bit of philosophy, but I think the trader was right. We are going to be empirical - that is, we're going to see *what works* and how to increase the probability that you're getting the right signals from the market. So no more philosophy. Let's take a look at the kind of charts you're going to be using.

Note for paperback readers: You'll be seeing the charts in black and white. It just costs way too much to print them all in color. But you need to see them in color - that's the way you'll be seeing the charts you look at on your computer screen, and if you have three moving averages, for instance, you need to be able to tell which is which.

Therefore, I would recommend you please go to my website: www.az-penn.com and enter your best email address that I should send the colored images document to.

Some Examples of Charts

If you haven't seen anything other than a normal stock market price chart before, let's open your eyes to the kind of extras you're going to see.

To get started with, here's a Google Finance chart. It just shows the price. (There's quite a funny story that goes with it - if you typed 'sell' into Google, it showed the Apple share price. Once it was brought to Google's attention, it somehow stopped working.) Time runs along the bottom axis, and the vertical axis shows the dollar price. Simple. And... not all *that* useful. Generally, it will simply show you the price at each point in time - each minute, each hour, or the closing price each day. That's it.

Now let's look at how a technical analyst might draw lines on a price chart like that one. This one below is what the old guy with the four pencils and the ruler spent his time doing. It looks pretty rough, right? It's not very easy to read, it uses a slightly different charting method than we use nowadays, and it goes back to 1974, when computers were huge things that filled a couple of rooms and used punch cards, and only NASA and the Tax Department could afford them.

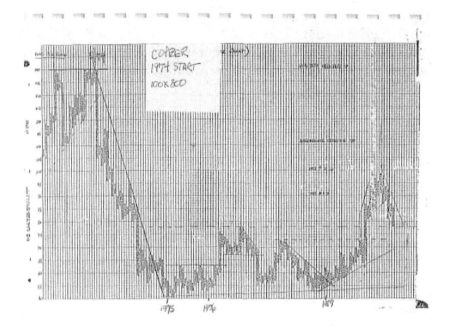

But we still draw trendlines the same way! Drawing trendlines is an art, not a science - it's how your individual gut feel and your experience as you learn more about TA will help you - but the idea is to get a line that summarizes price performance, so that when the share price crosses that line you can see the trend has changed. That breakout is a signal for action. As you can see here, the results were quite dramatic!

As well as drawing trendlines, nowadays computing power allows us to draw other indicators such as moving averages (the average of the last x days' trading), Bollinger bands (a representation of the volatility of a stock, that is, how much prices vary on a given day), and other more powerful indicators.

But using the market price to summarise a whole day's trading behavior is like asking someone what they did at the office today, and them answering 'work'. It's not really all that descriptive. So a slightly more complex charting method shows a bit more. OHLC - Open, High, Low, Close - shows you a bit more information. You get a series of vertical lines, one for each trading day. The vertical line shows you the total range of prices traded, so you can get an idea of whether the market was all over the place or whether the prices were all in a pretty tight range. The little flag on the left is the open and the little flag on the right is the close.

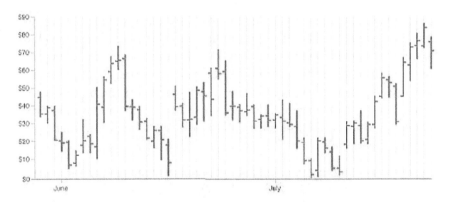

In the chart above, look at the second line. It's small, so prices were pretty close to each other. The left hand flag is lower than the right hand so we know the price closed (right) higher than it opened - that's also why the line is colored green. Then look at the next line. Red - it opened and then fell, and look, the close line is right at the bottom of the range. It's quite a big range. That must have been a dramatic day's trading! So you get a lot more feel for the market out of this OHLC chart than you did just out of a simple daily closing price chart.

As well as capturing prices, TA can show us other information, and it can perform statistical interpretation of price movement. For instance, volume charts show how much stock was traded each day. If I told you that the big change in the ninth bar of the chart - that huge leap up - happened on a day when millions of shares were traded, would you take it more seriously than if only a few thousand shares changed hands? Definitely, a movement that happens with lots of volume is a movement that lotss of people participated in - so you'd be right to take it more seriously.

Computers can also subject prices to manipulation, creating a momentum indicator - that is, how fast prices are going up or down and whether that movement is accelerating or decelerating.

And now for something completely different - the next picture shows you a candlestick chart, displayed on a screen with another indicator below it. Candlesticks take a bit of getting used to, but they show a lot of information, and they often give very clear signals. Using two indicators together, the way the candlesticks are used with a line chart below them are also very common. For instance, some chartists put a lot of faith in using two moving averages and noting any place that they cross as a price signal. Or the second indicator might be used as confirmation - for instance, if there's a signal in the candlestick chart, you can use a volume indicator to check that it's 'real' (i.e., that it has a high probability).

At this stage you may be looking at these charts and thinking, "Hey! Let's get started!" or you may have your head in your hands and be thinking, "I'm never going to learn all this." Well, everyone starts somewhere. And one of the reasons I wrote this book is that there is a huge information overload out there on the internet right now. Some of the information is good, some is so-so, and some is downright awful, and if you get started without knowing the basics, then one of two things will happen; you'll find out which is the good information the hard way, or you'll give up before you do.

So we are going to take things gently, we are going to take things systematically, starting with the easiest stuff and going on to more advanced techniques, and I'm going to keep us organized and focused.

Chapter 1 Quiz

1. Why does technical analysis work?
   a) Because mathematical formulas are built into the stock market.
   b) Because charts represent human behavior, which is predictable.
   c) Because share prices obey natural rules like the tides or seasons.

2. Which of these is not a kind of chart?
   a) Candlestick
   b) OHLC
   c) CCTV

3. What is the difference between fundamental analysis and technical analysis?
   a) One is only for traders, the other for investors.
   b) One is about a company as a biz, the other looks only at the share price.
   c) One is easy, the other is difficult.

4. You can learn everything you need to about technical analysis on the internet.
   a) Probably, but it will be more costly and very frustrating.
   b) Yes, of course, it's all out there and easy to find.
   c) What's the internet?

5. Are you going to read chapter 2?
   a) Yes.
   b) Yes.
   c) No, I'd like to watch some paint dry.

Quiz Answers are on page 256

2

Chapter 2: Basic Concepts of Trend

What is a Trend

Traders often say, "The Trend is Your Friend." If a given trend has become established, you can piggyback it in whatever direction it's going. And generally, traders only trade *with* the trend. So if a trend is going up, you only trade bounces, and if it's going down, you'll generally trade it by going short (that is, selling stock to take advantage of the dips). The idea is that even if you don't execute your trade particularly well, the trend will help you out and usually ensure you don't make a thumping loss.

A trend is quite simply a direction of price movement. For instance, prices may be trending upwards. That doesn't mean you'll get a price rise every day, but it means that the price will tend to rise over time. For instance, in an upwards trend, you might have closing prices for a bit more than a couple of weeks that went something like; 50, 52, 51, 51, 54, 53, 56, 56, 57, 56, 59, 60, 59. You can see that sometimes prices are up, flat, or even down, but they are moving up on the whole. That's a trend - a general direction. There will be oscillations within the trend, but the trend itself remains unchanged.

That means that you can trade these oscillations within the trend; as long as the trend continues, if you buy when prices are trading lower than the trendline, and sell when they're above the trendline, you'll make money. Trend trading strategies are very common and can be nicely profitable.

Trends often reflect a certain market sentiment - that is, if investors feel the economy is doing well, earnings are going up, the future will deliver better earnings still, there will probably also be an uptrend. But trust what you see on the chart, *not* what you see in the newspapers or on the bulletin boards.

I also need to give you a warning. Traders also sometimes say, "Is it a trend or will it bend?" That's why in technical analysis we need to be able to recognize trends, but we also need to be able to recognize signals telling us that trends are about to end or even reverse. (These are breakouts, and we'll talk about them in the next chapter. But for now, let's go with the flow and stick with the trend.)

Trend has Three Directions

Okay, this is pretty simple. In the words of "those magnificent men in their flying machines," there are three directions:

- UP
- DOWN and
- Flying around - or what traders call 'sideways'.

If you know the lyrics of the song, UP and DOWN are exciting - UP-tiddly-up-up and DOWN-tiddly-down-down - and the 'flying around' or sideways bit is not really emphasized. It's the same on the stock market. UP and DOWN will make you money. They're good strong trends. Sideways, also known as 'ranging' or 'consolidation', can be a big problem, and a market with a sideways trend is hard to make profits in. (On the other hand, when you get a breakout from a sideways trend, you'll notice!)

You'll see many times throughout the book some of my handout slides - yes, they're all drawn with my interactive whiteboard pen, but the good thing about the slides is that I've removed all the distractions that you get on a regular share price chart. No dates, prices, moving average lines, volume bars, whatever - just the trend!

A proper uptrend has increasing highs, but it also has increasing lows. And while a downtrend will hit ever-increasing lows, it should also see each bounce achieving a lower and lower level. Sideways, on the other hand, price movement can be anywhere - sometimes within a really tight range, sometimes just looking chaotic on the chart with prices all over the place.

Technical analysis can help you identify trends and give you good reliable signals when a trend is coming to an end.

Trend has Three Classifications

As well as three directions, the trend has three classifications, or time zones:

- Short term - less than three weeks
- Medium term - a few months
- Long term - six months to a year.

Each market has its typical way of defining these three-time classifications. Futures markets such as commodities futures tend to have shorter timescales, and equity investors have longer timescales, but you'll get the feel of whichever market you trade after a while.

A short term trend can be part of a medium term trend, and a medium term trend can be part of a long term trend - in other words, trends can come nested inside each other. Within a long term bull market (a market in a long term uptrend), for instance, the S&P may have shorter term uptrends separated by short term downtrends - rallies and dips. A longer term investor who is a less active trader may see a continuing uptrend, where you, as a shorter term trader, can see a pronounced short term downtrend.

You might use different trends as different signals.

- Long term trend: okay, there's a trend here, so this is a stock I want to look at. And it's a long term uptrend, so I will generally be buying stock when I think there's a medium term uptrend.

- Medium term uptrend: this gives me my profit expectation. Suppose we're trading low in the long term trend, I can guess where the stock price should be headed within that trend. For instance, in a long term trend where recent high were around $62, and it looks like if it continues it would get to $65 quite easily, and the price is now $56, I have a $9 a share profit potential (and $6 profit potential if the trend fades).

- Short term uptrend: this gives me my timing. So I've got that medium term trend in mind, but when is the best time to get in? When I see a real short term tick up that says to me this is the right time to initiate that short position.

Some people like to look at super long trends, like the idea of Kondratieff waves and 40-year cycles, but those are outside the scope of this book.

Support and Resistance

The trends we want to look at go up and down, and so do their trendlines. But we can also draw some really important straight lines on the chart, and these are called support and resistance lines.

You'll often see a share price exhibit a particular pattern of nearly getting to a price and then refusing to go any further. It's a bit like watching a child playing at the seaside, running down the beach towards the sea, but as soon as a wave comes, running back up the beach squealing happily so her toes don't get wet. Share prices behave just the same way!

A share price might keep falling to a particular price but then rising back again - that's a support line. It's likely that if the share price approaches that line, it will bounce off it again, so this *supports* the price. On the other hand, a share price might keep testing a high, but it never crosses that level - that's a *resistance* line, and the chances are, if it gets to it again, it'll not manage to maintain enough momentum to push its way through.

Here you can see my handouts. I promise you I had not been drinking when I made this one! See how the share prices just touch the resistance and support lines. (A channel has a resistance line at the top and a support level at the bottom - you can make some neat short term trades inside a well-established channel, but the most profitable trades you'll make are on breakouts - which we'll talk about later.)

RESISTANCE

SUPPORT

CHANNEL

For instance, look at the way in the chart below. The AT&T share price in the second part of the chart keeps coming up to $29.50 and just falling back again. At the beginning of January 2021, it gets from $28 to $29.25, but it doesn't manage to stay there. Then it gets to $29.75 about 25th January, and then it falls off, then it gets there again about 17th February, and again, it falls off. That's a resistance line, a kind of tidemark. You could put a ruler on the chart and draw it across, and there you have your resistance line.

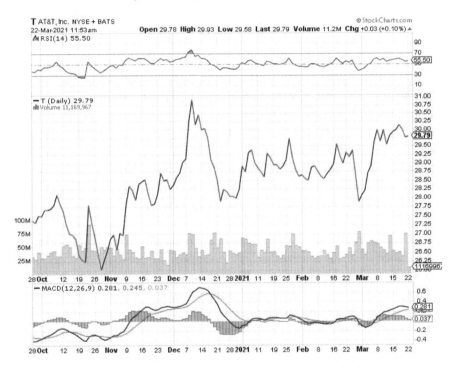

Now the stock has finally managed to push through to $30. It has actually gone through the resistance line... but I'm not sure I'm convinced. I'd want to see another indicator confirming that before I consider it a proper signal. (We'll look at those other indicators in Chapter 4)

But there's another interesting thing; it does look as if the stock has formed a support line, too. Have a go at guessing where it is - and I'm going to give you a clue, again you'll be looking at the more recent half of the time period. Can you draw a straight line which the price approaches, but won't go through? I reckon it's at about $28. Look, it's there just before that bit spikes up, then it falls back to it after the spike, then again at the beginning of March, and every time it bounces.

Now the support line is interesting because it says if I buy at $29, I probably only have a dollar downside, and I know that if the share price goes below $28, then it's time to take that loss and get out.

Why do support and resistance levels work? One reason is 'anchoring', the way that certain information gets stuck in our minds. Investors and traders often remember the price they bought or sold at, and a lot of investors say, "I'm not going to sell till I get my money back". If a lot of them bought at $52 and the price went down temporarily to the mid $40 levels, then when they see $52 again, they'll sell - which by the rules of supply and demand, will cause the price to stop rising. That's a resistance level in action.

The more times a share price unsuccessfully tests a support or resistance line, the stronger that support or resistance becomes. Buying close to support or selling close to resistance makes a good trade, as you'll capitalize on the bounce. But you'll want to put a stop-loss just below a support line (or above resistance) to make sure that if there's a breakthrough, you cut your losses and make a quick exit.

By the way, if a share price does break through a resistance line, that old resistance line will now become a support line. And if a share price breaks through a support line to the downside, that support line will now function as a resistance line preventing the price from rising past it.

Trendlines

It's not always easy to see the market trend. If there's a lot of price movement, you may be able to see that the market's in an uptrend, but not how steep the slope is or how fast prices are rising. You're seeing all the noise, and that makes it difficult to see the signal - the real trend. Drawing trendlines on the chart can help you visualize the trend.

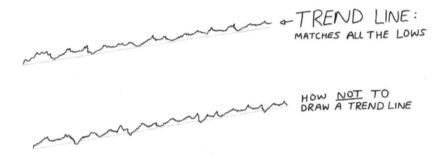

Basically, if the market's in an uptrend, then you're going to try to find a line that it keeps coming back to at the bottom. Find the lowest points that the price hits, and join them up. You are lucky. The software will do it for you - or at least help you do it - whereas this was a pencil-and-ruler job well into the 1980s. So what you should have is a chart that now looks as if all the peaks are 'sitting' on a line of support.

For a market in a downtrend, you're going to do things differently. You're going to draw a line that goes through the highest highs - the places that the price gets to when it bounces, but then runs out of steam and falls back.

Okay, with support and resistance, I showed you my hand-drawn pictures first. This time let's jump right into the real world and look at Amazon. I went on StockCharts and I just couldn't believe what a great example of a channel I'd got, so I stuck it into my drawing software and put in the trendlines - the real trendline is the straight one underneath, that's pushing it upwards, but you can also see there's a straight resistance trendline at the top. (The other two curvy lines are Moving Averages, which we'll cover later on)

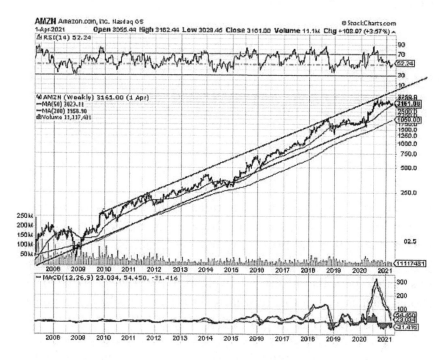

A trendline shows you very clearly the direction in which the market is moving and the speed of the move. It also acts as a support of the resistance line; for instance, in a downtrend, if the price goes towards the trendline (which is above the price bars), then you're getting to a decision point where it will either fall back again, or make a breakthrough.

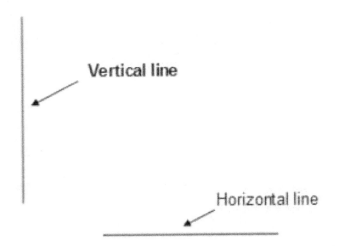

What you're doing is not very different from drawing support and resistance lines, but you're trying to get a slope instead of a horizontal line. The chart we just looked at is horrible for trying to draw a trendline, although it's got good support and resistance, so let's try something with an uptrend.

Here's Realty Income, where you have quite a lot going on, but I want you to look for one very clear uptrend. Just look at the candlesticks and ignore the other lines on the chart for the moment. They'll be covered in a future chapter. But this is the kind of thing you'll see when you open a charting package - this one comes from StockCharts - and you need to get used to focusing on the lines that matter first, and then to look at the rest. Get some practice by grabbing a straight edge and trying to find the line of best fit - that's the trendline. (The trendline is *not* shown on this chart, you have to draw it yourself — but if you want to see a live visual demonstration on how to draw a trendline correctly, then I would recommend you watch my *free bonus companion masterclass*, as that covers this topic in a lot more detail to help your understanding.)

You see from the dip in the share price in early 2021 (down to 11th January) that it quickly establishes an uptrend, and if you draw a line under the lows, although it heads higher, and then back, it doesn't break the trendline, it keeps bouncing back from it and making higher highs (that is, every little spike goes higher even if it falls back a little in between) all the way through January and the first part of February. Let's assume you got in around $58 in mid-January because you waited a little while to be sure it was a real uptrend; the stock would have gone to $63 (around 14th February) before finally breaking the uptrend by dipping to about $61 towards 18th February. That's $3 a stock profit, or 5% in about a month. You might have done a bit better than that of course, if you didn't wait for the sell signal, but got out nearer to $63 a few days earlier.

One way of thinking of the share price is that it's connected to the trendline by a rubber band. It can get further and further away from the trend, but the stretchy rubber band will generally keep pulling it back. If it hits the trendline, it'll usually bounce. But as it gets close to that trendline, you're going to want to watch out - this is a dangerous time, and it's also, for some traders, an opportunity, as there could be a breakout.

Occasionally you might need to redraw a trendline. It may become steeper or it may, on the other hand, become less steep as price rises decelerate. That doesn't necessarily mean the trend has ended. However, when an uptrend becomes very steep, that could suggest the kind of manic frenzy that often accompanies a market top, so beware of trading in such conditions and keep an eye out for bearish signals (that is, signals telling you the price is going to fall) such as a drop in momentum or moving averages.

Trend Channel

We already saw how if you connect up the highs and the lows, you can create a wide bar with roughly parallel lines, as we did with Amazon. These two lines define the trend channel. I actually like trend channels a lot as a way to trade, but you do need practice in drawing them properly.

There are several things you need to know about trend channels.

- The longer a channel continues, the stronger the trend. (Remember that Amazon trend! Over a decade of it!)
- If a trend channel is combined with a strong trading volume, it's more reliable than if trading is weak.
- If the price breaks out of the channel, it is likely to move quite significantly in the direction it has now established.
- A narrow channel doesn't give you much room for trading - if a stock is always trading within about 2% of the trend, that limits your potential profit. On the other hand, a wide channel, where the stock has some volatility within the overall trend, gives you a chance of larger profits.

If you get a good horizontal channel, running all the way across the page instead of up and down, this is one of the few times it's worth trading a stock that is not in an uptrend or a downtrend. You may have a stock where, for instance, a certain level of dividend yield means income investors tend to buy whenever it comes down to the bottom of the range, and sell when it gets to the top - you don't need to know the reason, just trade the channel. Buy on the bottom of the channel, sell at the top.

Channels are also really useful for setting your stop-losses and profit expectations. If you buy at the bottom, you're looking to exit at the top, but you should also set a stop-loss just below the bottom of the channel. If you've got it wrong, that stops you from being caught by an unexpected breakout.

By the way, you can even sometimes see from a channel how long the share price usually takes to move from bottom to top of the channel. That gives you a good idea of how long your trade will last so you can time it nicely!

Besides simple price channels, there are other kinds of channels, which use volatility rather than price indicators, such as Bollinger bands. But for the moment, let's just stick with the price channel; that's quite enough to get your head around!

Now go and find a few stock charts, and see if you can spot some price channels. See how many times the price bounced around within the channel and work out if you could have made a profit by trading it every time the price touched, or nearly touched, the bottom line.

Divergence

Remember, "is it a trend or will it bend"? Divergence is one way to tell. Now so far, we've talked about the trend, the channel, support and resistance. You can make nice profitable trades by using them as your guide. But sometimes prices break out of their trends.

There are quite a few reasons that might happen. For instance, you sometimes see that if a stock gets promoted to a major market index, and big investment funds and Exchange Traded Funds have to buy the stock because it's in the index. Or a stock might have a profit warning which the market wasn't expecting, and the price goes way below the range. Or a war might break out, or there could be unexpected political news that drives the markets higher or lower. You might also see the end of a big investor exiting their position - for instance, with some IPOs, the end of a lock-in period may see some of the sponsors, founders or management selling out. Or it may happen "for no reason".

Well, the reason is really that every time the trendline was tested before, there were buyers or sellers at the right price to send the stock back up. And this time, there weren't. And if that's the case, that quite likely reflects a slight change in market sentiment, and there are a few ways you could pick that up *before* the breakout. That's where divergence comes in.

When you're looking at your price chart, use a momentum or trading volume indicator (like an oscillator) running beneath it. (We'll take a good look at those and the way they work later - for the moment, don't worry about what they mean, just look at the pictures.)

Usually, you'll see the two lines run pretty much in the same direction most of the time. But if you have an uptrend, and the oscillator is headed downwards, that's a *negative divergence* and it suggests that the uptrend might not continue.

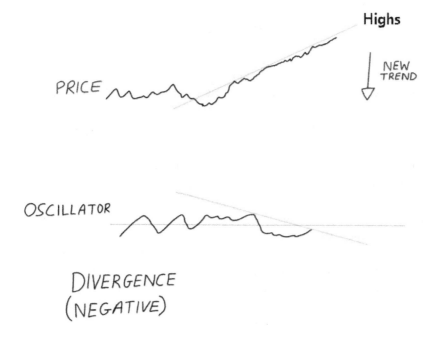

On the other hand, if the price just made a new low, but the momentum indicator is headed up, that suggests prices might rise - *positive divergence.*

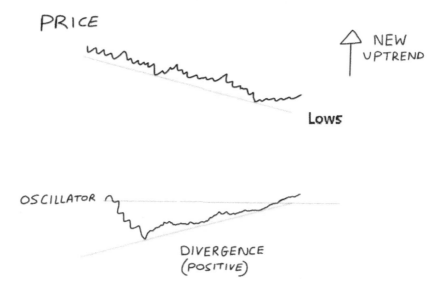

What you're seeing in the case of negative divergence is that while the price trend looks as if it's continuing, it is decelerating or falling behind the market. So that's an indicator that your price trend isn't as strong as you think it is. But you don't need to pay attention to it all the time - just if:

1. Your price is hitting new highs/lows,
2. Or you think you've got a double top or bottom forming (and we'll talk about those later).

To check if you really have divergence, connect up the highest highs, or lowest lows, and connect up the lines for the indicator for the same period - joining highs to go with price highs and lows to go with price lows. If the slopes are the same, great. If they're moving in opposite directions, you have divergence.

Divergence is not a signal - it doesn't tell you to trade. But it *is* an alert - that is, when you see divergence, if you're risk-averse, it's time to exit your position, and if you're a risk-on kind of person, it's time to stick close to your trading screen and watch that stock like a hawk.

Chapter 2 Quiz

1. The trend is your ....?
   a) Friend
   b) Opposition
   c) Share price

2. How many directions can a trend go in?
   a) Two
   b) Three
   c) Fifteen

3. What can divergence tell you about a trend?
   a) It might not be as strong as it looks
   b) It's going to reverse immediately
   c) Nothing

4. What is a support line?
   a) A horizontal line that shows where share prices have often traded, on a lower level than the share price now
   b) A trendline that shows how fast share prices are going up
   c) Similar to a VPL

5. What is a trend channel?
   a) A channel made by the trendlines that connect tops to tops and bottoms to bottoms, within which the shares trade
   b) Fox News
   c) A sideways trend.

3

Chapter 3: Recognising Breakout

So far we have talked about trading within a range. That can be really profitable and it can also be quite a low risk, low effort form of trading if you identify the right stocks and keep an eye on the patterns.

But if you want to hit the big time, you want the runaway profits that come with a breakout. Remember that "ball on a rubber band" idea I used when I talked about the share price and the trendline? What happens when the rubber band breaks? The ball goes way, way up into the air (or, of course, if we're talking stocks, it could also go in the other direction) - that's a breakout! Compared to trading the range, trading a breakout is like jumping on a train when it's already started moving.

Just so you know: a breakout can happen in either direction, up or down - it's simply breaking out of a pattern.

A breakdown, on the other hand, only goes down.

Breakout

A more technical description of a breakout is that it's when a stock price moves outside an established channel, support or resistance line, with increased volume. (The increased trading volume is required to show that it's a real breakout and not just a fluke.) Breakouts move to the upside, and they move fast.

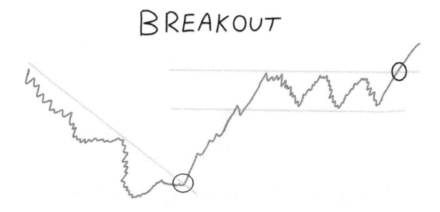

A genuine breakout is a big, bold move. If you're looking at a candlestick chart, you'll see a big bodied candle closing well above the resistance level. If all you see is the price just poking over the edge of the resistance level, that's not a real breakout - it's a fake-out. If you see the price getting near to the resistance line, but it hasn't gone through it yet - it's a fake-out. Wait for the line to be broken before you trade.

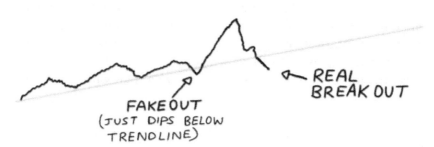

Note by the way that a breakout can happen even in a bear market, that is, a market that is in a major downtrend - there won't be so many breakouts to trade, but stocks that have the strength to move against the market are stocks that should really get going once they start, so you will still get that speedy rise.

Your signal is simple - it's the first time that the price breaks out of the channel, or breaks the resistance line, *and closes above it.*

How do breakouts work? One way they work is what's called a lockout rally. Imagine you have a well-known stock that's had bad results for a couple of years, it's taken a bit of action, and it's stopped going down but it hasn't begun to move up yet.

Everyone is thinking it will soon be time to buy it again, but they haven't bought it yet; they're waiting for something. And for whatever reason you get a little buying - maybe one brave fund manager, maybe a couple of brokers getting in - and it goes through the line, and now all those people who haven't bought it have a massive feeling of FOMO (which, as if you didn't know, means Fear Of Missing Out). It's motoring, so it must be time to buy, so they buy, so it goes up a bit more, so more people buy...

At that point, of course, the short term traders are already getting out with their profits!

How to find breakouts

If you're looking for breakouts, you won't find them. What you're looking for is the pre-breakout pattern. You're looking for stocks that are trading in a fairly narrow channel, that are trading in a really boring way - almost so the candlesticks fill the channel. You're looking for stocks that are range-bound. That is, stocks that are stuck in a range, which keep bouncing from top to bottom and back again without ever going anywhere. This kind of build-up is absolutely classic. It's like a pressure cooker - when it goes, it's going to explode.

You can also look for stocks that are close to their 52 and 26-week highs - this information is easy to find on any finance site. If stocks are trading at a high for the period, they're also going to be close to a resistance level or close to the top of the trendline. That means they'll either be close to a fall back down again into the channel, or they'll be ready to break out. By looking for stocks that are close to a high, you've cut out all the stocks that are not really going anywhere much, so you've reduced the number of charts you need to look at before you find a good breakout pattern emerging.

Of course, you can also look for stocks close to 52 and 26-week lows. That might catch the 'bouncers'.

Draw your resistance lines on the chart - even if they were last hit some time ago - and keep monitoring those stocks every time the price gets towards that resistance line. Use a volume indicator too - the best stocks for a breakout are those that haven't traded in much volume. You're looking for a market where investors have got bored, and they're not doing much - when you get the breakout, that's when they will get interested again! Then you will see the volume accompanying the share price move, which is how you know it's for real.

Another good potential configuration is where you see a resistance level that has been repeatedly tested by sharp spikes. You're looking for the share price to make big spikes, to make a big jump to test the resistance level, and then for it to fall back really steeply. You don't want to see gentle waves; you want to see a spiky mountain landscape of strong rallies that quickly reversed.

Or if you're a beach bum - you want to see big surf, not nice gentle waves. These spiky, punchy price movements show that the resistance level is a good strong one. It's as if the share price took a real run-up, but it still couldn't punch through the wall. So that's a tough wall, and any breakout that makes it through the resistance will be a massive one. The bigger the breakout, the more money you'll make on the trade.

Further good signs that a breakout could be coming are:
- The channel grows narrower
- A build-up period in which prices form a tight cluster
- Trendlines which make an ascending triangle - the lows are getting higher, but the highs have been on the same trendline
- The resistance level has been tested unsuccessfully several times.

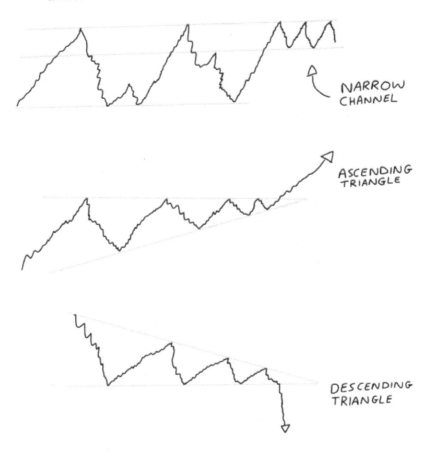

NARROW CHANNEL

ASCENDING TRIANGLE

DESCENDING TRIANGLE

The longer the build-up, the bigger the breakout. Once you've found your targets, plan your trade in detail *before* any breakout. I'm going to talk about trading tips later - but you should always plan your trade so that when the breakout comes, you can act real fast. Remember, breakouts are fast.

What do you do if you miss a breakout? If it was preceded by a really good consolidation period (trading within a limited price range), and has made a definitive move to the upside, you should jump in even though you're a bit late. You'll probably use the techniques you already learned in the chapter on trends to spot the right place to enter your position, as well as to set a good stop-loss. Or if it looks as if it's a pretty small breakout, you could wait for the price to test the line that was the old resistance level, and has now become a support level, and you could buy it then. Happily, you do quite often get a second chance!

Breakdown

What's a breakdown? It's just a breakout, except that the share price goes down instead of up. So it will usually be announced by a descending triangle in some cases - lower highs, but the lows are forming a horizontal line. Like a breakout, it's usually on high volume and will lead to a large price swing, and usually then into a new downtrend. It can often be very quick, which is why you need to set up your trendlines and then monitor them whenever you see a potential breakdown trade setting up.

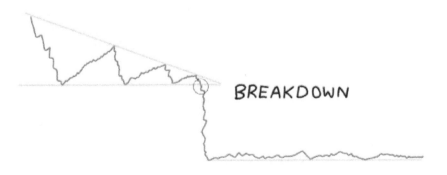

Looking for a breakdown by just looking at loads of charts is like looking for a needle in a haystack. On the other hand, if you have collected half a dozen charts that show tight consolidation build-ups and descending triangle trendlines, you pretty much know one is going to show up - but you have to be ready to act when it does. (That might mean actually watching your screens, but it could also mean setting up stop-limit orders with your broker and just letting them run.)

However, taking advantage of a breakdown isn't as easy as trading a breakout because you need to be able to short trade or trade options. Not everyone is happy trading short. (There's a subsection on this coming up.)

If you do go short, the best way to set up the trade is to put a sell stop-limit- order just below the support level. That is, an order which specifies a price at which the order becomes valid, *and* a price limit after which it is no longer valid (e.g., "Sell 100 IBM *if* the stock price falls below 90 but *not* if it goes below 95.) It's a good way of entering a breakout or breakdown trade. But if there is high volume and a lot of price action, you might not get your order filled. So waiting for a retest (or another chance) of the trendline that has now become a resistance level might give you a better price - *if*, of course, there is a retest. You can never be sure.

As always, decide your exit strategy before you enter the trade. Many traders use the moving average (which we'll talk about in the next chapter) - once the share price closes above the moving average, it's time to quit. (Think about that for a second; the moving average shows the average of prices for the *last* 20 days, let's say. As the share price falls quickly, it will fall *below* the moving average, because the moving average still has all the higher prices from previous trading days in it. As long as the price is still falling quickly, that will continue to be the case, but the moving average will eventually catch up once the fall decelerates. At this point, the stock *might* rebound, but even if it doesn't, the easy gains are gone and you can find a better trade elsewhere. Anyway, we'll talk about this again next chapter when it should make more sense to you.)

Channel Break - some trading tips

Let's look at a typical channel break and see how to trade it. Technical Analysis will give you good trading ideas, but you also need to learn *how* to trade. And if you haven't been involved in the stock market before, or if you've always been a buy and hold investor making simple market buy orders, you have a lot to learn.

First of all, you need to work out your profit target, and this will probably (though not always) also be your exit point. This is something buy and hold investors never bother with. It's easy with a channel break, though; look at the width of the channel, and if it's $6, then add $6 to the price at the resistance line, and that's your immediate profit target. If you're trading a round lot (100 shares), that's a total $600 profit.

Your goal should be to stack the odds in your favor, so usually, I like to see a stop-loss that's half the size of the expected profit if the trade works. In this case, that would be $3. If the stock falls to $3 below the resistance line, you're out. You've lost $300. This seems like a reasonable balance to me, risking $300 against $600 with a good chart formation that has something like a 70% probability.

In fact, let's just multiply the probabilities to see how good it is;
$600 x 70% = $420
$300 x 30% = $90

So if I'm right about that probability, then I have an expected value of $420-$90 = $330. It's positive. But even if the probability was only half - now come on, do the numbers. It's still a good chunky positive number. What we calculated here was what statisticians call the *expected value* of all the probabilities, and you need this number to be a positive one. If it's negative, what you're making is not a trade but a gamble.

Don't just set the trade and run away. Keep monitoring it. In particular, you should be watching the volume indicator - if this is a genuine breakout, then you'll see the sellers coming in and the volume increasing. So you might get to your original exit point, and say that having reconsidered the situation, this looks like a massive breakout. In which case, set a new stop-loss, and you might even decide to scale in, that is, increase your position by buying more shares.

But if you do scale-in, remember to reset your stop-loss. With a breakout into a bullish trend, you may have this setup:
- You entered the position at $70
- Expected profit $6 (using the channel range) = $76 share price
- So the stop-loss is $3 = $70-$3 = $67
- The price quickly gets to $73, you can see a lot of volume in the market, so you decide to scale in. If you keep your stop-loss at $67, your potential extra profit is $3 (from $73 to $76), but your potential loss is now $6 ($73 all the way down to $67). So you need to pull your stop-loss up higher, to say $71, so your expected return is still greater than your possible loss.

Also, remember how we talked about different lengths of a trend? A breakout could just be one breakout in a series. Look at the chart of Mattel above, and you'll see that there are three series of consolidation/build-up phases, tight channels of trading, followed by breakouts. Can you draw the rough trendlines and work out the dates? (C'mon, this is what you're going to be doing every day as a trader.) Okay… Consolidation from late January to the middle of April, then a breakout (or breakdown); more consolidation till the middle of June when there's another breakout; then more consolidation through July, with a bit more volatile price action this time, and then a breakdown just before the beginning of August.

If you're a long-only trader, this chart is no good for you. But if you can go short, whether your broker lets you sell short (and effectively 'lends' you the stock for the meantime), or whether you can take out options, then this is a great chart. It's particularly good because you have these short-term big steps down. Going short costs money, and options have expiry dates - so you're looking for *shorter term* trades as well as simply going short.

The first breakout in mid-April went from $25 to $21, then the second one in June went from about $22 to $20. But the third one in late July started at $21, and the downtrend ran all the way to below $15 by mid-September. The final breakout in mid-November leads to a severe downtrend in December. If you'd made good money on the first breakout, you might have said, "right, I'm done with that stock". You would have been wrong. There were another two good chances to make almost the same profitable trade, and the last was the best.

Hey, what was that gap up in November 2017 though? Apparently, the stock had got so low that there was talk of bigger toy company Hasbro buying it, and the stock jumped - but as you can see from the end of the chart, nothing happened.

The 'gap' by the way is when prices open above the previous day's closing price, with nothing in between. You'll quite often find it relates to corporate news, whether that's a takeover rumor, as here, or an earnings surprise.

Short Selling

If you want to make the most of breakdowns, you're going to need to be happy short selling or using instruments which allow you to replicate a short sale.

Basically, short selling is selling a stock you don't own. It's as if you promised to deliver a new smartphone to a friend of yours, anticipating you can get it at money off on Black Friday. You charge your friends ten percent less than the retail price, you get the phone at 40% off and keep the change (though possibly not your friend). Short selling allows you to make money out of a forecast that a price is going down. If you'd shorted Nasdaq just before the tech crash, you'd have made a huge return, but a lot of traders just take 4-5% on each of their shorts.

The risk, of course, is if you'd sold your friend the smartphone at ten percent below retail, then found out that the version he wants has just had a price rise and isn't in the Black Friday sale, you'd lose money because you'll have to buy it at retail and he's still going to want that 10% off.

Shorting is not that easy to do as a retail investor - institutional investors like big mutual funds, pension funds or hedge funds, and bank trading desks, make more use of it, often for portfolio protection rather than trading purposes. However, there are a few ways you can go short the market.

- If you have a margin account with your broker, and permission to short, your broker will 'lend' you the shares in your margin account and then sell them on the market on your behalf. You will at some point either close the trade at a profit, close it at a loss, or possibly have to pay a margin call to keep your trade going if it's out of the money at the time (which is why you need a tight stop-loss).

- For the market as a whole, or individual sectors, you could buy an inverse ETF (exchange-traded fund). This kind of fund delivers the reverse of the market return, so if the market goes down, the ETF goes up. You buy and sell them just like you buy and sell a share, and they are low-cost funds, so you won't lose a load of entry commissions like you would with a mutual fund. This is my preferred choice if I see a good short trade in the S&P, for instance.

- You can also use options. Frankly, there is a whole lot of very specific knowledge that you need to trade options - for instance, they come with expiry dates, so their value varies according to the time you have left as well as the price of the stock. Unless you are mathematically minded and willing to get to grips with the specifics (and take a look at the Black-Scholes formula if you're tempted), leave them alone.

- Finally, you *could* use something called a Contract for Difference (CFD), unless you're in the US or Hong Kong. However, you may find in other jurisdictions they are only available to certain investors - professionals, high net worth individuals, and those who can display a high level of market expertise. Frankly, I would avoid them till you've got several years of profitable trading behind you. Even then - be careful.

Please let me emphasize that while stop- losses are important for all trading, they are *especially* important if you go short. If you buy a stock at $600 and it falls, the most you can ever lose is $600 a stock. That's it. Wipeout. But your house, your car, your collection of Pokémon cards, none of that's on the line. Nor are your other stock positions. I *have* been completely wiped out on one or two stocks (both, as it happens, involved corporate fraud), but I lived to tell the tale.

On the other hand, how high can a share price go? $100? Higher. $500? Higher. Tesla has been as high as $900. Want more? Berkshire Hathaway trades at $380,482.75. There is, effectively, no limit to how high a share price can go. That means if you go short, there is no limit to the amount you could potentially lose. You could lose your shirt - your house, your savings, the rest of your portfolio, the lot.

So if you go short, make sure you have your trades thought through in advance, including your stop-loss, and don't let anything prevent you from using that stop-loss. That stop-loss could just save your life.

False Breakout

This is the biggest problem with breakout trading - there are simply too many false breakouts. And that's one reason I've emphasized probabilities and stop-losses because not every breakout trade will work, so you need to minimize the impact of the fake-outs. That's in contrast to trading *within* a channel, where your profits will be more limited, but you have a slightly better probability.

This is why you need a good trading strategy - you'll need to maximize your profits *and* make sure that you control any losses very tightly, because the win/lose ratio is probably not going to be as good as with range trading.

One indicator you need to look at is volume, and there's actually one in particular which is useful for breakouts - Volume weighted moving average (VWMA). In the case of a fake breakout, it won't do much at all - in the case of a real breakout; it will accelerate upwards, giving you confirmation that you've made a good trade. VWMA also gives you your exit level, as once the price falls below the VWMA - indicating that the balance between buyers and sellers has tipped - you have exhausted the short term profit potential of the trade.

It's worth keeping an eye on the news pages by the way. If a breakout happens along with fundamental news, such as a positive earnings surprise or a new product launch, it's probably a real breakout - and some serious institutional funds may back it.

Plus - don't give up! This could be part of the consolidation, the build-up - the last unsuccessful test of resistance before the *real* breakout. Patience is well rewarded.

Stop-losses

Set your stop-losses tight for breakouts. If a breakout reverses, it could be fast and hard. The ideal for a breakout, though, is that if you've read the signals right, it should make money from the moment you enter the trade.

So most traders put a stop-loss just below the resistance line. If the price falls back here, it could fall away pretty sharply back into the old trading range, so stop yourself out of the trade. But remember that stocks will often retest the level they have just broken within the first few days, and then rise again - so don't set your stop-loss at or above the resistance line, just a bit below. Only take your loss if the stock closes the day below the line.

Chapter 3 Quiz

1. What's a stop-loss?
    a) The price at which you will exit the trade if it goes wrong,
    b) An insurance policy,
    c) A kind of option.

2. What is a gap?
    a) A clothing store,
    b) When the stock opens much higher or lower than yesterday's closing price,
    c) The difference between the bid and ask price for a stock.

3. What indicator can help you tell the difference between real and false breakouts?
    a) Volume
    b) Moving average
    c) 52-week high-low

4. Define a break-out.
    a) A stock price breaks out of a trend channel or other pattern within which it has been trading,
    b) The Great Escape,
    c) The same as a gap.

5. Which of these is not a way of shorting a stock or index?
    a) A call option
    b) An inverse ETF
    c) Selling short on margin.

4

Chapter 4: The Four Types of Indicators You Need to Know

This is the chapter that's full of all the jargon you've been dreading. RSI, stochastics, MACD, oscillators, Bollinger bands - it's all here. This is a tough chapter to get through, and it's also going to be a long one, but two things will make your life easier.

First, you can divide all these indicators into four main families; an indicator will show you:
1. Trend,
2. Momentum,
3. Volatility, or
4. Volume.

A lot of them are just refinements of another indicator in the family. For example, once you understand what a trend indicator is for, it's easy to understand another trend indicator and what in particular you might use it for. It's like looking at a toolbox full of different tools - when you realize that all of them are either spanners, chisels, screwdrivers or drill bits, and they just happen to come in slightly different sizes and shapes, but each type of tool is used for the same kind of job, then life gets considerably easier.

Secondly, once you start trading, you'll soon find that you are spotting more better trades using some indicators than others. That lets you concentrate on a smaller number of useful indicators. So although you might have, let's say, fifteen sizes of spanner, you know there's one that fits almost every job you need to do on your sports bike, and another that you need for the Shimano gears, and the rest get left in the box almost all the time.

I should give a special mention to oscillators here. Basically, to oscillate means to swing, and the idea of an oscillator is that it's an indicator which swings around a central zero line. It may be expressed as a percentage or go from -1 to +1, and it can be derived from all kinds of calculations, but oscillators are broadly speaking only interesting when they do one of two things: (1) go to extremes, or (2) cross over the central line. They take a bit of getting used to.

You'll also find that some indicators will actually deliver you trading ideas, but other indicators are useful mainly as confirmation, or as advance alerts. For instance, I'd never expect a volume indicator to give me a trading signal, but if the volume isn't there to support a breakout, I probably won't make the trade. So you won't be looking at all of these indicators all the time - just the ones that give you the signals, and once you've got a signal, then the other indicators come into play to tell you if it's real or fake.

And a little extra tip - if you open up a charting program while you're reading this chapter, get a stock chart up, and then call up each of the indicators (usually in drop-down boxes), you'll get a feel for how the indicators look "live".

I like using StockCharts. As you can see from the image below, you get lots of options, for instance, 'range' means you can select different date ranges, whether you want a month or ten years. You can define 'type', candlesticks if you want, or a single line, or OHLC, whichever you find gives you the best feel for the price movements.

Under 'Overlays', you can get moving averages and Bollinger bands, and a load of other more advanced stuff. You can have three moving averages or just two.

Then 'Indicators' has drop-down boxes letting you select plenty of indicators, including most of the ones we'll be talking about - RSI, MACD, Chaikin Money Flow, Force Index, and so on. So there's a lot of power in this platform for you to explore.

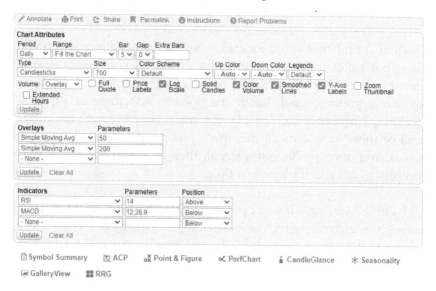

P.S. In Class 5 of the free bonus #1 companion masterclass, I demonstrate some practical ways of how you can use some of the indicators discussed in this chapter with real life chart examples. I would highly recommend you watch the free masterclass video after you finished reading this entire chapter by visiting: www.az-penn.com.

Trend indicators

You might well be able to look at a chart with the naked eye and spot the trends. But there's a lot of 'noise' in a stock price chart. Trend indicators use mathematical formulas to smooth out the noise and display the underlying trend in share prices in a way that makes it easier for you to pick up what's really going on.

Note that trend indicators always lag the trend, because they use past pricing data. For instance, a 20-day moving average uses the past 20 days' prices, so it will move more slowly than stock prices if they change direction. Trend indicators are trend *following* indicators, not trend *setting* indicators. That is, they won't tell you what's *going* to happen - they tell you a trend has already started, which can give you really strong trading signals. So they are not a faster way to get into a trade. They are best to trade in trending markets. In a sideways market, they're not all that useful, and if you try to trade a sideways market with them, you'll probably lose money.

Simple moving averages (SMAs)

A simple moving average just takes a number of time periods - say 10 days (which is two working weeks); it adds together the closing price for each day and divides by ten. So it's the average price of the stock over the last ten days. You can calculate it over any period - 20 days, 200 days, a year (though a year is probably not very useful for a trader). Or rather, you can get a chart package to calculate it for you, these days.

Why do we use simple moving averages? We use them to take the 'noise' out of the chart so that you can see the trend more easily. The idea is similar to trendlines, just a bit differently executed. But you should look at SMAs together with the price chart, because it's when you put the two together that you get the best information - and when you use two SMAs together, you can also get some interesting information.

For instance, when the price dips below a moving average, that's a sign that the stock might be breaking downwards. In this sense, an SMA can be treated a little like a resistance or support level. As a rule, in an uptrend, the price should be above the moving average - if it breaks down, this could be a strong signal that prices are shortly going to head downwards. But it's not got the best probability, so check with another indicator before you do anything about it.

The strategy of using crossing moving averages

Another way of using moving averages is to take two averages of different lengths, and to look for a significant crossover. All technical traders have their favorites; some like to use the 10 and 20 days MAs, others prefer 50 and 200 days, longer-term averages.

When the shorter-term MA crosses over the longer term, it gives you a bullish signal - the 'golden cross'. It's telling you that over the shorter period, on average, share prices have been trending higher than over the longer term. You might not see that so clearly from the actual price line, if the prices reported have been volatile. If the short term MA crosses to the downside, you have a 'death cross'. Prices are trending lower. That could be a good sell signal.

The problem, of course, is that while moving averages clarify what's happening, because the majority of a moving average is made up of older price data, they have a built-in time lag. And if a stock is trading in a range, in a fairly choppy way, you may find that the averages keep crossing over without delivering you any real information.

Look what happened here - this is a chart from Finviz, showing Graybug Vision. Look just at the end of February and you can see the purple 20-day average crosses the orange 50-day average, and keeps heading lower. At that point, Graybug was already down on its highs, but look how good a predictor that 'death cross' was in predicting the downtrend in the price.

Some traders use a three-MA system with a short, middle and long term MA, for instance, 5, 21, and 50 day averages. The trend is defined by whether the fast MA is above the middle MA (which shows an uptrend) or below the middle MA (which shows a downtrend). The signal is shown by the middle MA crossing the slower MA to the upside (that's a buy signal) or to the downside (that's a sell signal). You close your trade when the fast average crosses over the middle term average in the 'wrong' direction. I'm using the terms 'fast' 'middle' and 'slow' because for a day trader using 5 as the fast average, 21 might be his slow average, while for a medium term trader; 21 might be the fast average, and 200 the slow (using 21, 50, 200).

By the way, put some time into finding out which averages work best for you.

The three-average system can be confusing so let's just think about it with regard to a single buy trade. When the fast average is above the middle and slow averages, recent prices are rising. That might be just a temporary uptick. When the middle crosses the slow average to the upside, it shows that prices over the past month are now rising above prices further in the past, too.

That suggests a more continued trend. But if the fast average falls back below the middle average, it means the trend has decelerated, the last week has shown prices falling compared to the last month, so it's time to sell. (However, in *The Way of the Turtle*, Curtis Faith back-tested different strategies, and he found that while triple-MA trades have a higher win rate than dual-MA trades, they are not as profitable.)

As you can see from the chart below, you have a pretty messy and complex chart to read. Personally, I prefer the simplicity of just two MAs, but as they say, your mileage may differ. The zigzag line is the OHLC (Open-High-Low-Close) price line, and you then have a fast moving average in pink, a medium term moving average in yellow, and a slower moving average in light blue. You can see the fast MA sticks really close to the prices, while the slower MA is very sluggish and takes a long time to pick up. Notice that when the other two averages cross the slower MA right at the beginning of the chart, a strong uptrend starts, and you'd buy the stock here.

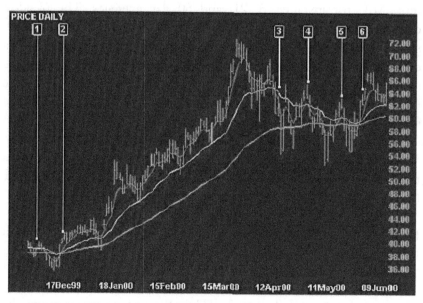

Now, if you hold on to the stock till the top, you'll see you wouldn't actually sell at the top. Instead, you'll lose some of your gains till the fast average falls below the medium one at point 3. But still, look how much you have made on the trade. From about $40 all the way to $54. That's a long term trade.

You could also take the 'swing' trades when those two moving averages cross over again; the trade at 4 doesn't work out at all, but it looks like the trade at 6 is a good one.

Remember, all your trades don't have to be winning trades. If you make 50/50 good trades, but you have tight stop-losses and let your profits run, you'll make money.

If you like to use MAs, you might play about with different lengths of time for your key MAs to see which work best for a stock or commodity you're interested in, or what's working best in the market at the moment. This does change from time to time as market conditions change and as other traders refine their technical analysis.

Exponential moving average (EMA)

The EMA takes the time lag problem and applies a bit of further mathematical manipulation to give the figures a recency bias, by giving more recent prices more weight. This makes them more timely, and many traders prefer them as the signals they give are likely to be slightly earlier than with the SMA. 12 and 26 day EMAs are particularly popular.

The EMA isn't 'shorter term' than the simple moving average, because all the same data is in there. The 12 day EMA still contains all 12 days. But it just gives a bit more weight to more recent ones.

In terms of all the kinds of signals you can find with EMAs, using them is exactly the same as using the SMAs. Why not try both to start with, if your charting package gives you a choice, and see whether it makes much difference which you use? It might be a good idea to 'backtest' - run both on charts for the past few years, and see how they compare in terms of how many trades you would have made with each, and how much you would have made in profit.

Moving Average Convergence/Divergence (MACD)

MACD develops the idea of a moving average a bit further still by adding even more math. It shows the difference between two different moving averages, whether they're getting closer together or further apart (the Convergence/Divergence in the name). And then we can get even smarter, and show a moving average of convergence and divergence.

Just so that you understand the calculation (you'll never have to do it, the software does it for you), we start off by taking a 12 and a 26 day EMA. When you eyeball the chart and look at those two moving averages, what you're doing is assessing the difference between them visually. MACD does this a different way by looking at it mathematically.

The MACD takes today's value of the 26-day EMA and subtracts it from the value of the 12-day EMA. That is today's difference between the two. Going forward, the same calculation gets done every day, and then you have a time series (a line of data) showing whether the difference between the two averages is getting smaller (convergence) or bigger (divergence).

So far, so good. But now to take the 'noise' out of the data, we make a moving average of the MACD. Typically, it's a 9 day EMA. That's then plotted on the chart and this is what we use as a 'Signal line'. And just to add some more visuals, the raw data of the Convergence and Divergence is often plotted as a histogram - a bar chart using the same space. Both the lines and the histogram use the same centerline, representing zero - both moving averages in sync with each other.

Okay, you don't necessarily understand why it works, but let's look at *how* it works.

The chart below shows what happened to Intel shares. I've blue-circled the two interesting indicators here. The MACD chart is at the bottom. First of all, the MACD heads up to the top of its range, having crossed the center line just about the beginning of 2021. So crossing the center line was the first alert, then moving up, about 22nd January. And then just before 16th February, the 50-day moving averages crosses over the 200 day in the price chart. That's the final signal that we have an uptrend. The MACD would suggest to buy at about $56 around 22nd January, and the stock runs as high as $63 before losing its momentum.

The MACD can give us a couple of useful signals. First, when the MACD line crosses the centerline. If it heads above it, buy; if it falls below it, sell. Secondly, when the MACD line crosses the Signal line (the average of the MACD, remember); if the MACD is headed up, buy, and if it heads down, sell. A rapid rise or fall in the MACD is also worth noting; it is likely to indicate that the stock is overbought or oversold, and that the current price trend will slacken off.

Although the histogram is not there to give you signals, it's a useful indicator for confirming other signals. When the blue bars are far below the line (in the negative numbers), prices are trending down; when the blue bars are above the line (in the positive numbers), the stock is in an uptrend. If you follow the 'humps' in the histogram, you also get a good sense for where the market could face a decision point - though you'll need to look at other indicators to see what that signal is. Here, for instance, you can see that the 'humps' are starting to build up from mid-November before the stock price makes its run up from 23rd November into early December. The histogram indicated the stock was already in an uptrend, though looking at the price chart you might not have got the idea.

Average Direction Index (ADX)

The ADX is an indicator some traders use to measure the strength of a trend. It was originally used in the commodity markets, though now it's used in other markets as well. I'm not going to go into how it's calculated; the formula is complex, with two different factors (sometimes also shown as separate lines) showing +DI and -DI - direction upwards and downwards, and these are then smoothed again to produce the ADX figure. Readings below 20 show that the trend is weak or non-existent; readings above 40 show a very strong trend.

If you spot an interesting possible breakout on the price chart, check out the ADX. Very often, a low ADX will give you confirmation that the existing trend is weak, and that gives a breakout a good chance of succeeding. But remember - the ADX says nothing about what direction the share price is headed!

Not every chart service gives you ADX. StockCharts does - here, it's the line above the price chart (the blue and red lines are moving averages). So let's see what the ADX tells us. A very weak trend at the beginning, and you can see from the chart that the price was just dodging about, going nowhere. Then a much higher ADX as the price went up after Nov 16th, but although the price kept going up, the ADX flattened out after 7th December. And then you have some sideways trading and the ADX flattens out again and tells you there's no strong trend; so if you spotted bear signals in any other indicators right then, the ADX would have told you to go along and take the trade. But the ADX *doesn't* see the bounce up in March coming, and right now in April it's looking weak even though (without looking too closely) some of those candlestick formations are suggesting we might have a bounce coming. So, you see, ADX can be useful, but don't rely on it. It's just sometimes, if you like, the tie-breaker when you can't decide whether to trade or not.

Force index

The Force index includes price *and* volume factors, so it doesn't just look at what price stock was traded at, but also at how much stock was traded. So if the shares go down $2, but only a few are traded, it shows a lower number than if the shares fall $2 on very heavy volume. The daily values are smoothed into an exponential moving average, usually over 13 days, and then it's shown as an oscillator - a line that moves above and below zero. When it heads above zero, it's showing an uptrend (higher prices, more volume), and below zero, it's showing a downtrend (lower prices, less volume).

Because it includes the volume of trading, as well as the price, it sometimes captures information you wouldn't get from a purely price-based indicator. For instance, if prices are still moving higher but the Force index is falling, then the volume must be dropping. That might suggest buying interest is fading out, and if this continues, it could eventually lead to the market topping out. But while the Force index is a useful confirmation for price signals, relatively few traders use this indicator to produce signals itself.

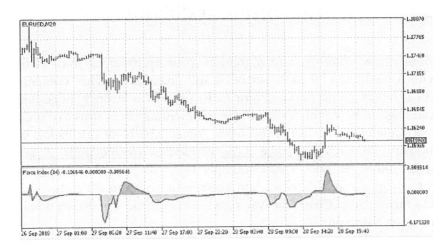

Here you can see the Force Index under the price chart. It's interesting how it shows the short term moves pretty well (first quarter of the chart) - look at the way it starts heading down at around 27 Sep 05:20, just before that big fall in price - but it has nothing at all to say about the longer term trend. And the second big blue peak doesn't give an advance warning of the rise in price; it happens at the same time. In fact, as a chartist, the big thing I see looking at that chart is a long term downtrend that I think is going to continue after what looks like a false breakout on 20 Sep 14:20, and the Force Index doesn't add anything to my knowledge. It's very much a short term indicator in my book, and this may be why many forex traders love it, but rather fewer equity traders seem to use it apart from a few day traders.

Momentum indicators

Momentum indicators aim to replace your eyeballing a price chart with something a bit more scientific and quantitative. They compare prices now with past prices, in order to show how strongly prices are trending. You could look at the momentum indicators as your speedometer - how fast is the stock going? The basic calculation is; momentum = (closing price today divided by closing price x days ago), and sometimes that's multiplied by 100, to deliver you a percentage figure. It's easy. And you're not going to do it, because let's face it, StockCharts' or Ameritrade's data banks can do it a whole lot faster than you.

But just as an illustration; last week the stock was at $50, and it's gone up to $75, momentum is 75/50 x 100 = 150% (or 1.5 for some indices). If the stock last week was $50 and now it's at $25, momentum is 25/50 x 100 = 50% or 0.5.

You may have guessed, if the stock price is flat, this index would give you 1, or 100%.

Momentum indicators won't usually give you signals, but they are useful as confirmation for your trading ideas. For instance, you can confirm a breakout if the momentum indicator has moved from the 98-99% range to 101% or 102% - the momentum has changed, that is, the stock's changed direction. If it keeps picking up further, that confirms your breakout will keep going. Use them to cut down the number of breakout trades that are stopped out when they turn out to be fake-outs, and you can increase your winning percentage considerably.

Momentum indicators are also interesting when they show *divergence*. If a stock price is still going up, but the momentum indicator is showing that it's putting the brakes on, that's a danger signal. It's like a train slowing down, which usually means there's a station coming up! If the share price is still headed lower, but the momentum indicator is coming back towards 100%, that shows the momentum behind the fall has started to fade away.

That's like a downhill skier slowing down as they come to the flat area at the bottom of the mountain. A breakout could be imminent - but that's where my analogy falls to pieces, because share prices don't get chairlifts...

When I started doing TA, I found these indicators were the most difficult to get my head around, even though my background included plenty of data manipulation and stats. I didn't find them as intuitive as, say, price charts or candlesticks. So if you have a tough time with some of them, you're not the only one.

Stochastic

The word 'stochastic', if you look it up in the dictionary, doesn't suggest this is a great indicator; 'stochastic' means "having a random probability distribution that can be analyzed statistically but not predicted precisely." And we're interested in predictions, so just how useful is a stochastic indicator going to be?

However, the stochastic is quite a good speedometer for stocks. Its inventor, George Lane, actually saw it in those terms - if a rocket is going to come down to earth and crash, it has to slow down at the top of its parabola. Planes only stall when they go too slowly.

How it works is by measuring the price range over a specific time period (typically 5 days). It compares the closing price each day with the absolute high and absolute low of the whole five days. So when it's at a high value, it means prices are closing towards the top of the range; a very low value means there's a high downside momentum. The Stochastic doesn't show 'oversold' or 'overbought', though - it simply shows the speed of price rises. As a comparison, imagine yourself going at 120 mph in your car - that's a high speed, but it doesn't mean you're immediately going to slow down. You might keep going for quite a while.

It *is* a really good confirmation for breakout signals from the price chart. If the stochastic keeps moving up steeply, it suggests the trend will continue - so if you bought on a price signal for a breakout, and the price has gone up, you should keep your trade running, perhaps scale in, and pull your stop-losses up to take account of the new entry price.

Another kind of signal is given when the price has been going up and up, but the stochastic starts to trend downwards. Even if this is quite a small divergence, and the stochastic line is just sagging a little bit, then you might want to look for a reversal. The stochastic is telling you that things are slowing down - and while that might just mean the price rise becomes less steep, if the stock has had a lot of buying interest, and risen quite steeply, the stochastic could be warning you that things are going to get bumpy. If there's no buying pressure left, the stock might fall quite fast.

The same signal works the other way around if prices have been coming down, but you see the Stochastic lift up - reversal could be on the cards. This is probably the one time that the Stochastic gives a good signal rather than just a confirmation.

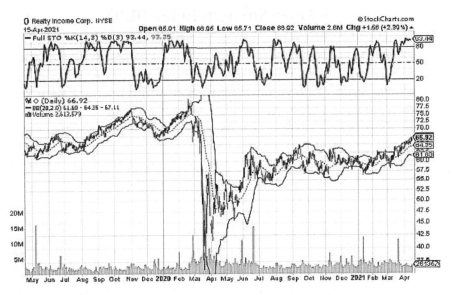

This chart shows the full stochastic at the top. Realty Income is one of the most well-regarded US real estate stocks and pays big dividends. Look how much the stochastic swings. Interestingly, the big moves into negative territory often come before a downturn, and the big swings upwards just before an uptrend. (Of course, you have to remember that the huge downturn in March was event-driven; this was the start of the Covid-19 pandemic in the west. I don't think the stochastic is really predicting that! But if you'd taken notice, you would be a bit richer, anyway.)

Relative Strength Index (RSI)

This index measures the ratio of upwards to downwards price moves. It doesn't look at how big the rise or fall was, but simply whether the stock closed up or down on the day. So, for instance, a 10-day RSI starts by looking at how many days was the stock up? 7. And down? 3. (If the stock closes level on the day, it gets a zero for that day.) Then the figures are averaged, so we get plus 7/10 and minus 3/10. (That's a simple way to do it. Other people use EMA and advanced statistical smoothing methods, which are only going to confuse you, so let's leave that out.)

And now all we have to do is calculate the ratio between the up and down moves, RS, and then the $RSI = 100 - (100 / (1 + RS))$.

If you've followed that, then you have probably guessed that the index goes from 0 to 100. If you haven't followed it, it doesn't matter. You've got the idea, anyway; the RSI is a measure of how often the price is rising, against how often it's falling. Usually, stocks will trade somewhere between 30 and 70 on the RSI, and that shows a reasonable balance of buyers and sellers. But an RSI above 70 shows that the stock is probably overbought - so the price could be about to fall - whereas if the index is below 30, the stock is oversold, so the price might be about to rise. (Some traders prefer to use an 80-20 range for their trades, which gives them fewer but higher probability signals.)

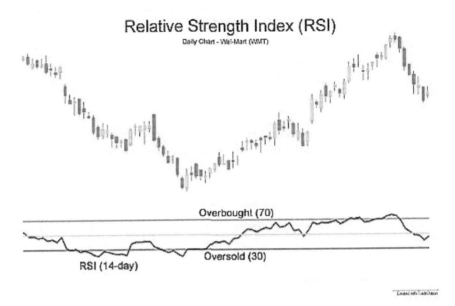

In the chart above, you can see how when the RSI dips below the 30 line the first time, the price stages a small rally, but the second time it's for real - too many sellers have been in the second stage of the downtrend and when there's a breakout, it really moves fast. Then when the RSI gets close to 70, there's a small dip, but it isn't till it crosses over the 70 line that the price really tanks. By then, just too many people have bought in, some have bought too much stock, and the moment the price decline begins, they 'catch a cold' and sell. You might like to think about the RSI line having just crossed over the center line (the straight line in light blue); will it stay around that level? Could it be heading for oversold territory?

What do we mean by 'overbought' and 'oversold'? When a stock is overbought, it may have had lots written about it in the press, many investors have been buying, the price has kept moving up, but now, everyone who wants the stock has got some. There are no newer buyers to push the price up. And a few of the early buyers might want to take a profit, which would be a catalyst for a downwards price move. With 'oversold', the stock has seen many sellers who want out, maybe because of poor earnings performance or a dividend cut, and now everyone who wanted to sell has sold. If a few contrarian buyers enter the market thinking the stock looks cheap, it could rise.

RSI is particularly good at picking up the bottom of a long fall or the top of a spike, where the price chart might not be telling you anything useful at all. If you want to get in towards the bottom of a market correction, watch the RSI! If you want to avoid being stuck with too much money in the market at the very top of a bull market, watch the RSI!

Most traders use the 14-day RSI. Depending on the time periods you prefer to trade, you might pick 9 (for day traders) or 30 (for medium term traders).

There are several ways to use RSI. First, it gives you a good feel for trends. If the RSI breaks its trendline, this might be the first indication that a reversal could be on the cards *before* seeing it in the price chart.

Secondly, you should look for RSI divergence. Look to see when the RSI is doing the opposite of the price line. When a price makes a higher high, look for the previous highest high, and draw a line connecting the two. Now look at the RSI underneath on your price chart, and do exactly the same - look for the most recent highest high, which may not be exactly underneath the share price's high, and draw a line connecting it to the previous highest high. Now look at the direction of the two lines. If they're going in the same direction, that's great. That's the way you'd expect it to be - the price is going up, and the stock is closing most days up rather than down. But if the RSI line is headed downwards, and not up like the share price, it's a bad sign - you have what is called bearish *divergence* and that's a good sell signal.

Price Rate of Change (ROC or PROC)

This is another oscillator, an indicator that goes from 0 to 100 and back again. (Most of these oscillators are 0-100, but they could be expressed as 0 to 1 as well - we just use 100 because it's easier to read than having decimal points all over the place. 77 is easier than 0.77 and it uses less ink. Or fewer pixels.) Think of price charts as a map; oscillators are speedometers.

It shows the rate of change in the price over a period, with a bit of smoothing - unlike the stochastic which measures the price compared with the price *range*.

ROC is centered on a line representing zero, so it shows how much prices are increasing (above the line) or falling (below the line). Usually, it's calculated on a 9- day basis; 14 and 25 are also used. There's probably a good reason for this, but it seems to be lost in the mists of time. When you're looking at a particular stock or market, find out which is the best for your needs. A very volatile stock might be better analyzed using one of the longer ROC periods, like 25 days.

This chart is for UK stock Superdry and comes from LiveCharts. I've deliberately taken out all the information except for the ROC at the bottom and the price line. You can see how the ROC shoots up at the start of the chart in mid-November, but then falls towards the centerline zero in mid-December.

If you sold when the ROC had got to 20 in early December, you'd have sold pretty close to the peak of just over 280p - if you waited till ROC crossed the center line in mid-December, you'd still have got out at 240p before it the price fell back to 200p in mid-January. Later on, the next move up happens just as the ROC line crosses zero again, at the beginning of February.

ROC is a nice timing tool to use within trends and to confirm trading ideas. Some short term traders like to trade when the ROC crosses the centerline. But for this to work, you should either have your moving averages in a bullish formation (i.e., the short term above the longer term average), or you should see the averages moving towards a golden cross.

Or you might already have seen a golden cross in your moving averages, towards the bottom of the recent trading range so that you're "buying the dip", in which case you can check with the ROC. If the ROC is weak, but it's rising, that suggests things are speeding up, which will help the price move higher.

You can also look at ROC divergence the way we looked at RSI divergence. And it's worth noting that both for the market and for individual stocks, an ROC that stays well above 50 could indicate you're moving into bubble territory, so it can be a warning sign.

Chaikin Money Flow (CMF)

This oscillator aims to measure buying pressure, or accumulation, against selling pressure or distribution. Chaikin oscillates between +100 and -100 (or +1 and -1). Chaikin differs from ROC or RSI because it builds trading volume into the equation as well as price and gives more weight to price movements that occur on strong trading volume.

With some charting programs, the zero line Chaikin shows as red, above as green. A stock that you're looking to break out or continue upwards is more likely to do so if the Chaikin band is mainly green; if there's a lot of red in the Chaikin band, you might want to reconsider that trade or cut your initial position and set a tight stop-loss. On the other hand, if you see lots of red in the Chaikin oscillator, and you fancy shorting a stock - that red is a good sign!

But even if you don't get the traffic light signals, Chaikin usually gives a strong visual signal as you'll see a really big hump of bars if it is strong.

Chaikin divergence can sometimes give you a good idea of a stock that's looking exposed. If a stock price rallies, but the Chaikin indicator is still in the red, that means the rally is based on very little volume. A pullback is much more likely when that is the case. On the other hand, if the Chaikin oscillator is nice and green, it's likely that the rally will continue.

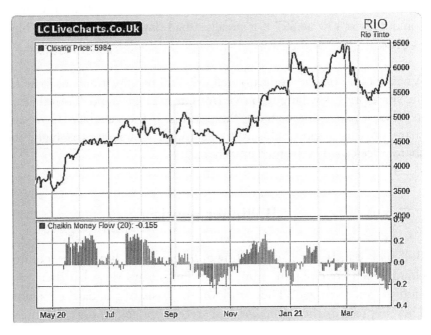

Another UK stock - this is global miner RTZ. If you look at the rallies that I've marked in yellow, the Chaikin Money Flow tells me that they're not really supported by much money. So I'd expect them to fade out, and they do. On the other hand, the rise between November and January is, at least at first, quite well supported by the CMF, so if there's a golden cross in the moving averages too, it may be worth going along for the ride.

Volatility indicators

Volatility indicators have a different focus from momentum indicators. They don't tell you how fast prices are moving, but how jerkily - whether the share price is making smooth progress, or whether it's all over the place. High volatility shares tend to be ones where no one is really sure what the price ought to be - they might shoot up from $100 to $115 one day, and fall to $90 the next - whereas a low volatility share might trade around $100 all the time, sometimes as low as $97 if it's really a bad day, or maybe just as high as $104.5.

What does a volatility indicator tell us? Technically, it tells us how far the share price is willing to move from its average trend. Turn that on its head; it tells us how strong the trend is. If the volatility is low, the share price is sticking closely to its trend. If volatility is high, the share price could be headed anywhere.

Bollinger Bands

Bollinger Bands are usually shown as two thin lines or a colored cloud which envelops the price chart. I've always regarded them as a kind of 'price sausage'. They work on the basis of standard deviation. They represent the *distribution* of recent prices about the mean (average). That means that they adjust to changes in price volatility. Remember, if the price is jumping around a lot, it has a high standard deviation, and if it's pretty flat or in a stable trend, it has a low standard deviation.

The top band is one standard deviation *above* the moving average, and the bottom band is one standard deviation *below*. Since the share price is usually (though not always) somewhere inside, that gives you your 'sausage'!

Finding it hard to visualize? Okay, here's an example from Bigcharts. It's Proctor & Gamble over the last year. Take a look where there's a squeeze in the sausage, so to speak. July - a big squeeze followed by an uptrend. Mid-September, another squeeze followed by a small uptrend. Then the share price goes nowhere till the next squeeze at the beginning of 2021, and suddenly there's a new downtrend. Interesting, hm?

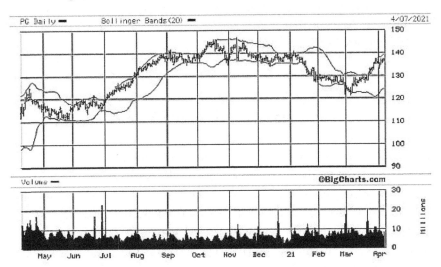

Bollinger Bands will not give you a signal. But they can help you assess whether a price signal is a good one or not. For instance:

- "The squeeze" - When volatility is low and the bands tighten even more, a sharp price movement becomes more likely. But that move could be in either direction, and there could be a false move in the wrong direction first.
- When the bands get really far apart, volatility is high and existing trends may break down.

- If prices are generally sticking to the top band, a stock may be overbought and there could be a downwards move in prospect. On the other hand, if prices are glued to the bottom band, and you spot a breakout on another indicator, the stock's likely to be oversold which means there could be a quick lift-off.
- Prices sometimes have a habit of bouncing within the bands, so if in a chart where a stock's behaving that way I see a bounce off the bottom band, I'll probably check out the top Bollinger Band as a potential medium term price target, and maybe the moving average as a shorter term target.

Worth knowing: Bollinger Bands have nothing to do with Bollinger champagne - except that if you learn to read them well, you'll be able to afford a few bottles of bubbly.

Average True Range (ATR)

The ATR shows you in a single line how volatility changes over time. Unlike previous indicators which generally take the closing price, ATR was designed for markets like commodities which frequently gap up or down, or make limit moves (that is, the exchange stops them trading if the price moves more than a certain amount). So ATR looks at the true range of price as being the greatest of these three comparisons:

1. the current high less the current low, or
2. the current high less the previous close, or
3. the current low less the previous close.

All these numbers are used as positive values (even if the biggest variation was downwards, it's not shown as a negative number). The average over a number of periods (usually 14) is then calculated.

Because it's shown as an absolute figure, you can't compare ATR between stocks. Google (Alphabet) shares are worth $2020 and can go up or down more than $50 a day; Cisco shares are worth $50 and don't usually move more than $1.5.

And because it's an absolute number, it shows *only* price volatility - high values could reflect prices are dropping or soaring; all you know from the ATR is that the movement was extreme.

If you see what looks like the beginning of an uptrend, check the ATR. If the ATR is increasing, that uptrend is getting some support. But if the ATR hasn't moved much, the impetus or 'push' behind the uptrend may fade away - this might help you decide not to make the trade.

Wow, look at that. Right at the start of the chart, Cisco started an uptrend in early November, and you can see the ATR shoot right up. It's really got some oomph. And then the ATR falls away in late November, even though the price chart is still in an uptrend for a while.

You wouldn't want to short it at the $43-45 price level where the ATR starts really falling away, but if you look at the return you'd get for holding on to the shares during December-January, and then think you could have had your money in a much more interesting situation like a massive breakout... as a trader you would want to be out of there and into the other stock, or waiting around two months until February for a bit more action in Cisco...

Volume indicators

Here's our last set of indicators. The previous indicators have all told us about the way the share price is behaving. Volume indicators, on the other hand, tell us nothing about price. They tell us how much stock is being traded.

You might think, "The price is going up! Why do I need to know how much stock is changing hands? That's nothing to do with the price!" But I can tell from my own experience, as well as many other experienced (and profitable) traders, that volume is one of the most important indicators of all. It's the lie detector of price trends. It's the fake-finder. It's the fraud-buster.

If an apparent price trend isn't accompanied by an increase in volume, it might be fake. If it is accompanied by very thin volume, it's definitely a fake. Learn to check the volume indicator just like you check your rearview mirror before turning left. It's a life-saver!

Intraday volume

If we look at the volume traded during the average day, it's not evenly distributed. From half to three-quarters of stock is traded during either the first or the last hour of the trading day - the open or the close. No one trades much at lunchtime.

At the open, traders are reacting to yesterday's close and this morning's news, or perhaps fundamental analysts have made calls in the morning meeting on a stock that announced earnings yesterday that are the reverse of the initial market sentiment. All this gets done first thing.

Then in the last hour, you've got traders squaring their positions, closing positions they don't want to hold overnight, and investors reacting to news that came through today.

That means if you're a day trader and you're trying to follow volume, you never really know what the volume for the day is going to be till the close. There could be high trade in the morning and then nothing all day.

You can have a good guess though. You know the average daily volume traded per stock. So you can split that up, about 40% in the first hour, 40% in the last hour, the rest spread (or perhaps a third in the first hour, to be conservative.) Then, if at the end of the first hour, a stock has traded 52% of its average daily income, you know it's well ahead of where it ought to be at this time of day.

Let's do a little charting. Go to Bigcharts or StockCharts, and I want you to get a five-day chart of IBM, showing the price hourly, and showing the volume. Can you see how the volume spikes up at the beginning and end of each day? Try it with Cisco or Microsoft. It should be about the same. The only time it's different is when you get a big announcement or news in the middle of the day.

Unless you're a day trader, other volume indicators are less work and will be more suited to your trading style than this one, though.

Volume by Price

Volume by price shows the amount of volume for a given price range. The calculation is based on every trade in a given period, at a given frequency, so you could have

- A six-month chart of daily closing prices,
- A two-week chart of price and volume every half-hour
- A five-year chart of price and volume each week.

You'll see the Volume by Price displayed as a bar chart with horizontal bars to one side of your price chart. Here's one from TrendSpider, a paid-for software that gives you alerts, scanning and the ability to backtest your trading rules as well as charting software. Here, the Volume by Price is shown by grey bars on the right hand side. What's the interest in knowing volume by price? It shows you how much volume has been traded *at a given price level.* That often turns out to be a support or resistance zone for the share price. Here, you can see that there are two particularly large bars that correspond to a support/resistance level.

And some charting software goes further - it colors the horizontal bars for Volume by Price in green or red. It assumes that if the price ended the day down, it was driven by selling, and contrariwise if the stock price went up, the bulls were in charge of the markets. So the longest bars show areas where there has been the most demand to buy (more green in the bar) or sell (more red in the bar) the stock over the period for which you ran the chart.

Obviously, for every seller, there's a buyer. But in any given market, you get a feeling for who's in charge. You may find it easier to understand thinking about real estate - when it's a 'buyer's market' prices are going up, everyone wants to buy real estate, if you put your house on the market, you might get competing buyers bidding each other up; when it's a 'seller's market' you'll be lucky to get people viewing and they'll probably ask for a better price, a new bathroom, or whatever. One side or the other is 'driving' the deals and that's what the green and red bars will tell you.

Accumulation/Distribution indicator (A/D)

This indicator shows the relationship between volume and price to determine the trend of a stock; the relation between price and demand may show accumulation (i.e., buying of stock) or distribution (i.e., more sellers). Basically, it's an application of the law of supply and demand by manipulating figures that we can easily get from the stock market. It's a cumulative value, adding the previous measure to todays to get the current value.

The A/D indicator is useful
- As a confirmation of trends, when it follows the share price closely;
- When it diverges from the price trend, and it suggests the price trend could change.

Be warned though that the A/D can peak or trough a month or two before prices do. So though you know prices are exposed, it's not a great indicator to trade on - it simply tells you that you should be looking for another signal, but when you do, it'll be a good one.

Using A/D together with the RSI is useful. RSI will show if the stock is likely oversold/overbought, and that may back up what the A/D indicator is telling you.

Take a look at March 8; Tesla shares hit a low, the A/D hits a low, the RSI just goes below 30 all at the same time here. So that says, hey, there's *gonna* be a bounce - and there is. And while the immediate bounce fades away a bit after hitting the 650-700 resistance level during mid-March, it does look as if an uptrend is beginning to establish with a series of steps up at the end of March. The A/D is a bit high right now but the RSI hasn't gone past 70 - if it did, I would definitely want to close out the trade, though.

On-Balance Volume (OBV)

OBV is a similar indicator with a slightly different approach. Instead of adding all the figures, it *subtracts* "down days" and *adds* days when the stock "closes up". What it's trying to do is to work out how much of the volume was driven by sellers, and how much by buyers.

The actual number isn't relevant - it depends on where you started. What's important is the trend, and the theory behind OBV. It's pretty interesting. OBV aims to pick up the difference between the big, institutional investors - professional fund managers, insurance companies, pension funds, and the like - and retail investors (whether that's the Robinhood crowd, buy-and-hold guys, or the kind of people who are stupid enough to take tips from taxi drivers).

When the price moves on slim volume, it may be driven by the Robinhood traders or a few retail investors taking a tip from CNBC. But when the price moves on big volume, it's going to be the big investors who are moving it. Ultimately they are the ones who move the market, so if you track what they're doing with the OBV indicator, you have the best chance of spotting the *real* price trend - what the smart money is doing.

That's the theory. Okay, we can all think of a stock where the mighty Wall Street hedge funds and the little retail traders had different views, right? GameStop - Redditors were buying like crazy and the hedge funds were going short. OBV doesn't really seem to do anything here. I really thought OBV would show all that big buying and selling peak to be on slim volume, but it doesn't. And I'm not really sure who was the 'smart' money here either, because if you were a retail trader who bought GME in November and sold any time since the beginning of 2021, you made a packet.

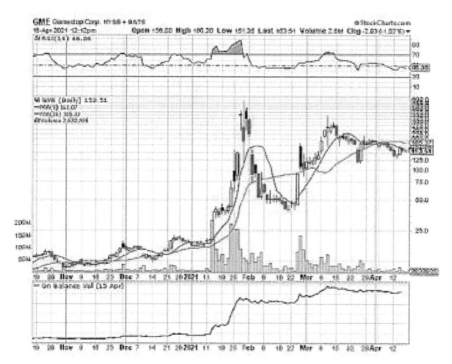

So you can see I'm not the biggest believer in this one - but it may work for you. You'll only find out by tracking it, along with all the other indicators, till you find out which one catches your eye most often and turns out to be giving you good information. I like moving averages and RSI best, and a friend of mine loves to have 3 or 4 oscillators open. He makes different trades, too, but we both make money. Watch out for spikes by the way. OBV can get thrown off course by the reaction to earnings or new product announcements.

A note before we go on

Okay, that's it for indicators. I bet you're feeling relieved! You may also be feeling a bit overwhelmed, and maybe some of those names and abbreviations are swimming around in your brain and getting mixed up. I packed into this chapter what takes many technical traders a good while to acquire. When I started out, I was using price and moving averages for a long time before I even discovered MACD.

So don't worry if you found this hard going. You can go on with chapter 5, which looks at patterns, so it's quite different - more visual, less mathematical and analytic - and come back to this chapter later. Or just stop reading for a while, let your whirling ideas settle down, and come back and read this chapter again.

Chapter 4 Quiz

1. Why are volume indicators so important?
    a) They tell you whether there is real money behind a move in the share price.
    b) They tell you whether you'll be able to sell your stock.
    c) They are just nice to know.

2. Why would you not go short if the A/D tells you we're at the top of the market?
    a) Going short is risky
    b) The A/D is often a month or so ahead of the trend
    c) The A/D is only a confirmatory indicator and doesn't give signals

3. What is RSI divergence?
    a. When the RSI changes direction
    b. When the RSI is trending in the opposite direction to prices
    c. When the RSI trades below 20

4. When the share price dips below a moving average, it's
    a) A potential bearish signal
    b) Just noise
    c) A sign of a breakout

5. Why is the ADX useful?
    a) It tells you the price trend doesn't have much impetus left in it,
    b) It tells you the price is going up,
    c) It tells you the price is going down.

5

Chapter 5: Continuation Patterns

Some types of patterns crop up again and again on price charts - like the cup and handle, triangles, and pennants. If you learn to recognize them, they can give a feel for what's likely to happen next. (I like to compare them to that creepy music in horror movies; it *might* just be there to get you on edge and Mom's going to come in with a cake, but then on the other hand, we know that *more often than not* it's the guy with the ax, the chainsaw or the knife.)

A continuation pattern suggests a price will continue in the same trend. It's a useful pattern to know. When you see a continuation pattern and it is completed successfully, the chances are good that the price will now continue in the same direction. But you do need to wait for the pattern to be completed, as some end in failure and trend reversal. Typically, you'll see the pattern building up, you'll see the completion and breakout, and you can then trade that breakout to catch the trend.

Continuation patterns are always most reliable when you see them within a strong trend - a small surfboard and big waves. If the share price is hardly trending either up or down, I wouldn't even bother looking for a continuation pattern. And a lot of them are prone to false breakouts, so remember to check for confirmation from other indicators.

Cup and handle

Cup and handle patterns are continuation patterns that you'll generally find in an uptrend - the 'cup' is a dip in the trend. The cup and handle pattern is difficult to describe and can be hard to spot, but you'll know it when you see it. (I think it looks more like a soup ladle, to be honest.) The first part is the 'cup', which is a price decline followed by an almost equal rise - if you draw a trendline freehand, you'll probably get some kind of parabola or U-shape. The next part is the 'handle', a triangle or sideways channel that should, as with normal cups, be smaller than the cup, and ideally remaining in the upper half or (even better) upper third of the cup. Look for a deep cup and a relatively shallow handle. But note that the handle can be pointing down, when you're expecting an uptrend to resume. That doesn't matter! The breakout will still be upwards.

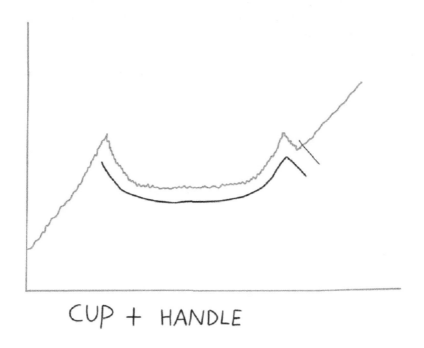

CUP + HANDLE

Never start trading with the 'cup'. The cup is just an alert that something is getting set up. It's the handle that tells you what's really going on. Let the handle get well established, and look for a breakout. When the breakout happens, it's time to trade. Most of the time, the cup-and-handle is a continuation pattern - it makes a pause in the trend, but then the share price rejoins the trend.

You're most likely to lose money on a failed breakout. Set your stop-loss at the bottom level of the handle, or at the most recent swing low within the handle. That means if, unusually, you've got a reversal, or if the breakout fails, you're covered. Meanwhile, your profit target is the breakout point, plus the total height of the cup. So if the cup is $30-35, and the breakout is $35, your target is $40. Your stop-loss will probably be around $33, so you have a 5:2 expected profit:loss ratio. That's not too bad.

Here's a real example, a cup and handle formation in McDonald's. On the left hand side of the chart you can see an uptrend, and looking at those candlesticks you'll also note it's almost entirely green - very few days closed down during the trend. Then it broke, almost exactly halfway through the chart at the beginning of November, and then after falling significantly it settled into a consolidation pattern forming the 'cup'. It hasn't really formed a handle yet, but that's potentially a nice deep cup if the pattern continues to work out.

Dead Cat Bounce

(I really hope you're a dog-lover!) A dead cat bounce (DCB) is a temporary uptick in a steady downtrend. The price goes up temporarily before the downtrend reasserts itself - a 'bounce', but not a reversal. Often, it's caused by bargain seekers thinking a stock must have reached the trough. Sometimes, traders who have been bearish simply want to cover their shorts and lock in some profit. So the price ticks up - but not for long.

Now here's the problem: how can we tell the real bottom from a DCB? You can't. This is why I don't advise you to short a DCB - if it turns out to be a breakout, you could lose a lot of money very, very fast.

On the long side, if you buy into a DCB, you risk seeing the stock price fall away sharply. (Of course, you should set a stop-loss which will stop you from being suckered into staying in the stock all the way down.) But if you *don't* buy into it real low, you'll miss the uptrend!

You can't tell the difference easily. So if you spot the DCB early, you can 'scalp' it - take a quick profit from the uptick and sell before the downturn resumes. A quick trigger finger and tight stop-loss controls are needed for this trade. A DCB can easily double the stock price before turning down again, so you might want to take partial profits on the upside - lock in a profit in case the stock turns down fast.

Your best bet is to build up your experience by paper trading till you have some gut feel for this play, and remember your trading rules. And remember, this is a short term play, and one which takes fast reactions. If you're more of a mid-term speculator, leave DCBs alone.

Triangle

This is a really common pattern to find, though it takes a little expertise to interpret correctly. The price trend starts to show convergence with lower highs, and higher lows - so that if you draw a line connecting all the highs, and a line connecting all the lows, you get a triangle. You're going to want to have at least two connecting points and ideally three so you can see this really is a triangle and not a random pattern. The closer the two lines of the triangle get, the more likely it is that you'll get a breakout, with the price breaking out of the triangle quite forcefully. That's the trade you're looking for.

Sometimes a triangle will be symmetrical. But it can also be an *ascending triangle*, where the highs draw a horizontal (or more gently sloped) line but the lows are rising - or it can be a descending triangle, in which case you have a horizontal line of lows and the highs are coming down to meet it. It is a medium term pattern, taking some weeks and in some cases even a couple of months to form.

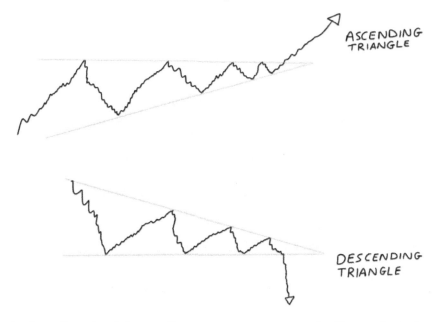

ASCENDING TRIANGLE

DESCENDING TRIANGLE

A *descending triangle* is a really strong pattern to trade. Remember, the price must already be in a downtrend. The triangle is just a consolidation within the trend. You're seeing lower and lower highs - buyers are unable to get the price going up. Meanwhile, the lows are providing a good solid support line. Once the price breaks below the support, you make your trade.

The chart above is one of the ones I found on Finviz when I asked it for descending triangles. The site automatically identifies patterns - they're not always 100% in my book, but sometimes they're real classics, and this I think could turn out to be a good trade... except that the price *wasn't* in a downtrend before the triangle got started.

The good thing about the triangle is that it tells you what profit to look for. Where the triangle started, measure the distance between the low and the highest price. That's your potential profit. Subtract that from the low, and you have your share price expectation for where you want to close the trade. So here as soon as the share price closed below the bottom line (and it hasn't yet), I'd want to go short, so a bit less than $15, and then looking at the difference between the blue line and that early December top, I'm looking for $1.50 profit - so a share price of $13.50 is my immediate target. Also, because it's not quite a classic pattern because of the uptrend, I'm going to look for some good volume backing the move downwards before I enter the trade. If the price bounces back just through the blue line, I'm not bothered, but I will set a stop-loss around $15.30 so my risk is only 30 cents a share against a $1.50 profit potential. I'm quite happy with that ratio.

Bullish flag

Bullish flags are some of the most reliable patterns, as long as your stock is in a strong trend before forming the flag.

A flag shows up when the trend pauses for a while and the share price trades in a tight range. It's called a flag because you can draw a rectangular box around it, like the shape of a flag. It might be moving upwards, downwards or sideways.

Bullish flags are only short term phenomena. One might last a few days or a couple of weeks. If you see what looks like a flag but the share price starts trading up and down in the range, it's formed a *channel*, which we already looked at and which is a longer term pattern. Note that flag patterns usually run in the opposite direction to the trend (imagine the center bar in the letter N).

Bullish flags are very quantifiable. The depth of the 'flag' which on the left I've shown here as x can be added to the breakout price to get your target share price. You'll enter a little above the line to make sure it's not a fake-out. And the stop- loss is just below the bottom line. (Just below, because some traders will try to "take out" the bulls by pushing the price just below the line before the price goes up again, so if you put your stop -loss actually on the line, you could lose what's actually a good trade. Taking a tiny bit more risk will deliver very significantly more return.)

Bullish pennant

Bullish pennants are the short term version of a triangle. The pennant is triangular, and they are both short-term signals. They typically don't last much longer than 10-15 days - 20 at the outside.

The pennant will form, typically after a big and fairly quick (steep) move in the price (which you see on the left). You'll then see prices consolidate into the pennant. You'll probably see this happen on lower volume, so it's worth checking the volume indicators for confirmation.

Now the thing that I particularly like about bullish flags and pennants is that when there's a breakout, it's a big one. They basically show the market taking a breather and drinking a Redbull before starting that uptrend again, and the uptrend is likely to be fast and furious.

Occasionally there will be a fake-out, so put a stop-loss just below the bottom line of the pennant. Meanwhile, your profit objective is the height of the 'mast' - the last strong move before the pennant started forming. So both your downside and your upside with this trade are easily quantifiable, and your upside will be significantly greater than the downside.

Look at the chart again and you'll see how I measured the height of the pennant where the pattern began, 'x', and then I've added this to the resistance line at the top of the pennant to give me my target price. I've shown you where I entered the trade, after the breakout, and where I would put a stop-loss.

Do remember that the target is an initial target. I won't necessarily sell at that point - I will take another look at the chart and reassess. If it looks as if the uptrend will continue, I'll set a new target and a new stop-loss. (The stop-loss is very important.) And maybe I will sell enough to cover my original stake, so my initial capital is recouped and all that's now at risk is the profit. But remember: winners run their wins, and only cut their losses, so I'm not going to be too cautious.

By the way, if you're still unsure on bullish flag and pennants, I would definitely suggest you watch my free bonus #1 companion masterclass because in Class 3 I demonstrate examples of both patterns with real life charts – which will hopefully help your learning!

Bullish falling wedge

Wedges are a bit of a refinement on the triangle. The market consolidates between two falling lines, with lower highs and lower lows. Both the support and resistance lines point downwards, but the resistance line is steeper, so you have what looks like the point of a pencil pointing downwards towards the right.

So it's not like the pennant which is pretty much even on both sides, and pointing straight forwards - I find it easiest to spot the difference not by looking at the individual trendlines, but by seeing where the formation is telling me to look.

If a pennant was a pointing finger, it would be pointing along the road (to the right), whereas a wedge is pointing at a plane (if its a bearish rising wedge) or pointing at the pavement (if its a bullish falling wedge).

Confirmation for the wedge also comes from volume indicators, as generally, there is less and less volume traded as the wedge develops.

Perhaps it's counterintuitive, but a *falling* wedge heralds a price break *upwards*. The pointing finger is showing you the *reverse* of the real movement! However, look at the downward price moves inside the wedge and you'll understand why - they are getting shorter and shorter, the price is falling a bit less each time.

By the way, make sure you really are looking at a wedge - it should definitely show convergence (lines moving closer together). If the lines are nearer parallel, it may be establishing a channel, and that's an entirely different thing.

Not all wedges end in a breakout. That's one reason you might want to wait till you see the actual breakout before placing a trade. If it's a genuine breakout, not a fake-out, you'll see rising volume as the price goes up, too, though it *may* retest the top line of the wedge. (Remember, when the price breaks through a resistance line, that line becomes the new support.) Some traders will actually wait for that retest before buying - the problem, of course, is that they will possibly miss the fastest and most profitable breakouts.

To calculate potential profit, look at the successive lower highs within the wedge. Each of those highs represents a potential resistance point. So if the breakout happens at $40 and the last high was $46, you have a potential $6 profit. If things are still going well at that point, you can hang on in and wait for the next resistance level. Some moves go back to the initial price at which the wedge started. But every time you decide to stay in the trade, raise your stop-loss to just below the new support level.

Bearish flag

It will not surprise you to know that these are just the reverse of a bull flag - a consolidation phase in a strong downtrend.

Here's a bear flag. It's a small pattern in a downtrend making a rectangle, and you're looking for the breakout.

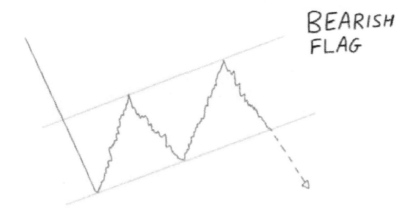

BEARISH FLAG

Bearish pennant

Here's a bear pennant. It's a small triangular formation and again, you're looking for that breakout that brings you back into the downtrend.

If you go short, you can capitalize on the big downwards move at the breakdown - but place a buy stop- limit order as a stop-loss just above the top line of the pennant, just in case.

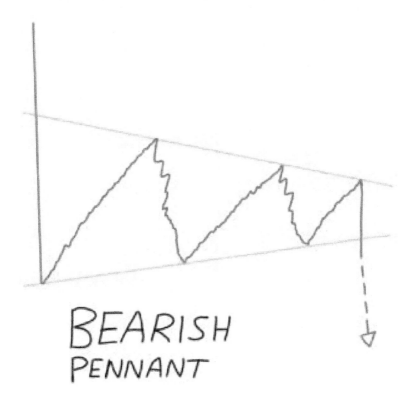

BEARISH
PENNANT

Below is a good chart example of a bearish pennant - Exide entered a downtrend late 2018, after what looks to me like a classic head and shoulders pattern (we'll look at those next chapter), but then look, it forms this upwards pennant in August 2019. Every time it gets to that bottom line there's the potential for a breakthrough, and look how fast it is when it comes. From $185 to $130 really, really fast. But of course, the price might have moved back up towards the top of the pennant one more time - even twice; so that's why you don't trade a pennant till the price has actually closed below the line.

In fact, you can spot quite a few different patterns in this chart—there's an uptrend from the beginning of the period to about October 2019, which I drew a line for. Also, I haven't drawn a line but perhaps you'd like to try to do so for the head- and-shoulders that forms between about April 2018 and April 2019. And then I have drawn a line for the downtrend, as well as for the bearish pennant pattern we already discussed.

Of course, it's easy to see all these patterns in hindsight. Would you have known what to do every time? Where would you have put your target price and your stop-losses? It's worth thinking about this every time you look at one of these charts.

Bearish and rising wedge

Remember that, counter-intuitively, a falling wedge leads to an upwards trend? A bearish wedge is one that is rising - and will probably lead to a breakdown. Apart from the fact that you'll have to trade short to capitalize on it, a bearish wedge works pretty much the same way as a bullish wedge.

BEARISH
RISING WEDGE

The stock should be in a long term downtrend. The wedge is pointing upwards (like the analogy I gave of pointing to a plane). And the break will be downwards. Because of the risk of going short, you need to be very certain with this wedge - check the oscillators, as those should provide confirmation. If they don't, rethink!

Problems with continuation patterns

Continuation patterns are not always reliable. Sometimes they in fact end in a reversal - something you may pick up by looking at other indicators, such as RSI or OBV. If a rising wedge occurs when a stock is in an uptrend, it could potentially be a reversal signal leading to a downtrend - the breakout will still be on the downside.

Another problem with these patterns is that they are often tested by false breakouts, which can lose you money if you get tempted to take too many trades or don't set a close enough stop-loss. If you are trading continuation patterns a lot, keep a good record of your trades and their success rate per pattern. That will help you understand which patterns and trading methods are working best for you. Depending on your particular trading style, that might not be the same patterns and methods that work for me or anyone else.

Chapter 5 Quiz

1. For a pennant to give a strong signal
   a) The share price should already be in a defined trend
   b) The pennant should be long and thin
   c) The moving average should be underneath the pennant

2. What's the importance of the 'handle' in setting your stop-loss in a cup-and-handle trade?
   a) None
   b) You should set a stop-loss at a swing low within the handle or at the depth of the handle
   c) You should set a stop-loss way below the handle

3. What is a dead cat bounce?
   a) Cruelty to animals
   b) A temporary reversal in a long term trend
   c) A form of flag pattern that fails

4. Ascending and descending triangles are
   a) Good patterns to trade
   b) Not very useful
   c) Totally subjective

5. A wedge
   a) Always ends in a breakout
   b) Never ends in a breakout
   c) Ends in a breakout if there's good volume towards the end of the wedge.

6

Chapter 6: Reversal Patterns

Just as we saw that there were patterns that usually end in a continuation of the price trend, there are also many patterns that often lead to a reversal of the trend. This is where to borrow a phrase I've used before in this book; you find out that it may be a trend, but it's gonna bend!

Obviously with a reversal pattern it's going to be either at the top or the bottom of the market - for the foreseeable future anyway. At the top, you have what's called a *distribution* pattern - investors and traders who own the stock are deciding to sell (distribute) it, and eventually there are more sellers than buyers. At the bottom, you have an *accumulation* pattern as market participants begin to accumulate the stock, and the power moves to buyers from sellers.

You *cannot* have a reversal pattern without a preceding trend. There has to be something for it to reverse. If you're in any doubt about what looks like a reversal pattern, just set the chart for a longer time period and check that the trend is there and firmly established before the pattern starts to form.

As with continuation patterns, reversal patterns can fail, so watch them carefully for the breakout and place your stop-losses sensibly. You'll also find that the longer a pattern takes to develop, the larger the move is likely to be once it does break out, so patience is a virtue if you're trading these patterns.

Bump and Run Reversal Bottom

Remember the cup and handle? This starts out looking a bit like it, with a pretty symmetrical dip forming a 'cup', but then it breaks out above the trendline. Other people have described it as looking like a frying pan, with the 'handle' out left, along the trendline.

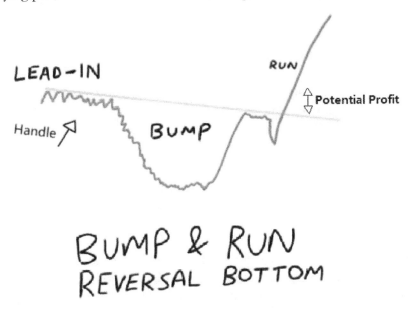

You'll find it in a downtrend, and you can draw the trendline along the downtrend - usually not a very steep one. It can take as much as a month for that trend to become established. Then you get the 'bump', cup, or frying pan, whatever you want to call it - the price drops quite steeply, then forms a nice round bottom, and starts climbing again. If the price closes above the trendline on the upside, it's a good buy signal, often signaling an upside of 50% or more.

This is a good quantifiable pattern, meaning that you can pretty much analyze how much upside you'll get out of the trade. If you mark the price at the top of the left 'handle', this is where normally you'd expect the price to rebound to if the bump and run makes a successful breakout. The bump (cup, frying pan) should normally be twice as deep as the handle, nicely defined, so you can see this pattern really clearly when it occurs.

And very often, the pattern delivers rather more than expected. So don't be too quick to sell - if the price is still running strongly upwards, supported for instance by high volume or by the MACD, use a trailing stop-loss and keep running your winner.

Tom Bulkowski discovered this trading pattern and according to him, it achieves its price target 76% of the time, with an average rise of 55%. That's a very good performance - most patterns have either a low success rate but high profitability, or a high success rate but lower profits. This one has both!

If you're a bit more daring and risk-friendly, you can also play this pattern by drawing parallel lines to the trendline, and buying on the way up when the price closes above one of those trendlines. How do you know how wide to make the trendlines? Simple - measure the highest to the lowest price in the handle, and that's your measurement for these trendlines. However, this trade doesn't have quite the success rate of waiting till the higher breakout, so you could get stopped out.

You may get a throwback, with the price falling back after the breakout. However, if you continue the main trendline, as long as the price doesn't close below the trendline, the breakout should still happen - you just need to wait for it. Only close the trade if the price falls below the trendline.

This is a really great trade for medium term long-only traders.

Bump and Run Reversal Top

Guess what? This is just the opposite of the Bump and Run Reversal Bottom. So it's a good trade for short traders.

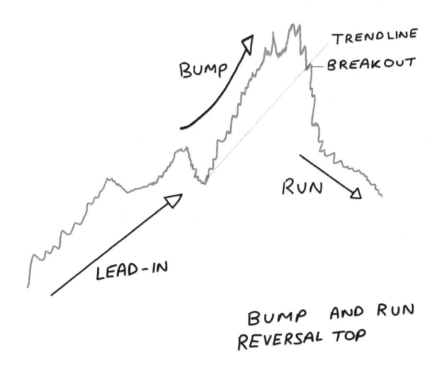

Let's just talk through how it works. The 'handle' or 'lead-in' sees quite an orderly trading, with the buyers setting the tone and the stock closing up most days in a fairly tight range. Then everyone notices the stock is doing well, and you get some people buying it because it's going up, speculating, more short-term traders getting into the market. Prices go up much more sharply and usually the volume increases, too - lots of traders jumping in.

And that's not sustainable. Right at the top you might get a double top, or just a very rounded top. And then people start getting cold feet. Some of the investors who held on to the stock all the way up the bump decide to take a profit. Some of the speculators who bought in right at the top are stop-lossed out. Others get scared and sell. And when the price breaks the trendline, you know that now things have got serious, and you go short.

As with the bump and run bottom, this pattern *can* see a retracement (temporary reversal). The retracement is rarely more than half the 'bump' size, but if you're trading short, you will be stopped out. Keep watching because if the price comes back to close below the trendline again, this is the real thing - and you should take that short again.

Another nice thing about bump and run? While it can take three or four months to set up the lead-in and the bump, the 'run' part of the pattern often takes just a few days to deliver you a significant profit, so your money is at risk for very little time. You just have to be patient watching the pattern and waiting for the right time.

Double and Triple Bottom

This is one of the first patterns I ever learned.

A double bottom looks like a letter 'W'. Up, down a bit, up a bit, and then down again. The psychology of it works like this: the price is trending down, with lots of sellers exiting the stock. Then a few speculators or maybe some value investors look at the price and think, "Hey, this is cheap," and buy in. But the price doesn't get very far. Sellers who missed their chance to get out earlier decide to sell, and some of the buyers look at the panic and think, "Okay, I'll take my profit before it goes down more". This selling drives the price back down - but only to where it was before, and now you have buyers again.

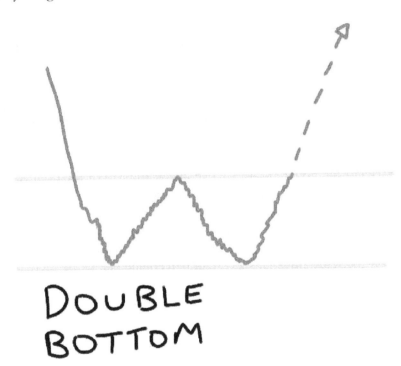

DOUBLE
BOTTOM

Now, of course the price could bounce around between those levels for a while, and if it did, it would form a channel. But you have two lines that you can draw across that W now (as I've shown with the light blue lines). First of all, the failed bounce forms a resistance line, so you can draw a horizontal line at the top of the bounce. And secondly, the two bottom corners of the W form a support line. So you can draw a line between them, too.

If the price breaks through the resistance line and closes above it, it's a buy signal. You can also quantify how much profit you expect to make. Measure the move between the bottom corners and the failed bounce, and you can expect to make at least 60% and possibly 80% of that as a profit, and fairly quickly, too. Of course, you're going to put a stop-loss below the resistance line, so if it does turn out to be a fake-out, you don't lose too much.

I like this pattern because it has a high-profit potential. That said, you'll find that you 'kiss a lot of frogs' in terms of price action that looks like turning into a double bottom and doesn't.

All is not lost though, because the share price might be forming a *triple bottom*. (Yes, that is a share price reversal pattern and not a rare medical problem.) This behaves similarly to a double bottom, except that it takes longer to get round to breaking out. Your buying signal - the price closing above the resistance line at the top of the bounces - is the same, and your profit potential is the same.

Be smart, though. Your profit potential is big, but just in case it doesn't work out that way, remember to place a *trailing stop* which will ensure if the share price falls a certain percentage below the high, you will still get out at a profit.

Double and Triple Top

Okay, a double or triple top is just a double or triple bottom the other way round. The difference is that to make real money out of this one, you need to go short - that is, sell shares you don't own. Then when the price has gone down, you close the deal by buying shares at the lower price. Not all brokers will let you go short.

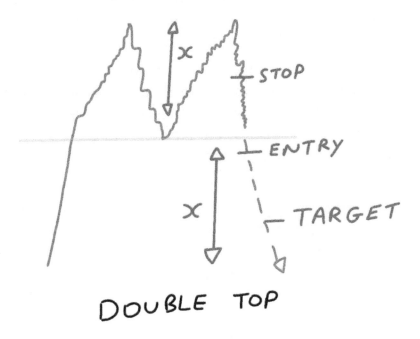

DOUBLE TOP

But double and triple top formations are also interesting if you have a longer-term investment portfolio as well as your trading portfolio. I don't think it's a great idea to "time the market" by trying to sell at the highs and buy back at the lows, but if you see a top forming, you might want to take a few profits, lighten up your more speculative positions, and maybe take a little insurance out in the form of a put option or an inverse ETF (exchange traded fund).

- A put option gives you the right to sell a stock at a given price. If the stock is trading at $242 and you think it's going to fall, you could buy a put option at $180. Traded options have an expiry date. Usually, you won't hold it that long, just till your trade works out.

- While most ETFs reflect the performance of a market, an inverse ETF gives you the exact opposite. If the market goes up, the ETF goes down. What you're interested in as a short seller is that if the market goes down, the ETF goes UP. Buying an inverse ETF can make you money if you trade a good strong breakdown.

At the same time, as an equity investor, if I see a double bottom forming, I know it's time to look and see if I can buy some more of my favorite stocks at a good value.

The chart below shows Jan 2001-March 2004 of S&P 500 (The months and years are shown under the volume bars, not under the price chart, which is kind of annoying, but you should be able to follow them.)

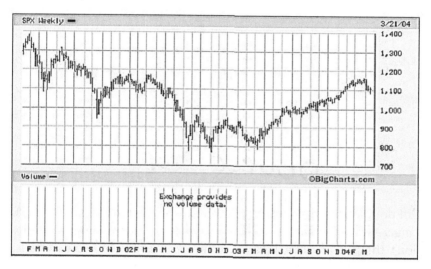

Look at how stocks come right off the top in 2001, there's a little retracement on the way down, but there's a clear double bottom in June and September 2002. You then see the price drop from about $1,000 to just below $800, then rises again, doesn't get much further than $950, then falls back. Then you have another failed breakout, you can see that resistance line at $950 holds, and the price comes back again - but it doesn't hit the support line, it turns before closing below $800 (there's just the little tail of the low below the line) and then it just keeps going up, fast to $1,000 and then all the way to $1,150.

By the way, sometimes you'll find a double bottom doesn't quite work out, but later, a second double bottom formation starts to show. Often, it will form with the same bottom, but the intermediate highs are lower than in the first pattern. This one could be the real deal, and with stronger resistance levels, when it breaks out, it could go up much faster than you'd expect. So never give up on your double bottoms! Keep following the chart to see what happens next!

And in fact, you might want to enter a limit order to buy just above the resistance line, so that if you're not trading all day, your broker will do the work for you. At the same time, enter your stop-loss order little way below the breakout level - always allow a little space, just in case there's a fake retracement. Here I would probably have thought about entering around $925 or a little higher, and probably I'd put a stop-loss around $880.

Head-and-Shoulders Top

First, I have to mention that this pattern has nothing to do with shampoo. What it does is to form a pattern a bit like a head-and-shoulders photo - a left shoulder, the 'head' in the middle, and a right shoulder.

If you want to trade this pattern, you need to go short - that is, either sell shares you don't have (so you need a broker who will let you go short), or use some other way of taking a risk on the price going *down*. When the shares hit your target, you make a purchase order, and buy the shares below the price you sold them. Neat.

You'll find this pattern coming after a strong uptrend. It's a medium to long term pattern - it's not going to play out in much less than a month. And if it's a real head and shoulders, you will see that after the higher 'head' formation, the share price will hit the 'neckline' already established between the left shoulder and the head, and bounce off it again. You can draw this neckline across the chart; it's usually pretty flat, but sometimes it has a slope. If it slopes downwards, it's particularly bearish.

So we now have a chart with three lines on it - the price, the trendline, and the neckline.

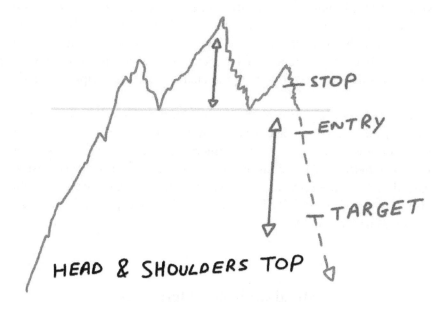

The low of the left shoulder doesn't usually break the trendline. So the trend is intact till you get to the head. When the share price comes down again to the neckline, it does break the trendline. So that's (probably) the end of the uptrend, but it's not time to buy yet, because the neckline provides resistance and the price will bounce off it to form the right shoulder.

The moment you're looking for is when the price comes down again from the right shoulder. (Usually, though not always, the shoulders are roughly symmetrical.) Keep watching till it closes below the neckline. It has now gone through the resistance level and its time to go short. At this point, your profit target is the difference between the top of the head and the price at the neckline - subtract this from the current share price for your close-out price. So, for instance, if the price got to $58, the neckline is at $50, then my target profit is $8, and my target price is $50-8 = $42.

There can be a retracement up to the neckline, but if it doesn't breakthrough, the price will fall again. That's why you should probably set your stop-loss slightly *above* the neckline, allowing for that little bounce - you won't be stopped out of a profitable trade.

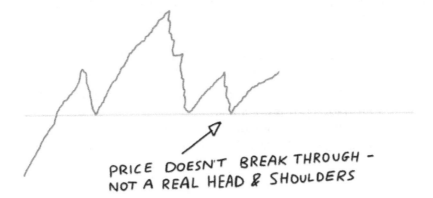

PRICE DOESN'T BREAK THROUGH -
NOT A REAL HEAD & SHOULDERS

Note that if the price doesn't actually close below the neckline, it's not an actual head-and-shoulders top pattern. Look at the chart above and you can see what looked like the real thing - but wasn't.

Some traders set their stop-loss at the top of the right shoulder, but that's pretty loose and you could lose quite a bit if the reversal doesn't materialize.

Head-and-Shoulders Bottom

You've probably guessed that this is the opposite of a head-and-shoulders top. The difference is that it comes after a downtrend, so it's a reversal pattern that will have the stock soaring upwards afterwards.

Head and shoulders formations are not equal. Their profitability is affected by a couple of factors:
1. The taller the 'head' in relation to the neckline, the greater your trade's profit potential.
2. A smaller right shoulder shows the stock is already losing momentum and is less likely to bounce out of the reversal.

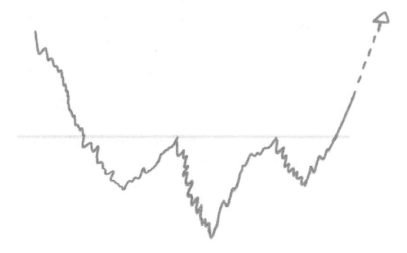

HEAD & SHOULDERS BOTTOM

You should also watch the volume of shares being traded. On a classic head and shoulders bottom pattern, the volume will increase and be really strong on the breakout. Strong volume tells you that the move is not a small correction, but a proper breakout with big funds behind it that should deliver you a good profit.

If the price is still dropping when you reach the target, don't get too greedy. It might be time to lighten up and take the risk out of your position by selling some of your shares, even if you don't sell the whole position. Take a good look at the chart before you make your decision, and in particular, look at the momentum indicators - if they're strong, you might be in for the ride, but if it seems like momentum is falling, it's time to exit your trade and book your profit.

Rounding Bottom/Saucer

We talked about the cup and handle formation, but the rounding bottom is just a cup. No handle. It comes when an existing downtrend slows down, bounces around, and creates a rounded trough with a flattish bottom. Quite a few chartists call this a 'saucer', as it is, usually, a bit flatter than a cup.

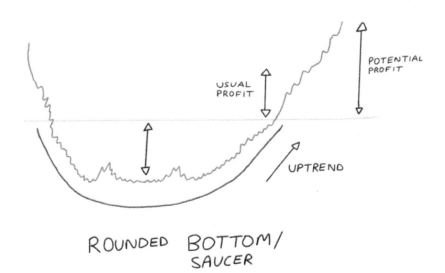

Drawing the neckline isn't quite as easy as with the preceding patterns. You're looking for the last proper price spike before the saucer started to form. This is one of these times that charting can be an art rather than a science; there could be several places looking equally possible, but most of the time, there will be one spike just a little more pronounced than the others. So get your ruler, or the crosshairs on your trading screen, find the spike and then draw horizontally across the whole chart so that the line crosses the top of the spike. Then you just have to watch till the price closes above the line, and buy.

It's also tricky to plot your target profitability. It's probably best to take about half the depth of the 'saucer' and then add that to the neckline - in about a third of cases the pattern captures the whole depth of the 'saucer' as profit, but you can't depend on that. So this pattern is more limited in profitability than other reversals, but to make for that it is quite reliable. I've shown both levels of profit target on the chart.

The price may retrace at the neckline before breaking through. But this is a pattern with a nearly 60% success rate if you get it right. The flatter the saucer, the more likely you are to get a good fast breakout. If you track volume, the volume indicators should follow the pattern of the saucer - high at the beginning of the decline, low in the middle where the price is drifting along, and then increasing as the price starts to go up again. That's a good confirmation for your trade.

This chart comes from tradingview.com, another source of charting, with a thriving community - one of the members suggested the gold price was forming a rounding bottom. It actually makes the point about the 'spike' much better than our drawing - you can see there are two highs before the bottom starts to form, and the neckline is drawn across from the second one. After that, we're definitely in the rounding bottom. But you *might* have seen the little spike that goes above the neckline, a bit earlier, as the beginning of the bottom, in which case you would just get into the trade a bit higher. (You can sign up for a free trial on TradingView if you're interested; it covers commodities, currencies and cryptos as well as equities.)

Where do you put your stop-loss? There's no really obvious place. Some traders put it at the midpoint of the saucer - that is, halfway up - but that only gives you a 1:1 risk:reward ratio. I prefer to put it just below the breakout, and I know another trader who puts it at the bottom of the breakout candle (yes, you have to use a candlestick chart to do that).

Like other reversal patterns, this can be quite a long term pattern. It's not for day traders, but if you're looking to trade positions and hold them for several months, this can be a useful pattern to look for.

Parabolic Rise or Run-Up

If you have done math to a high level, you know what a parabola is. If you ever played frisbee, you probably have quite a good idea. If not, I'm going to have to explain what 'parabolic' means before we start discussing the pattern.

A parabola is a plane curve which is mirror-symmetrical. Okay, if that doesn't mean much, let's try to make it easier. Imagine you have an ice cream cone. If you cut through it horizontally, you'd get a circle. If you cut through it on the skew, you'd get an oval or ellipse. If you cut through it from somewhere on the side to halfway through the top, you'd have a parabola - a kind of long thin curve. You would also have wasted a lot of ice cream.

I fully accept that this is not one of my most talented drawings, and I am no Michelangelo, but I hope you now have a good idea of what a parabola looks like!

You don't get to see the whole parabola in this reversal pattern, only half of it. And you see it upside down, like half a letter 'U'. There are two things to notice about this curve and that gives us two ways to trade it.

1. It's a bit like a series of steps, if you look at the candlesticks - particularly since on a candlestick chart each 'step' has one big, bullish candlestick at the start of it. Every time the price hits a high, it should be higher than the previous high, and the low in between should be higher than the previous low.

2. But the second thing that you really have to notice is that the curve keeps getting steeper and steeper. And there is a limit to how far that can go.

Short term traders often trade their way up the 'staircase' either using moving averages (buying when the price moves up through the moving average), or using flags and pennants, which we looked at in the chapter on continuation patterns.

But if the curve continues to steepen, at a certain point it's going up almost vertically. If you continued to draw the curve, it would have to go back in time, which is obviously impossible. People are buying like there's no tomorrow - people are buying in a panic because "if you don't buy it now, you'll never be able to get into the stock". They have FOMO big time. There is a bubble mentality.

Here's GameStop - it's not quite a classic 'staircase' though if you look at the candlesticks, the jagged price line in black and red on the chart, you can see a big candle starts one step up about 22nd December, and then there's another big step up around 14th January. And then there's another about the 24th January, and at this point, the curve has really steepened. Look back to the previous year and you'll see how the trend was running at an angle of about 20 degrees, maybe, and suddenly it's almost vertical.

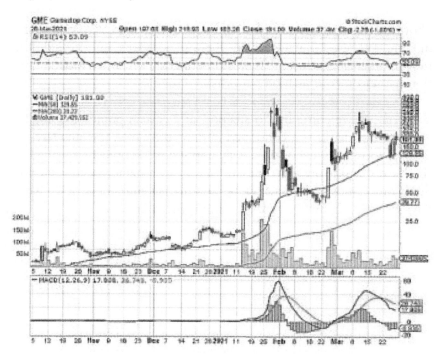

You *could* try to trade that steep vertical. Plenty of small investors did. For those who got out at the top, great. (And by the way, thiss chart also illustrates why going short is dangerous. Plenty of hedge fund managers would short GameStop for very good reasons. And they were *bleeding* money.)

Those who had been in GameStop since 2020 were fine too; maybe feeling a bit miserable that they weren't multi-millionaires anymore, but just ordinary common or garden millionaires, but hey, that's not so bad. But the little guys who bought in because they read about it in the press or on Reddit and got caught up in the excitement - they were toast, with a capital T.

Where do you go short? You have to draw a trendline using successive lows. When the stock price goes south through the trendline, catch the break. Weakening momentum oscillators might also confirm the trade.

Your target profit? Quite often, the share price will go all the way back to the beginning of the really steep part of the curve. And that's exactly what happened with GameStop in mid-February.

But you have to be careful with this one. Set a really tight stop-loss. Sometimes you get one or two big swings at the top. In fact, this is a lovely reversal to play as a day trader; I don't particularly like it, even though the potential rewards are very high, and if I do play this kind of curve, I don't keep my position open overnight. I'm just there to catch those big moves down, and as you can see, there were some very big moves indeed.

The other reason to be careful - look at the volume bars in that chart during late January. There's an awful lot of stock being traded; emotions are very high, some people are facing huge margin calls from their brokers. It's a very tough market to trade in.

Now you know both continuation patterns and reversal patterns. You can guess whether the stock will carry on in its current trend, or break out and reverse. We've talked about how to trade the patterns, and - an important factor - where to put stop-losses so you don't lose your shirt.

Most of these patterns are medium to long term. But in the next chapter, I'm going to take a look at patterns that are sometimes useful in the really short term - candlesticks. And this Japanese technique is a whole new ball game.

Chapter 6 Quiz

1. If a double bottom fails, and becomes a triple bottom instead, my target price and stop-loss will be
   - a) Half what I expected
   - b) Exactly the same
   - c) You don't trade triple bottoms

2. When you have a parabolic rise, you'd expect trading volume to be
   - a) Low
   - b) Normal
   - c) Extremely high

3. The flatter the saucer,
   - a) The faster the breakout
   - b) The less likely it is to be a signal
   - c) The more likely you are to spill your tea

4. Reversal patterns usually
   - a) Take longer to set up than they do to break out
   - b) Don't happen when the market is in an uptrend
   - c) Are exactly symmetrical

5. The Bump and run reversal is
   - a) Only for day traders
   - b) A good trade for medium term long-only traders
   - c) Almost never profitable
   - d) A bad car accident

7

Chapter 7: 16 Candlestick Patterns that Every Trader Should Know

So far, we've been looking at western style price charts and even where there are candlesticks, we've been looking at them over such a long period that we're looking at trends rather than individual time periods. But candlestick charts give you lots of information besides the trend - in the shape of the candlesticks and in particular very short term formations, maybe just a couple of days.

So this chapter is about candlesticks, and looking at the patterns that are really useful. There are six bullish patterns, six bearish patterns, and four continuation patterns - and if you didn't enjoy all that jargon in the chapter on indicators (RSI, OBV, MACD, ODX), I can promise you will find the names of the different candlestick patterns much more user-friendly and even on occasion quite humorous.

So what is a candlestick?

A candlestick is slightly different from the OHLC line that most charts show. It was developed in the Japanese rice market and it shows pretty much the same information, but in a format that emphasizes different facets of the share price movement.

The open-to-close range is represented in a big fat *body*. This has a different color depending on whether the share price went up or down.

- UP used to have an open white body with black outlines in old-fashioned charts, but now we have a full-color pixelated world; it might also be green.

- DOWN used to be an all-black body, but nowadays it's often red. Think of funerals, or think of red lights - the message is the same.

The body is the first thing you see, but you will also see little lines sticking out from one or both ends. Some traders call them the *wick*, other traders call it the original Japanese term, *shadow*. These show the intra-day high and/or low. If the day closed at the high, there is no upper shadow; if it closed at the low, there is no lower shadow.

I'm using my hand-drawn slides again. Remember green = up, red = down. A bit like traffic lights where green = go, red = stop. But if you ever look at older books on charting, you'll see the upwards candle as white and the downwards one shaded black.

(Just to refresh your memory: if the day closed at the high, what color is the body? If it closed at the low?)

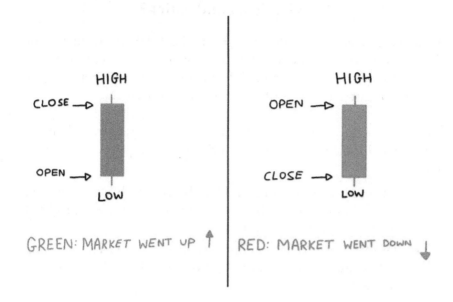

GREEN: MARKET WENT UP ↑ | RED: MARKET WENT DOWN ↓

So a great tall green-bodied candlestick with no top shadow and a short bottom shadow means the stock rose nearly all day, only dipped a really tiny amount below the open in trading, and then closed at a high. A short stubby red candlestick with a long bottom shadow and a short top shadow shows that the price closed the day not far from where it started, but after some big selling action pushed the price down - and that it never traded very far above the opening price.

Try drawing some candlesticks for yourself on a bit of paper and think about what they mean.

Now let's look at a few candlestick patterns. They can be a single candlestick on its own, or a series of candlesticks.

Six Bullish Candlestick Patterns

1. Hammer

The hammer looks like a hammer, with the head up. It has a short green body, no (or almost no) upper shadow and a long lower shadow. So that means the stock traded up (the green body), but didn't close far from where it started (the small body), but it went way down during the day (the long shadow) before closing up. This was a battle between bulls and bears, and the bulls won.

Very often, the hammer comes after a short downtrend, and it's a sign the trend will reverse, and the stock price will start to go up.

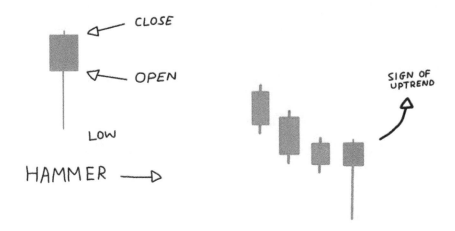

2. Inverse Hammer

The only difference with the inverse hammer is that it's hanging upside down - a short green body (the hammerhead) with a tall upper shadow and much shorter or no lower shadow. So here, the battle went a different way - the bulls tried to push the price up, the bears managed to push it down again, but the bears still lost, because the price ended up on the day. So again, it's a sign that the market could be set to go up in the near term.

Sometimes, you get two almost identical candles together at the top of an uptrend, though - a green and then red. That's an inverse hammer and then a shooting star, and this combination is called a 'tweezer top'. It indicates that a reversal is imminent and the market is likely to turn down. You can also have a tweezer bottom - just the reverse, showing the reversal is on its way and things should start moving up.

I should say I like the tweezers a lot. I've found them one of the easiest candlestick patterns to see, and they're also pretty reliable.

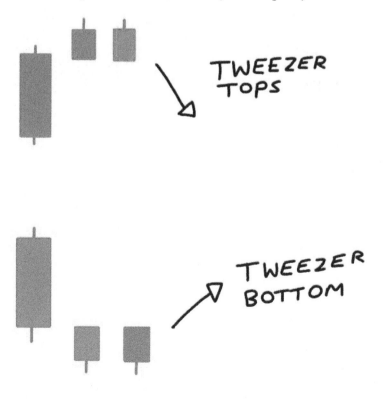

3. Bullish Engulfing

This has a small red candlestick that is completely 'engulfed' by the big green candle that follows it. The bottom of the green candlestick is either equal to or lower than the red, showing the share price opened at the same level or lower, but the price has really moved up and closed the day much higher. A victory for the bulls!

Again, bullish engulfing is usually a reversal pattern in a downtrend.

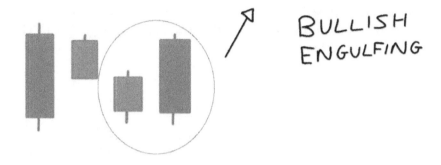

BULLISH
ENGULFING

4. Piercing Line

The first step with the Piercing Line is to find two big candles, a red one followed by a green one. They both need to be good long candles.

Now you need to look at their relationship. The green should be lower than the red - so that means the price opened lower than the day before, but rose during the day.

Next, you need to look at how far up the price managed to get. It needs to have closed more than halfway up the red bar. If it nearly got to the top of the red bar, that's a really strong signal. The downtrend should reverse.

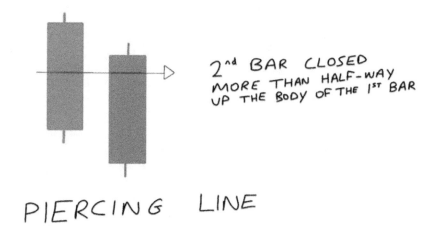

2ⁿᵈ BAR CLOSED MORE THAN HALF-WAY UP THE BODY OF THE 1ˢᵀ BAR

PIERCING LINE

5. Morning Star

Morning Star happens in a big downtrend and it is a sign of hope that the night will soon be over and the morning should be coming. We've had one-stick and two-stick patterns; this is a three-stick pattern, a small candle squashed in between two long ones. The first long candle is red, and the second one green - the end of the downtrend with a low close, and the beginning of the uptrend with a high close.

Imagine a 'star' between two mountains if you need help remembering this one. The best morning star pattern is where there's no crossover at all between the star's body and the bodies of the other two candlesticks (it doesn't matter if the shadows overlap). In other words, trading gapped down before the star, and gapped up after the star. That's a good bullish signal.

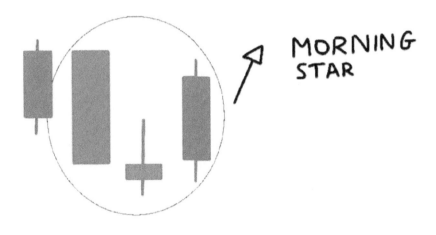

MORNING STAR

6. Three White Soldiers

Of course, nowadays this could be three green soldiers! It's another three-stick pattern, with three white or green candles marching uphill. They should, to form a really good signal, have short shadows. (Think about that; the price hardly fell or didn't fall at all below the open, and it closed near the high. So the bulls in the market, the buyers, had life all their own way.)

Three white soldiers are easy to spot because the candlesticks are long ones, and contrast with generally smaller and mainly red candlesticks in the run-up to the signal. It's a really strong bullish signal and definitely worth trading.

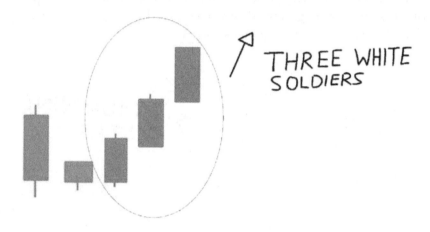

THREE WHITE SOLDIERS

Six Bearish Candlestick Patterns

1. Hanging Man

It would be quite easy to confuse the hanging man with the hammer. But the hanging man is red, with a big downside shadow. The day saw a big sell-off, and even though buyers got the price back up again, it was still down on the day.

Hanging Man is a reversal pattern. You'll find him 'hung up high', at the top of an uptrend, and he tells you prices are going to start going down. I mean, with a name like Hanging Man, you wouldn't expect it to be good news, would you? Again this helps us to identify him, because the hammer comes within a downtrend.

HANGING
MAN -
BEARISH

2. Shooting Star

This is quite like the inverted hammer. It comes at the top of an uptrend, and you'll see it has a tiny body and a really long shadow or wick at the top. And while the inverted hammer is green, this is red - it's a warning sign. (If you find the shooting star followed by an inverted hammer that looks almost exactly the same, though, you have 'tweezer bottoms', which sounds rather painful but is a good reversal pattern showing the market is likely to rise out of a downtrend.)

Let's explain what's going on when you see a shooting star. It gapped up, so the opening was just above the day before's close, and it went way up to the high but then came all the way - or almost all the way - back down again. And now here we are with the next candlestick gapping down; that's all we need to know. The new trend will be downwards.

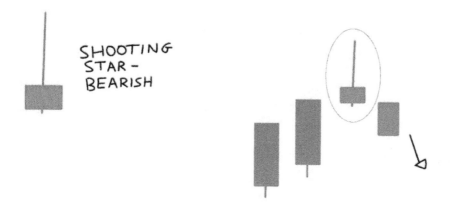

SHOOTING STAR - BEARISH

3. Bearish Engulfing

This is the other way around from the bullish engulfing. The first candle is a little green one, and the second is a big red one. The upwards movement has stalled, and the downtrend begins with a big move down.

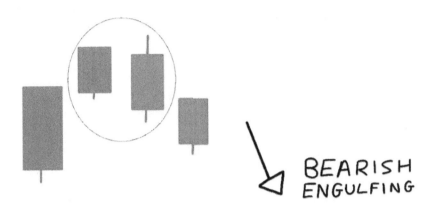

BEARISH
ENGULFING

4. Evening Star

The evening star is the reverse of the morning star; it tells you night is only just beginning.

It's three candles, just like a morning star; two big candles sandwiching the tiny one in the middle. First a big green one, then a little green one with hardly any body, like a twinkling star, and then the big red candlestick which tells you all you need to know. We're going down, down, down.

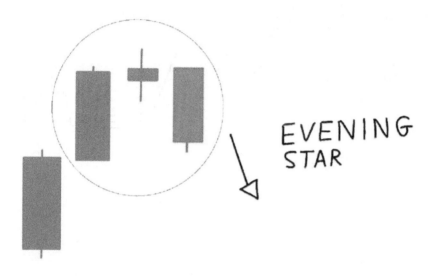

EVENING STAR

5. Three Black Crows

Three white soldiers showed you the market was going up. Three black crows are just the reverse. There are three big long black (or red) candlesticks in a row, each lower than the other. And you guessed it, they are not good news. (Unless you're short, of course.) The price is going to head downwards.

The only problem with recognizing the Three Black Crows is that nowadays they're quite likely to be red.

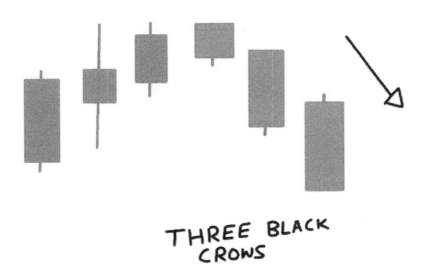

THREE BLACK
CROWS

6. Dark Cloud Cover

This is a nasty one. Look for two long candlesticks, one green and one red (Or white and then black.) The red candlestick opens above the top of the green candlestick, but it closes well below - more than halfway down the green candlestick's body. It's not just balanced the upwards movement but exceeded it.

If the next candlestick doesn't come back up again, or if it only just manages to close in the very bottom part of the big red candle, then you have confirmation that the trend is going to be downwards.

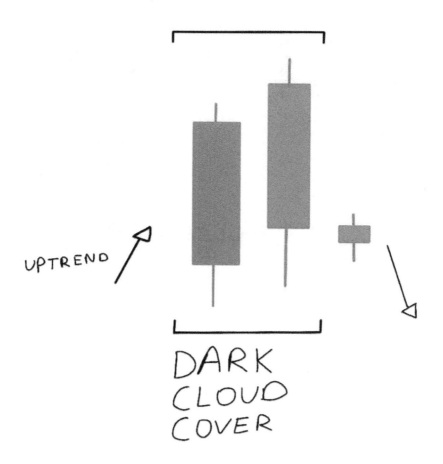

Four Continuation Candlestick Patterns

1. Doji

The doji is a funny little thing, like the 'star' in the evening and morning star; it's a candlestick that doesn't have much body at all, so it looks like a plus sign or a cross. A doji shows a day where the share price hardly changed at all.

While you find the doji sandwiched into the two 'star' patterns, on its own, it doesn't convey a signal; it's quite neutral unless it's in one of the other patterns.

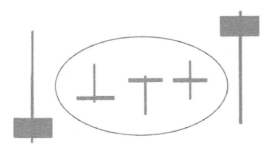

DOJI

2. Spinning Top

This is like a doji - a candlestick with hardly any body. But unlike the doji, it has really long shadows. That's why it's called a spinning top - it looks like a typical toy top.

Like a doji, on its own, it doesn't have a lot to say. With the spinning top, you can see that the price moved up and down a lot during the day, but closed not very far from where it started. So this could be a sign of consolidation, the market taking a breather, but things could go either way - down or up - once that period is over.

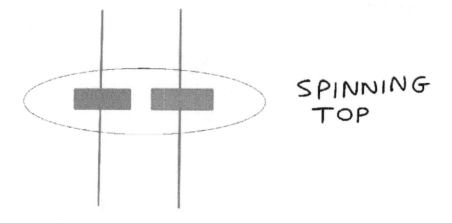

SPINNING TOP

3. Falling Three Method

Both the 'threes' are patterns that have three candlesticks of one color squashed in between two of the other color - green inside red or red inside green. In fact, you've got five candlesticks in all, so I don't know why it's not called "falling five".

Falling three has two great big red candlesticks on the outside. Inside, there are three, smaller, green candlesticks trying to break out upwards, but they fail, and the downtrend continues.

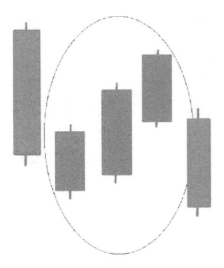

FALLING
THREE
METHOD

4. Rising Three Method

Rising three is just the other way around. Here, you have two big long green candlesticks on the outside, and three shorter red candlesticks are trying to break downwards on the inside. They don't manage it - the second green candlestick finishes higher than any of the preceding candles, including the first green one.

This is a good sign of an uptrend that's got a lot of strength in it and should stay intact for a good while.

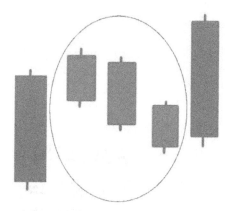

RISING
THREE
METHOD

And finally, the dreaded Marabozu!

The Marabozu is a particularly interesting candle since it has no wick or shadow at all. It's just a box. Either green or red.

That means the price did this;
- Green Marabozu - opened at its lowest and went all the way up to its high, where it closed.
- Red Marabozu - opened at its highest and kept falling all the way to the close.

So a Green Marabozu is a bullish sign, which can be either a continuation or a reversal signal depending on the trend. If it forms at the end of an uptrend, then the price will probably continue to go up; if it forms at the end of a downtrend, then a reversal is likely, with prices rebounding from their lows.

Conversely, the Red Marabozu is to be feared - it's a bearish signal. Avoid the curse of the Red Marabozu - unless of course, you engage in the black magic of shorting stocks!

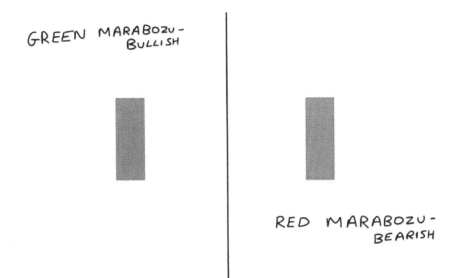

Let's just take a look at a practical example of candlesticks. Below is a chart for Oracle with what might be interesting candlestick patterns circled in blue. Can you see on 25th January and the day before, you've got those tweezer bottoms? The rise is very short term but it's definitely there!

Then at the beginning of March, you can see three white soldiers - although they're not, as they really should be, in a downtrend. Still there's a fast and furious rise just after them. (I think the gap down around 12th March was associated with a results announcement.)

Now there's another interesting series of candlesticks towards the end of the chart. Can you spot them? Which way would you trade?

It's another three white soldiers, I think. And I probably would be buying...

Chapter 7 Quiz

1. A candlestick's colored body shows
   a) The high and low of the day
   b) The open and close
   c) The open and the high

2. What is a doji?
   a) A candlestick with hardly any body
   b) A very long red candlestick
   c) A bearish signal

3. What is the opposite of Three White Soldiers?
   a) Four White Soldiers
   b) Marabozu
   c) Three Black Crows

4. A candlestick that is colored red or black shows that the price
   a) Went up on the day
   b) Went down on the day
   c) Did not move

5. Which of these are bullish signs?
   a) Hammer
   b) Inverse Hammer
   c) Arnie Hammer

8

Chapter 8: Avoid the Traps

Trading chart patterns always sounds so easy to do. Websites show you successful trades that were profitable, and you look at the pattern and say, "oh yes, of course, anybody could have spotted that", and it looks so easy.

It's not. First of all, you have to kiss a lot of frogs - that is, for every chart that shows you a meaningful pattern, you're going to see an awful lot of charts where there's no clear trend at all. Secondly, some patterns can be deceptive and set traps for the unwary trader. For instance, 'headfakes' often happen when you were expecting a proper breakout. And thirdly... some traders make life awfully difficult for themselves, whether through being too emotional, not setting stop-losses, not considering risk, or not knowing what some of the *bad* patterns look like.

So in this chapter, we're going to take a look at some of the traps. And then in the next chapter, we'll look at trading psychology, and that includes a few more ways that many traders sabotage their own performance.

Fake-outs and Fake Head-and-Shoulders

Sometimes the set-up looks great… but then the expected price movement fails to emerge. Prices move the 'wrong' way for your trade. These are like a "headfake". But there are ways to check them out and avoid a few of the fakes.

You may fall into the trap of looking at a head and shoulders formation without realizing that it's actually just a blip in a bigger trend. Always check your chart with a longer time period before acting on a trade.

By the way, remember to check the pattern against the big picture. In the chart below, you think you see a head and shoulders formation, but actually, it's happening within a major trend and the trendline, not the neckline, is what matters. Always remember to look at several different time periods - I always look at a month, six months, a year and five years, which may be overdoing it - so you don't get caught by a pattern that doesn't work.

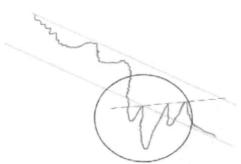

THIS LOOKS LIKE A HEAD & SHOULDERS BUT WHEN YOU LOOK AT THE BIG PICTURE ITS STILL IN A BIG DOWNTREND

Even if the price here had broken through the neckline, the top line of the downtrend channel would probably put up resistance, and that would limit your likely profits.

Or you may see the price come down to the neckline of the right shoulder, but not actually break through it. It might just dip below it in intra-day trading but still close above it. This isn't a proper breakout - wait for the price to close below the neckline before you buy.

In many head and shoulders patterns, there's a false breakout with a retracement before the real one. Sometimes, market practitioners are just trying to ensure traders with tight stop-losses are 'stopped out' before the price really moves. So don't put your stop too tight, and be ready even if it's activated to jump back into the next breakout.

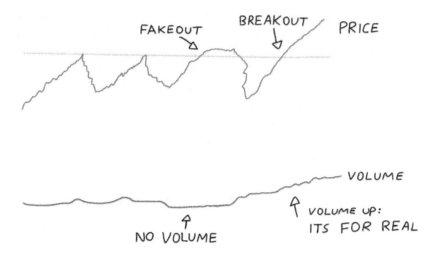

You also get fake-outs - for example, the price breaks the trendline to the upside, but then it falls back again, instead of giving you the expected breakout. You'll probably fall into that trap a few times, but some confirmations can help you avoid it:

- If there's a low volume of trading, it's probably a fake-out; breakouts have high volume.

- If the price is headed very slowly towards the trendline, it's probably a fake-out; breakouts have real momentum and tend to start with a really big move.

- A fake-out from a double top or double bottom is one that doesn't lead to the expected reversal - instead, you get a continuation. If you recognize it, you can simply reverse your trade - if you expected a double top to lead to a fall, and the price starts heading up, then stop the short and go long.

- Try placing your stops just short of the 'expected' price or just a little more. Double bottoms, for instance, are well known patterns and lots of traders will have stop-losses at exactly the same price, often a round number. If you stay away from that level, you may not get faked out if the market-makers try to "shake the tree".

No Trend at All

Almost every good chart pattern needs a good strong trend established for it to work. It is really, really difficult to make money trading when there's no trend. And the market can be trendless for 60-70% of the time. If you don't trade for nearly three-quarters of the year, how on earth can you make money?

Mind you, if you don't see any good trades in a sideways market, don't force the issue. It's always better to have cash sitting in your account than to waste it trading for the sake of trading. Taking a risk when you haven't identified a return is one of the dumbest things you can do.

Mean -reversion trades are probably your best bet. The concept of mean reversion is that statistical probabilities group towards the mean (average), so that if a price goes to an extreme high, it will probably fall back; if it goes to an extreme low, it will probably rise again. Even sideways markets have a range, though they don't have a trend, so identify that range and you've got a trading strategy.

But to carry out these trades, you need to get four things right:
1. Detect oversold/overbought stocks using momentum and volume indicators, not just price charts.
2. Buy stocks when they are trading on the low side of the range. It may be profitable to wait for a slight bounce so you know you're not going to get stuck in a downwards breakout that could cost you money. Your target price is not the other side of the range, but the middle (so your profit is half the width of the range).
3. Be careful with your stop-losses. If there's a breakout, you do not want to get hit.
4. If there *is* a breakout, it may be worth joining it. Again, be careful; set a tight stop-loss.

You will not make big money in sideways markets. You can make a little. If markets are range-bound for a long time then you may need to consider trading them, but to be honest, the risk-reward ratio is not that good, so I prefer to sit them out. Or you might look at another market to trade - foreign exchange, commodity ETFs, or futures; but to do that, you really should have already at least paper-traded these markets, or you could be jumping out of the frying pan into the fire.

Adjust Your Moving Averages

Most chart packages have already decided which moving averages to display. These are often, for instance, the 9 and 18-day averages, or 9 and 26 day, or 50 and 200.

But these might not be the best averages for you. Don't fall into the trap of letting a charting site decide which moving averages you should use.

For instance, if you've decided to become a day trader, you'll want to get something like 5-8-13 bar averages. You can get price bars for every hour, every five minutes, or every minute even, so you might have a 5-8-13 minute average instead of 5-8-13 days. Watch out though, because though in a good trend, they'll give you great signals; in choppy trading, they can be all over the place, and you're best declaring time out, going flat (closing all your positions) and going to get a coffee.

If you trade longer term, you'll want to look at longer term averages such as the 26 and 50 day SMAs or EMAs. 20/21 are good for swing traders together with the 50 day; the 200 and 250 period MAs go well as the slower average.

Remember, the EMA moves faster than the SMA, so it will flag up trades more quickly - but you pay a price for this, because it will give you more false signals than the SMA. If you're happy making a lot of trades and closing the bad ones quickly, use the EMA, as it will get you into a price swing more quickly; but if you want to trade longer term, and keep your positions longer, then SMAs will give you winning trades that are slightly less profitable, but fewer stopped-out trades and fewer trades overall.

One of the reasons MAs work is that nearly everyone uses them. So while you might think it's fun to create a 34-day moving average, it might not give you any useful, actionable information. You can try it, backtest it on a few charts and see. But I doubt you'll actually find that it's a secret weapon. I've tried a few and they've never worked out.

And lastly, moving averages just don't work in trendless markets. When the market is ranging, don't try to use the MAs for trading ideas - they're going to be all over the place and will only get you into trouble. Wait till you can see a clear trend again.

Risky Symmetrical Triangle

We've looked at ascending and descending triangles, which can give you a great trading signal. But sometimes the trendlines form a symmetrical triangle. The highs are getting lower, and the lows are getting higher, and when the two lines meet, *something* has got to happen. The trouble with this formation is that it's super risky. The chances are 50% it'll be up, and 50% it'll be down, and at a guess about 90% that it'll be fast and furious.

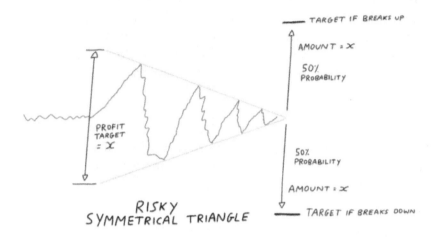

RISKY SYMMETRICAL TRIANGLE

As I've stressed repeatedly, the trend is your friend, and trading a market that's not got a clear trend is tricky. And by definition, with one trendline going up and one coming down, with the symmetrical triangle, you have a trendless market - *unless* there's a really good strong moving average line, for instance, in which case you have a 50-60% chance that the breakout will be in the same direction. But there's also a good chance that there will be a fake-out first (usually with low volume while the real breakout will see an increase in trading volume).

So if you're risking on one of these triangles, it may be better to wait till the breakout and new trend is clear - and keep your stop-losses tight or the price could run away from you in the wrong direction. In fact, prices quite often gap up (or down) from these formations, so even your stop-loss may not help you.

Your profit target can be measured by taking the depth of the triangle when it began to form, and adding that to the breakout point. Your stop-loss should be at the last point at which the price touched the bottom line of the triangle. Since this is a 50-60% probable pattern, you're going to want a better than 2:1 risk/reward ratio for it to be potentially profitable. I wouldn't take it on much below 4:1, personally.

But you can ride the trend if you look at the moving average. As long as the price stays above the 20 or 50- day MA, you can keep your trade moving and bring your stop-loss up to date with the moving average every day. That way, you'll be stopped out automatically if the trend changes. A trailing stop like this is a great way to run a longer term position.

Super Rocket Stock

One of the big dreams of the stock market is the one stock that will make you your fortune. "If I'd put every penny in my IRA into this stock... if I'd mortgaged my house and bought this stock... If I'd maxed out my credit card to buy this stock..."

Point one: do not trade anything other than *risk capital*. That is money that you know you could afford to lose. If you lost your house and your pension, and owed the credit card company $50,000, you would be in dire straits. Don't go there.

But secondly, this dream is exactly that - a dream. Shares do not go up and up and up. They go all around the houses.

Let's look at Cisco - a 'rocket' of the tech boom. If you bought and held Cisco at $1.92 in 1994, you would have made a load of money. If you'd bought it at $15 towards the end of 1998, you would have seen it soar to over $80 - and then fall back to below the price you paid for it by the end of 2002. Now, it would be worth $50. (This chart's from Bigcharts. Their data goes way, way back. Not all chart sites have such good long term data.)

Plenty of gurus are keen to sell you their 'rocket stocks'. They'll use a combination of different approaches - analyst upgrades, earnings surprises, charting, trade volume. And they perform okay - for a while. But the problem with analyst upgrades is that analysts usually base their estimates on what the company tells them, and few analysts want to get out of step with a rising market - they fear if they call the top and the market keeps going up, they'll be fired. And the problem with 'rocket stocks' is that there are many other people who have got in at the same time, and the same price, as you. If things go wrong, they'll chicken out.

These stocks are often really speculative, like GameStop, for instance. I'd call Tesla a super-rocket - it's been driven by having a great story and a charismatic CEO, but it hardly makes any money, and competition from companies like Toyota, Volkswagen and Renault is heating up. (Incidentally, Volkswagen is up 62% from its lows. Good money for those who caught it.)

That means there's nothing to keep the share price from falling off a cliff. I know that we're talking about technical analysis and not fundamentals, but with stocks like this, I worry that the market is full of people who've heard the story but don't really understand the numbers. That pushes the stock up, and up, and up - and if you remember the parabolic rise? That's the trap.

Long Candles

In the chapter on candlesticks, we looked at several signals involving long candles. But sometimes, a super-long candlestick can be a trap. It looks like a bullish signal - and for a little while, it is. But while the share price may test resistance above this long candle, it's usually a bull trap and the share price will, after a while, come back to earth. And it can hit the ground hard.

Why does this big candle happen? New buyers are coming into the stock thinking that it's making a breakout. Maybe some big players are pushing the price up. What's important is that this long candle doesn't sit nicely among the other candlesticks - it's isolated. There may even be two big candlesticks.

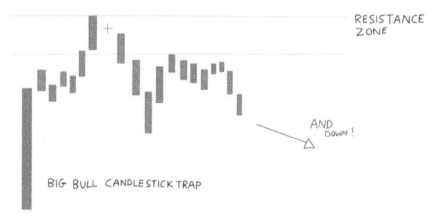

Maybe you missed that signal, and you're sitting in the trading range on top. You'll often get another chance, because a huge candlestick with a big upside shadow or wick will fake a breakout from the trading range. Novice traders will look at a big white or green candle and say, "Yay! Breakout!" Experienced traders will look at the big shadow on the upside, and they know that it means the market was trying to push prices higher and higher, but *it wasn't working.*

However, you should always check signals on a longer or shorter timeframe. For instance, a green/white weekly candle with a huge upper shadow looks as if the market tested the highs and couldn't sustain them. If you look at the daily candles, though, you may find that you have a pattern that is trading within the expected channel - up to the topside trendline and then just a small correction. In that case, don't get suckered - if you are long on the stock, it's still on course.

Lack of Discipline

The worst trap that most traders face is a lack of discipline. That might mean not getting up to catch the market open, not setting stop-losses, or not taking a trade where all the signals look good because you don't like the stock. Once you've decided on a trading strategy and on which signals are the ones you're going to trade, stick to your strategy and system. Chopping and changing loses trader's money...

... and that brings me to the next chapter, which is not technical, not about charts, and not about prices. It's about trading psychology - the psychology of other traders, but most importantly, your own.

P.S. Before we go onto trading psychology, if you are finding this book useful so far - I would really appreciate if you could spare 60 seconds and write a brief review on Amazon on how this book is helping you. It would mean the world to me to hear your feedback!

Chapter 8 Quiz

1. If you want to be a great trader, you have to kiss a lot of:
    a) Boys
    b) Girls
    c) Film stars
    d) Frogs

2. Three of these signs would tell you the 'breakout' is a 'fake-out', but which is the signal you can rely on to tell you a stock is going to break out upwards?
    a) The share price is moving slowly towards the resistance level,
    b) The share price goes above the resistance level in trading but closes below,
    c) The RSI looks overbought,
    d) The share price moves on big volume.

3. Rocket stocks are so called because
    a) They build space exploration equipment,
    b) They are rock solid,
    c) They are expected to go up like a rocket,
    d) Rocket rhymes with 'Reddit'.

4. How can you make money in sideways markets?
    a) Mean-reversion trades using oscillators,
    b) Head and shoulders formations,
    c) Candlestick charting,
    d) Shorting.

5. What is the worst problem which loses traders money?
    a) Worry,
    b) Lack of discipline,
    c) Setting stop-losses too tight,
    d) Not setting stop-losses tight enough.

9

Chapter 9: Trading Psychology

Trading isn't just about spotting the right chart patterns and making the right trades. It's also about what's going on in your own mind.

After all, the whole reason charting works is that it shows, in the aggregate, the sum of human behavior. Most of those humans will be prone to just the same emotions that you are - greed, fear, anxiety, excitement, doubt, and so on. But most of them don't make money trading.

In fact, statistics show that 80% of traders give up within a year. But then, 60% of new restaurants fail in their first year and 80% within 5 years, and you wouldn't think that was such a risky business as trading the market, would you?

So this chapter is about trading psychology, and mainly about you, and how you can stack the odds in your favor by understanding how the market tries to trigger a reaction, and how you can resist the reactions and emotions that will lose you money.

The Basics of Trading Psychology

I had a friend at university who was way, way better than me at math. He would have been a huge help to me when I started doing technical analysis. He could spot data patterns just from printed numbers - he didn't have to see a chart - and he came up with amazingly different ways of looking at common statistical problems.

Unfortunately, he got stressed out very easily. He flunked his first-year exams. He saw a psychologist, and the university said okay, fine, we understand, come back and we'll pretend it didn't happen. He just about managed through his second-year exams, with a lot of help from his friends, but when it came to finals, he just went missing. He couldn't even bear to turn up to the examination hall.

He didn't fail because he couldn't do the work. He didn't fail because he was stupid. He failed because he couldn't control his own fear.

He would never have made a trader.

If you are trading, you have to be able to overcome your emotions. The market can terrify you. During the tech crash in 2001, you could see some people were shell- shocked. They just couldn't think. Some of them panicked and sold everything. Some of them tried to put their heads in the sand and pretend it wasn't happening. Neither of these was a great strategy, though one or two of the people who sold did manage to get out of the market at a profit. They were too scared to think.

And the world is full of people who sat on massive paper profits for years. I had a friend who'd gone to work for a start- up, got shares in it, then it floated and she got shares, and they kept going up all the time, and she was a multi-millionaire... and then the tech crash came, and she was only 'just' a millionaire.

"Hey," I said, "I think you should sell your shares."

"You're joking! They were $152 last week and they're only $100 now; I'm going to wait till they hit $150 again and then I'll get out."

"They're not going to hit $150 again."

I could see her thinking that I was pretty good at this stock market stuff, and maybe it would be worth following my advice.

"What did you pay for them, anyway?"

"Nothing."

"Right, so you make a profit anyway."

"Yes, but they were $152. I just don't want to settle for less."

If I remember right, I convinced her to sell half of them. I hope she did. The share price kept going down all the way to single figures.

That's greed, and that's the second emotion that really ruins traders. (Plus, what she was doing was 'anchoring', which we will get to later and which is another thing that can really mess with your mind.) Greed can make you double up a position when your risk management rules are telling you that you're already running enough risk there. Greed can make you double down on a losing trade, lying to yourself that it's going to go back up. Greed can make you refuse to implement a stop- loss (which is why you should always enter a stop-limit order at the same time you make your initial trade).

To get back to charting, technical analysis can show you when other people are being greedy. Remember the parabolic rise? That's people getting greedy. It can show you when other people are getting fearful. Many breakdowns happen because people get scared as soon as they see their shares fall, and scramble to sell - and all the while the price is going down. Your edge is that if you can read the charts right, and stay unaffected by market panics, you can make money out of your trades.

So to be a successful trader, you need to neutralize fear and greed. There are several ways to do this.
- Zen: train yourself not to feel fear and greed.
- Discipline: feel fear and greed but then follow your trading system.

- Self-analysis: work out why you feel what you do about the market.

But in the end, you have to neutralize these emotions. That's what this chapter is about.

How to Get in The Mindset of a Successful Trader

Fear is a natural reaction. So is greed.

- You're crossing the street and a truck comes careering towards you. Fear says, "get out of the way!" And fear is right.

- You go out to a restaurant and just the wonderful aromas coming out of the kitchen make you feel hungry. Greed says, "Order *all* the dim sum!" Greed is right!

But these reactions are not necessarily good ones on the stock market. Let's do some thinking through them, and you need to do the thinking before you start trading, because once you're in the middle of the market, you're not going to have the time to think.

You have a losing trade. You've started with $1,000. You lose $25 or $50. What are you afraid of?

- "My first trade is a losing one; that shows I have no chance of ever winning." Hey, remember we looked at how your profit reflects the *profit potential* of each trade, multiplied by the *probability* of that trade being correct? You will *inevitably* lose some of your trades. It's a bummer that it's this one, but hey.

- "I was dumb to make that trade." No, you had good reasons to do it (well, I hope you did), but the stock market just moved the other way.

- "I'll lose all my money!" At $50 risk at a time, assuming you always use a stop-loss and you lose every trade and your stop-loss comes into play, you have to make 20 losing trades without winning a single one before you lose all your money. With only a $25 risk, you'd have to make 40 losing trades. This is what finance theorists call the risk of ruin - and this is why you have stop-losses.

There's another time people get scared. That's before they make their first trade. They sit on their hands. This would be right if the market is trendless, but otherwise, once you've identified a good trade, you need to make it.

- "I'm scared to make this trade." Have you looked at the chart? Is the signal clear? Did you get confirmation from another indicator? Have you identified your profit potential and your stop-loss? Is the money you're putting in less than 5% of your portfolio? So what do you have to be afraid of? Do it.
- "If I lose this trade, I'll lose my mojo." We already went through this.
- "But now it's for real." Er, yes, it is. Just remind yourself about the first time you did something you enjoy that felt a bit dangerous at the time - rock-climbing, surfing, playing a saxophone solo, whatever. For that matter, standing up and learning to walk!

Overcoming greed is actually easier because a lot of the time, your stop-losses will do it for you. If you set a trailing stop-loss for every trade, it will signal you when the price momentum has stalled and it's time to jump ship. Just obey the system. But you might also want to think:

- Do I need every single penny? If a stock goes from $408 to $525, but I'm only onboard from $415 to $501, does it matter? Or if I didn't get out at $525, and now it's $499 and my stop-loss is activated? I'm still making a lot of money. Not getting greedy is just about having *enough* on your plate.
- It's easier to make money when the move has momentum behind it. That means taking your profits out of the middle of a big trend is less risky than the profits at either end. Maybe not such a big profit, but a lot more bankable.

- There are thousands of stocks on the market. You'll do hundreds of trades, maybe thousands. This one doesn't have to make your fortune all on its own.

Now I will confess that when I'm on eBay and the minutes are ticking down on the auction for something I really want, my palms get sweaty and my heart beats a bit faster. But that's in my personal life. When I'm trading, I make my orders and that's it. So yes, you can *learn* to change your responses, and to take greed and fear out of the equation.

By the way, if you wanted to trade stocks because you think the stock market is exciting... please, don't. Using real money trades to prop up your ego or get an adrenaline rush is dumb. Take up an extreme sport instead; it's cheaper.

How Does Bias Affect Trading?

There are several kinds of biases that affect us when we make decisions. For instance, if as an investor I buy a stock, then a few weeks later I read that some famous investor bought into it or that Goldman Sachs issued a buy recommendation, really I ought to be asking, "Why did they do that? What are they expecting? Do they see the same value that I do, or is there something I missed?" Instead, I go, "Oh look, I made a good decision; other people are doing the same."

That's an example of *confirmation bias* - we notice and value information that confirms our existing beliefs. Sometimes we go a step further and indulge in *motivated reasoning*, which was described by Ted Seides in his book *Capital Allocators* as "confirmation bias on steroids". When we do this, we use our bias to argue against or discredit information that doesn't fit our views. The problem is, sometimes that information is right and we're wrong.

Commit yourself to look at and consider opposite views. When you're looking for confirmation of a trading idea in your second indicator, be tough - don't treat it as 'compliance', just ticking the box, but really have a good look and think about whether it really backs up the signal you think you've found. When you hear talk about a different way of looking for trades, or using different indicators, don't switch off and say 'That's not my way' - listen, question, think. It might still not be for you - but keep an open mind.

Representative bias is rather similar to confirmation bias. If you go to the Kentucky Derby twice, and both times you get the winner because you bet on a horse with a name beginning with B, does this mean the same strategy will work next time? But often, traders are inclined to copy trades that have been successful without thinking about *why* those trades were successful. So be careful not to get into this kind of lazy thinking; work out what you did right and *why* it worked.

Tribe identification can be a kind of bias that you don't even notice. You might say, "I'm a value investor", or "I'm a day trader." That ought to just be a description of your usual strategy, and perhaps it goes a bit deeper, if you've put some work into examining the philosophy of investing. But if it means you're trying to fit in with some idea of "being a day trader", particularly if you're part of a crowd on Reddit or Facebook and you're doing stuff that they do, because they do it - that's a bias. So is just blindly trusting gurus, whether they are called George Soros, William Eckhardt, Curtis Faith, Warren Buffett... or even A.Z Penn!

And then we have *hindsight bias* which is really a devil to deal with. Hindsight is always 20:20 vision, as they say; if a trade went wrong, it was the fault of the market, and if it went right, it was you being a trading genius. Keeping a detailed diary of *why* you traded as well as your trading records in cold hard cash is really important, both as a tool of education, and in keeping you clear of hindsight bias.

By the way, thinking in probabilities helps keep bias at bay. That's why I've stressed, all the way through the book, that you should have thought through the probability of a trade going the right way, the profit potential, *and* the risk that you are running.

If you make several losing trades, but all of them had a 70% chance of working out, and there's a 4:1 ratio between the profit potential and the risk - then you've only lost 4% of your total portfolio, you are doing things right. You had a streak of bad luck. Anybody can have a streak of bad luck. (In case you wondered how the 4% was calculated, it's $1,000/$50 x 20%).

On the other hand, if you tried to make the same trade you did last week, a stock that went from $40 to $50 and fell back to $40 so you're buying it again, without looking at whether the trendline has changed, what the moving averages are doing, whether the profit potential is still the same, and what the probability is this time around - you're doing things wrong, even if it works.

In the long term, discipline will win. In the short term, try to stay unbiased, and free from fear and greed.

7 Tips to Avoid Emotional Trading

1. Have good strong trading rules. Never take a trade that doesn't have the required profit/loss ratio. Put your stop-loss in place when you enter the trade. Know how long you are prepared to give a trade to work. Never bet the bank. Have the whole trade planned before you execute it.
2. Have patience. Wait for the right trade. There are 2,400 stocks on NYSE, 3,300 on Nasdaq, 832 on Euronext Paris, 2,483 on London, and that's before we talk about markets like Tokyo or the Australian or Canadian exchanges, currency trading, commodities, treasuries, corporate bonds, munis, or other instruments you could trade. There are enough trades out there in the world - you don't have to take a lousy one just because you haven't seen anything good today. Take a break instead.

3. Look after your personal life. If you have family, remember to spend time with them and not glued to the screen all the time. Participate in group activities and keep yourself physically active - do a sport, go out hiking with friends, whatever. Good traders do have addictive, obsessive personalities, so make sure that you don't let that side of you take over your entire life.

4. Plenty of traders like to be macho, but that's so last century. Look after your mind by doing breathing exercises, yoga, Tai-Chi, meditation or some similar calming and focusing exercise. It will help you keep your mind open and free from distractions, which is exactly what you need to spot trading patterns. Hey, there's even an app for all these!

5. Don't rationalize your losses ("it would have worked except that this happened"). Don't get angry. Don't think that losing means you're a bad trader; losing is part of the trader's life. Losing is not a judgment on you; your business plan accepts that you will have times when the market turns against you. You are not a fool for making that trade, it had the right ratios but the probabilities just didn't work out this time. You lost. Put it behind you. Get on with the rest of your life.

6. If you're feeling ill, or if you have a hangover, or if something else is on your mind (a break-up, an ill elderly parent or child, your tax return needs to be done) - don't trade. You will not be able to concentrate properly, and if you make bad trades while you are in this state, it's going to make things worse.

7. With any one trade, remember how much of your money is *not* in this trade. How much of your money is *not* at risk. Even if it sounds like a lot of money, remember that according to your trading rules, it's a tiny percentage of your total. Your lifestyle, your house, your entire net worth, is not at risk on this single trade.

And a bonus tip: FOMO is your enemy. Do not ever, ever let it get a hold of you. Fear Of Missing Out is not a valid reason to make a trade. It might be a valid reason to climb Kilimanjaro, visit Las Vegas, or do a parachute jump, but it's not a reason to trade.

How to Control Emotions While Trading

I'd like to quote a really successful trader, Victor Sperandeo, or 'Trader Vic'. In *Methods of a Wall Street Master*, he says: "When you make a trading decision, you should feel absolutely confident that you are right, but you must also recognize that the market can prove you wrong."

It's not easy. But remember that you are playing *probabilities*. You are making an educated and properly thought-through speculation, but things can happen that are outside your control. You cannot possibly know 100% of what's going on or predict 100% of the price movement, but if you know 80%, that's enough to be confident that you're making a good decision. But if the other 20% turns out to be different from what you expected, be flexible enough to change.

(A builder friend told me the way he thinks when he's looking for a renovation project. "I take a good look. Roof's good. Floor's good. No cracks in the walls. What needs doing? New electrics, new boiler, redecoration. Then I allow 20% for the fact that something's always going to go wrong." That could be the rotten floorboards that he couldn't see because they were hidden under a carpet, or the fact that the old wallpaper won't come off without wrecking the finish. That's not dissimilar to how traders think.)

Remember that every trade *is just one trade*. In your trading plan (which we talk about in Chapter 11), you actually expect a certain number of trades to fail. And you have an explicit rule against betting the bank. And you use stop-losses to get out of failing trades before they lose you too much money. So how bad is a single trade? It's an annoyance, but it isn't a wipe-out.

To get the emotion out of your system. Close the trade, then do whatever makes you feel better. For one trader I knew, he said throwing his telephone at the wall. He stopped doing that when smartphones got too expensive. Another trader I asked said, "Yeah, if I lose, I shout '**** you!!!!' at the screen. I know it's not logical and the market can't hear me, but it gets it out of my system."

Or you may not feel much emotion at all, in which case, close the trade, and get on looking for a better one right away.

Keep meticulous records - and a diary

You need to keep good records if you're a trader. First of all, at some point, the tax authorities are going to get interested in what you've been up to. Secondly, you need to be absolutely clear on your own risk position at all times.

But as well as just keeping your trading records, keep a trading diary. You should include the following sorts of information in it;

- How did you feel today? Tired, had a cold, felt great, a bit low on energy? Was there anything in particular on your mind?
- What trades did you look at and decide not to do? Why? (And to be a perfectionist, come back and see whether you were right to stay out, and note the details.)
- With the trades you committed to, what made you decide to do so? Did you have any niggling doubts or were you 100% certain? Did you get worried about them at any point? Were there any problems with execution?
- Did you get stopped out of any trades?
- Did you scale into any trades? Were you right?
- What was the market overall doing that day?
- What were the big headline items in the papers?

Looking back at that diary over a month can give you some good information. You traded a lot more shorts when you had a toothache, for instance. You missed some good head-and-shoulders trades, but you were right to turn down the channel trades. That tells you that you've got a good feel for head- and-shoulders, maybe do a little more work on those patterns and get more confident with them. You may find out you do better in a downtrend than you do in an uptrend.

As for the headlines - I find that sometimes 'Super Bowl = Kansas City Chiefs win' or 'Twitter suspends Donald Trump's Account' mean I can zero in on a day much more easily than if I just had the date. And sometimes ('Gulf War starts' or 'Brexit Referendum') the headlines will be one of the things that affected the markets.

I am glad I kept a diary because I had a quite aggressive medication for a bug that I'd caught for a few weeks a while back. After a week of trading, I looked at my diary. My trades were way out of line. I had one big winner and a whole load of bad trades, and a couple of bad trades where I had forgotten to put a stop-loss. I actually made money for the week, but it was clear that the medication had fogged my mind up. Until I finished the course of medication, I stayed away from the market. Without my diary, I might have kept trading - and I might not have been so lucky with the next couple of weeks.

Finally, analyze all your trades, particularly losing ones. Why did a trade go wrong? Did you miss something that you should have noticed? Perhaps you didn't check the volume indicators to confirm the price pattern, for instance. Did you break one of your trading rules? Did you set your stop-loss wrong? Was your order badly executed because you were trading an illiquid stock?

Analyzing your losing trades should teach you to trade better. It should also stop you feeling aggrieved or aggressive or depressed about losing trades - you know why you lost, so that's a mistake you're aware of and can learn from. And analyzing your wins? The same - why did it work? Did you take full advantage of the price movement? How can you make it easier to spot situations like that in the future?

Sticking to it

The real differences between someone who is going to win at trading and someone who is going to lose are very simple. The winner

1. Has a plan,
2. Puts the plan into effect,
3. Sticks to the plan,
4. and keeps going.

That's it. As you know if you've ever made New Year's Resolutions like "I will go to the gym," "I will not eat more than 1600 calories a day," "I will practice my guitar playing" ... making the resolution is the easy bit. Sticking with it is the hard part.

Don't just learn the stuff in this book and make one or two trades. Have a plan for how many trades you're going to make, at what risk/reward level, with how much money. Don't just paper trade forever; when you understand what you're doing, make real trades with real money. And then keep going.

You might still fail. But if you don't do these four basic things, you have a 100% probability of failure. If you do them... you might actually succeed.

Chapter 9 Quiz

A slightly different form this time. Get a piece of paper and write down your answers.

1. How well do you handle fear? Think of some situations in the past when you've been afraid.

2. What New Year's Resolutions have you made and broken, or made and kept? Have you successfully changed a habit, like giving up smoking?

3. Do you make a lot of plans that you don't carry out? When was the last time you achieved something you had planned for a while?

4. Are you good at budgeting, doing things on time, getting your taxes filed? If not, what kind of difficulties are stopping you from being better?

5. Do you care more about being a success, or about other people seeing that you're a success? Why?

Have a good think about the answers. You may learn more than you expect, and the information could make you a much better trader.

10

Chapter 10: Ten Top Tips for Each Aspect of Trading

Ten Top Tips for Successful Technical Trading

1. Be selective. Only use indicators and patterns that you are really familiar with and used to using. Paper trade till you narrow down the indicators that work with you, and stick with them. Know what kind of stocks or indices you want to trade, and stick to them. If you want to introduce other markets or techniques, do the work, paper trade on them first, make sure you don't have too broad a focus.

2. Watch out for 'real world' events. Always know when Fed decisions, earnings releases, payroll numbers are coming out. If you think they will move the market, you can choose to go flat (close all your trades).

3. Don't rely on the naked eye. Just looking at the price chart is not TA. To do things properly, you need to know the patterns, you need to use the indicators, you need to draw trendlines. And that leads on to...

4. Always identify your profit and stop-loss levels and make sure the odds are stacked in your favor. Traders don't buy a stock "because it's going up" or "because it *will* go up", they buy a stock because they've identified a price point that it has a certain probability of achieving according to the patterns and trends they've identified. Plan every trade properly.

5. Protect your downside. "Scared money never wins" so never place a trade that could lose you more than 10% of your total capital. Use trailing stop-losses to protect winning positions that you've decided to let run. Use tight stop-losses on trades that could go against you.

6. Run your profits. Never close off a trade because it's in the money. If the trends are intact, then keep running your profits (and keep looking, never just trade and forget it). A good trader can make money with only a 40% win rate if all the winning trades return high profits. Use a trailing stop-loss to protect yourself, and if the risk gets high, take some money off the table, but run your profits.

7. Backtest your strategies, patterns, indicators, or at least test them by paper-trading for a while. Don't go straight into the market and trade. You can also refine your strategies and indicators - making quite small changes can have a big impact on the outturn.

8. Look at multiple time frames before you trade, so that you can identify the long term trend as well as the short term opportunity.

9. Have discipline. If your strategy is "buy every time the 50-day moving average crosses the 200 day, as long as the momentum indicator looks good", then do it every time. If you have a stop-loss, always use it. Don't overrule trades that fit your strategy because you have a 'feeling' about them.

10. Keep a journal. You can look back and see *why* you traded as well as what you traded and the outcome of the trade. Are you learning from your mistakes? Equally important - are you learning from your successes?

Bonus tip - keep learning, and keep refining your techniques. Sometimes markets change a little, and just tweaking your strategy can increase your profits. Sometimes a new indicator has advantages over the old version. Sometimes you'll read a book by one of the great traders and almost everything in it will be stuff you know, but you'll just get one piece of information that's new and that really makes a difference.

Ten Top Tips for Working with Indicators

1. Learn to recognize patterns. If that means printing out price charts and drawing all over them with a Sharpie - fine! Use a ruler and two different colored pencils. It's a bit subjective, so check up later whether your patterns worked out. If you just can't 'see' a particular pattern, concentrate on ones you can spot easily and that work for you.

2. Use trendlines, support and resistance. Again, if it means drawing on bits of paper, go ahead and do it; it will be worth it. These lines will tell you how much potential profit can be made, where to put your stop-loss, even - well ahead of time - where you might want to re-enter the trade.

3. Back-test or paper trade. Do this before you start trading, and do it if you ever want to introduce a new indicator or pattern, or try a different style of trading. Now, you may not be the kind of quantitative rocket scientist who's going to invent new indicators and tweaks and backtest them over 20 years of data, fine. But if you're not, at least spend a few weeks doing honest practice paper trading and making sure your new whatever-it-is works.

4. Don't run before you can walk. For instance, learn to read a candlestick chart, preferably by looking at a stock you know. Talk yourself through what's happening in each candlestick. Then what happened the next day. Then the next. Now look for the patterns - hanging man or shooting star or hammer. See where they worked and where they didn't. Get a feel for the charts. *After* that, you can start adding complexity.

5. Make sure that you know which indicators can actually give signals, and which are only for confirmation. If you expect the volume bar to tell you whether to buy or sell, you're never going to make money. Get a feeling for which confirmation indicators work best with the kind of signals you're using.

6. Use convergence and divergence. Often, an indicator's best signal is the fact that it's running *against* the price trend (divergence). Even just looking at volume - if the volume traded is falling but the price is still going up, there can't be many buyers left in the market. The day the last buyer has filled his or her boots, the price is going to look exposed.

7. Don't buy someone else's system. You're a human being and that means you are unique. If you make it as a trader, that uniqueness is your edge. Pick your own rules and your own indicators. If you like to make lots of small trades, don't go for a system built on following really big medium term trends, because it's never going to feel right.

8. Remember that no indicator will ever be right 100% of the time. This is where your trading record is important, because your % of winning trades and your % return with any indicator will dictate whether it's working for you or not. If it's only right half the time, but when it does it doubles your money, and when it doesn't, you're stopped out at a tiny loss, then it's worth using!

9. You don't need to understand how an indicator works (mathematically speaking) to be able to use it. I drive. I have no idea how my car works. I couldn't repair it myself, but I know how to drive it and that's enough for me. On the other hand, if I didn't know how the steering wheel worked, you're right; I'd be in trouble. If you have an indicator that you just can't get to work for you, then junk it.

10. Indicators come and go. Sometimes everyone wants to trade a new indicator and MACD is yesterday's news. But a bit like fashion, eventually, what goes around comes around.

Bonus tip: There is no secret 100% reliable indicator that will double your money every month with a single trade. Indicators like this exist only in the realm of marketing, and they are there to make someone else money - not you.

Ten Top Tips for Making Your Trades

1. Make sure you have a trading system and trading rules. These can be simple. In fact, it's best if they are as simple as you can make them. What signals do you trade on? What confirmations do you use? How much risk will you take with each position? How tight a stop-loss will you use? Write them down and make sure you can see them.

2. Get an online broker who is responsive and fast. Do some proper research and look at user reviews before you decide which to use. I have one broker who gets good prices but regularly takes fifteen minutes to fill an order; I only use it for investment, not for trading. It helps if your broker allows you to use stop-limit orders so you can set trades up to run automatically if the price hits your targets.

3. Many brokers have a demo system, so you can practice using the system to enter orders without putting your money at risk. It's worth using it extensively to make sure you understand the functionalities and any quirks it may have. If there's no demo system, it's best to start with a few small, simple trades rather than go wading in with a big and complicated set of orders.

4. Use limit orders to ensure you don't get put into a trade at the wrong price. If your trade had a profit expectation of $5, but you're put in $1 higher than you expected, you've lost 20% of your profit.

5. I've said this before, and I'm saying it again: ALWAYS set a stop-loss order at the same time you make your trade.

6. Don't trade stocks that are illiquid (have a low volume of trade), don't trade OTC stocks, don't trade stocks that have a widespread (i.e., the difference between the price you can buy at and the price you can sell at will take a bit of bite out of your capital). If you can't afford to trade round lots (100 shares), you may find it useful to use a broker that offers fractional trading.

7. Use a no-commission broker and make sure they don't have hidden charges. This will reduce the frictional cost on your trades.

8. Always check you have the right security and the right amount of shares. Double-check that it comes out at the amount of money you expected. Sometimes there will be two classes of stock for one company, or 'fat finger' has you getting quoted for 10,000 shares instead of 1,000, so always double-check before you confirm the order. (Don't ask me how I know this.)

9. Ensure your broker is regulated by your country's financial regulator. Check it out and make sure your money is secure with it. There are many sharks around - some very shady companies indeed, some of which make a habit of suddenly disappearing without a trace - particularly when it comes to non-stock assets like forex and commodities.

10. Make sure you have a laptop as well as your main computer, and a mobile (or a broker that uses a mobile app). If your main computer crashes, or your broadband provider has an outage, you're not going to lose your trading access or be stuck in a trade you wanted to get out of.

Bonus tip: choose a broker that doesn't have an account closure fee (or has a very low one). If you just can't get on with their order entry system, or if their service levels start to fall, you can make a quick exit without paying through the nose for it.

Ten Top Tips for Being Aware of Disruptors

The stock market *usually* follows its regular course depending on the laws of supply and demand, and the psychological probabilities of human behavior. But there are a few things you need to be aware of that can disrupt the usual price evolution of a stock and that can affect a market in ways you were not expecting. So watch out for these items on the financial calendar - and generally.

1. Corporate earnings releases. You *might* decide to trade the release because you have certain expectations - but you *need* to be aware that the results will be coming out on a particular day. If you're trading a stock, make sure you know the next results date.

2. Ex-dividend dates. When a stock pays a dividend, there is a particular date on which the shares go from trading *with* the right to receive that dividend, to trading *without* the right to receive it. The share price normally adjusts by the amount of the dividend. Again, be aware of the date!

3. Economic stats such as non-farm payroll figures, housing starts, and so on. This is one time that reading the financial pages pays off - because normally, they're not a big deal, but occasionally, the market is getting a bit worried about, say, housing starts, and if the number is the wrong one, the market can be spooked. So it pays to know if there's a particular focus on any one statistic.

4. Central bank announcements are always important, whether that's the regular Federal Reserve announcements, monthly Bank of England meetings, European Central Bank, or Bank of Japan - whichever of these markets you're trading. If you're trading ETFs, then you need to keep an eye out, as though individual stocks may be less affected, the broad index is likely to move.

5. Keep an eye on stock splits. Sometimes, chart packages fail to update, and it looks like the stock halved overnight - in fact, there's just twice as much stock in issue, and the system *should* eventually get round to showing it.

6. One wise trader once said the best way to trade the market is to look at the cover of all the magazines, and go short whatever's on the front. *Time* and *Newsweek* and *The Week* are all showing cryptocurrency headlines? Time to give up on Bitcoin! While that's not really a trading strategy, there's a grain of truth in it - avoid sectors that are being hyped.

7. Elections can move markets. However, they don't always move markets in the way all the experts say they will. Watch out for stocks that have a political sensitivity, though - for instance, with the increasing tensions between the US and China; I gave up trading Taiwan Semiconductor. I have better things to do than keep an eye on what's happening with US-Taiwan-China relations.

8. Personally, the moment I hear that a stock is the subject of takeover rumors, I stop trading it. The trouble is that technical trading works when 'all other things are equal', but if a bid comes way above the current share price, all trades are off. And if the bid doesn't come, that could see the share price tank. Some traders love this situation and believe the charts will show them what's going on, but my gut feeling? There are too many ways I can lose.

9. Okay, a slightly different kind of disruption. The week that stocks rallied after the big Coronavirus crash, Robinhood had an outage. If you only used that broker to trade, you couldn't take advantage of the bounce. If, on the other hand, you had a second account ready with, say, Fidelity, and enough funds in that account, you'd still have been able to trade. It's worth having two brokers just in case.

10. And as I mentioned in the tips for placing trades - make sure your own kit has redundancy. That is, if one computer or device goes down, you have another. If your cable, broadband and Starbucks Wi-Fi goes down, you have mobile data access.

Bonus tip: if you have a cat, do not leave your computer and keyboard unattended even for a moment in a room to which the cat currently has access. Don't ask me why. Just don't. A friend tells me the same is true for toddlers.

Chapter 10 Quiz

Ten top questions. There are no right answers, but there's time for a bit of self-reflection.

1. Why do you want to make money as a trader, instead of doing a job, writing a novel, becoming an entrepreneur, or investing long term?

2. What do you think is likely to be your worst fault as a trader?

3. What do you think you'll enjoy most about trading?

4. How much time are you planning to invest in your trading?

5. What markets do you want to trade? Why? (OK, I know it's cheating to have two questions.)

6. Have you already selected a broker or opened your brokerage account? If not, why not?

7. How will you make sure you're aware of disruptors?

8. How will you record your ideas and your trades?

9. What is your definition of success as a trader?

10. Exactly how much money could your cat cost you, and is it worth it?

I would just like to mention before we go onto the final chapter on Designing Your Trading Stategy, if you are finding this book useful so far – it would mean everything to me if you could spare just a few seconds and <u>write a brief review on Amazon</u> on how this book is helping you so far.

11

Chapter 11: Designing Your Trading Strategy

However good your recognition of patterns and your analysis of what's going to happen to the share price, you need to be able to execute trades successfully if you're going to make money. And you'll also need a trading strategy - an overall idea of how much risk you're taking, how much profit you ought to make for that level of risk, how many trades you need at what level of profitability and the probability to make your desired return.

It's basically a business plan. You'd expect anyone who's starting up a sandwich shop to have a good idea of how many sandwiches they're going to sell, how they're going to price them, what wastage they'll be left with, what their staff and rent costs are, and what profit they'll make. But a lot of traders get started without a business plan. They only have a few ingredients - hope, a bit of charting ability, and some money - and frankly, being a successful trader with those ingredients is like trying to make a sandwich with just ketchup, butter and mayo!

So in this chapter, let's talk about how you're going to set yourself up. What kind of charts you're going to look at, what kind of trades you want to do, the costs of doing business (yes, you'll have costs!), and how to work out your objectives.

Objective - turning $1,000 into $10,000

That sounds like a lot, but of course, that depends on how long you take to get there. If you left $1,000 in the bank at a 1% interest rate, you'd get there... in over 150 years. On the other hand, if you wanted to get to $10,000 in three months, you'd need to make a return of 23.3% on your money every week. That's not a lot, is it?

Okay, that *is* a lot, given the average return on the stock market is around 8% a *year*. But if you think about it, trying to make $1,000 into $1,233 in a week sounds less of a challenge than $1,000 into $10,000, doesn't it? (You might also like to know that Tony Sperandeo, in September 1982, grossed $880,000 on trading capital of $1 million - an 88% return in one month. He did have quite a few years of experience as a trader behind him at that point, though.)

You probably will take a bit longer than a few months to turn your initial $1,000 stake into $10,000. It might take you a year to get there. Meanwhile, if you'd left your money in the bank, you'd have $1,010 - ten bucks more than you started with. So okay, this is certainly an objective that's worthwhile, and that rewards the (controlled) risks you're going to take.

So the next thing is to think about your risk appetite. Because supposed to get from $1,000 to $10,000 over a year, you'd need to make around $750 a month ($750 x 12 = $9,000).

You could make that up in different ways:

1. With ten trades, of which only two win, but they make $375 each because you chose really strong breakouts (and tight stop-losses on the other trades), or
2. With ten trades of which fifty percent closed out at a small loss, and the other half made a bit more than $150 each.

Or, of course, any number of other combinations. For the sake of simplicity, by the way, I assumed you split your money into $100 stakes and only make one trade per stake. You might easily have traded more often than that. And in situation (1), with those two really strong breakouts, you probably should have scaled in on them, using what you had left from the losing positions to increase your winnings if the chart pattern showed the breakout was going to form a continuing uptrend.

Now that's just an example. You are going to have to think about how long you want to work to get there, how much time you have to give it every week, how often you're aiming to trade. But you'll be putting the numbers together that way - looking at how many trades you make, how many you win, what's your average win and average loss. That's basically your business plan.

But however great your risk appetite, **don't ever, ever bet the bank**. Divide your stake into at least ten lots of $100 each - some active traders work with an even more restrictive regime and never trade more than 5% of their money on a single trade. (However, they are willing to scale in - that is, if a trade is already profitable and the trend appears established enough to deliver a further profit, they might increase that stake, but only to a limited extent.)

Win rate/profit potential

Your success as a trader depends on two things; the first is your win rate (the number of winning trades as a percentage of all trades), and the second is the average amount you win (less the average amount you lose). That's how some people make money playing blackjack - they count the cards, work out the percentages, play a small amount for every losing hand and when they think the cards are coming out in their favor, make a much bigger bet. So they lose 90% of the time but make it all back in a couple of hands - at least, they do until the casino gets wise to it, and then it's time to call it a night.

Let's look at the win rate first. Technical trader Michael Masters claimed a 70% win rate, according to Jack Schrager in *Market Wizards*. No doubt you're hoping to claim that kind of a win rate. It would be easy to make money if you lose less than a third of the time, right?

But Vic Sperandeo, not a purely technical trader by any means, claimed that his win rate was only 40-50% - sometimes, he lost more often than he made money on a trade. And yet, he was regarded as one of the real Wall Street genius traders.

So although you need to know your win/loss ratio, that's only the first half of the equation.

Let's suppose your win rate is only 40%. You need to make sure that your wins make a lot more money than your losing trades lose. This is where your risk reduction rules come in. There are a number of factors here;

1. How much capital you place on any one trade,
2. The profit potential of a trade,
3. The loss potential of a trade.

Let's talk about (2) and (3) and how they relate to each other. I hope you noticed that when I talked about patterns, I often gave you the way to work out your profit potential.

It's systematic - draw those resistance and support lines, measure the depth of your triangles, count on the share price going exactly where the chart says it will. 'Hope' is not a word you're allowed to use - quantify the expected profit using the chart.

Now let's look where you need to place your stop-loss. Again you're going to do that by looking at the chart. And so now you have the expected share price, let's say, of a successful breakout, at $325, and if the breakout doesn't happen, you've placed your stop-loss just below the support line, at $285. You can buy the shares at $298.

So now you can work out your risk/reward ratio. This is where technical analysis really helps you. If you are a fundamental, long term investor, you *do not know* your risk/reward ratio; you can guess it, you can reduce risk by, for instance, buying established companies, which don't have too much debt and are unlikely to face major product liability lawsuits, but you can't quantify it. As a technical analyst, you can. You can measure the expected profit and the potential loss for every single pattern.

So for this trade: expected profit is $325 - $298 = $27, and the potential loss is $298 - $285 =$13. Your profit is twice as large as the loss, a 2:1 ratio. If you have a high win rate, you can be very profitable. But if you have a lower win rate, you need to be more demanding; the way Vic Sperandeo made his money was with a low win rate but an expected upside of 4 or 5 times the risk.

Remember that as a trader you need to think of the return on risk, not the return on capital. You may be buying $10,000 worth of stock, but if you have a stop-loss, that means you will sell out at $9,500, then you only have $500 of risk.

One thing is sure, though; if your risk-reward ratio is 1:1, that is, you're willing to lose a dollar for every dollar of potential profit, you are really unlikely to make a living trading! You would be surprised how many traders start off doing 1:1 trades, or even worse - usually because they are not actually working out the risk/reward ratio on their trades.

But how do I know my win rate?

Aha. You have guessed the problem.

Well, let's think of it this way. First of all, you have an idea, most likely, of whether you want to look for a few potentially highly profitable trades, or whether you want to be pretty continuously making small profits and turning your trades around. And you can also look at the probability of the types of trade you do - some patterns are more reliable, others have bigger breakouts but are likely to work out less often.

You still don't *know* your win rate. And that's why I'm going to suggest you should paper trade for a month first. I know, you want to get into the market and make your money... you're afraid of missing a profitable trade and a big uptrend... Remember, the trend is your friend, though, and FOMO is your enemy. Have patience and do your paper trading, find out your strengths and weaknesses, and most importantly, your risk/reward ratio. Then you've got a plan that, hopefully, is robust enough to withstand the worst the market can throw at it.

Changing the scale of your trades

Suppose you do exactly as we suggested and you turn your $1,000 into exactly $10,000. Will you still be making $100 trades?

I hope not. Because by the time you have a decent size portfolio of say, $100,000, you're going to be frazzled. There just won't be enough trades in the marketplace for you to make a return, and you'll be back to making the kind of money that passive buy-and-hold investors make. A mere 8% a year? Phooey!

Almost every successful trader changes the scale of their trades according to two factors;

1. The size of their trading portfolio,
2. Their form.

Obviously, by the time you've got a $10,000 portfolio, you should be placing $500 or $1,000 trades (depending on whether you want to move to the 10ths or 20ths of the portfolio). Scale up again every time your portfolio size doubles up. With a portfolio of nearly $2,000 you can make trades of $200, not just $100, and your risk profile per trade hasn't changed.

You should also change the scale of your trades according to your recent form. In particular, if you're making a typical number of losing trades, reduce your trade size. Randy Mackay, a hugely successful trader in the currency markets, was very careful about risk management. If you're losing, he always said, drop your size from 5-10% to 4% of your capital, or even 2% - make tiny trades till you get a winning streak again.

One trader quoted in Jack Schwager's *The New Market Wizards* even says that if he has three losing trades in a row, he calls "time out" and paper trades for a while till he feels his trading instincts are back on form.

He's actively engaging in risk reduction - minimizing the number of poor trades he's likely to make and maximizing the good ones. Sure, he's not making money while he paper trades, but he's not losing money, either.

So this is another element of your risk reduction plan. Think about what rules you want to put in place here. Above all, resist the temptation to make bigger trades when you have lost money, in the hope that you'll win it back. That's not how things work. Remember that you should always cut your losses and run your winnings - scale up your winners that are running strongly in a good trend, and chop your losers. The same applies to your form; trade a bit more money (don't get stupid!) when you're on winning form, and when you're doing poorly, stop yourself losing more money by trimming your trade size back.

Personal taste is important

There is no one size fits all rule. You may want to be able to trade full time within the next year. Or you may want to get started in a much gentler way, or to concentrate on longer term trades and only do maybe one or two trades a month. You may decide that you prefer fundamental analysis and investing in value stocks, but use what you've learned in this book to choose the best entry points and spot when the charts are warning you there may be trouble ahead. You won't make such fat returns, but if that's your style, you can still improve your investment.

Introspection pays dividends. Think about what you really want to do. Think about your strengths and weaknesses, think about how much time you have, think about your motivation. That should all feed into your trading plan.

What kind of trades?

While there are certain things that all good traders have in common, most will agree that to be a great trader, you need to find a way of trading that works for you.

For instance, what's your average holding period? For some traders, it's 3-4 weeks. For some, it's minutes. This might have to do with the hours you can commit to trading, but also, you may prefer to look at longer term charts and try to find major breakouts that can run for some time, and make fewer trades but with larger potential returns. Other traders like to make lots of small profits.

If you have a really mathematical turn of mind, you may want to trade options. If you are more of a visual person, and a lot of technical analysts are, you're probably happier trading the stock.

You may also, if you have a background in economics or you've been a fundamentals-driven investor before with success, find that a hybrid trade is your best trade. That is, you're already getting some ideas from the level of stock valuations or the way central banks are behaving, but while you allow that to suggest the kind of trade you should be looking for, you use TA to pull the trigger.

What kind of indicators?

You may also find certain indicators flag up trades instantly the moment you look at them, while others, no matter how much you try, don't make any sense at all. You should definitely *try* every kind of indicator and trade, but if you fall in love with candlesticks and they give you great, profitable trades with a very low failure rate, then stick with them.

But remember that as well as knowing how to get trading signals, you need to have a confirmation step in your trading rules. So if the candlesticks are giving you a hanging man, check the volume indicators and the moving averages just to make sure you're still happy with the trade.

And now… make your rules.

Making your Trading Rules

This is really important. Sometimes, if you're a successful trader, you'll just get a gut feel, "Hey, this market feels really trembly and on edge and it's overvalued, and I should really go short, because it's going to tip over and crash hard."

You might be right. You might be wrong. But you still don't bet the bank. You still apply your trading rules! That's why it's important to formulate good strong rules. Write them on a postcard, make them into your screensaver, have them on a post-it on top of your monitor, whatever you need to do. Here are mine:

1. Look for strong price signals: channel breakout, head-and-shoulders, good range trades. (I used to include Golden Cross, but it let me down once too often. Maybe I should give it another try, as that was a few years ago.)
2. Always confirm the price signal with another indicator (RSI or volume).
3. If in doubt check a third indicator. If that is not conclusive, don't trade.
4. Ensure the potential profit is at least 2x the stop-loss level, 3x or more if possible.
5. Trade in lots of [5% my portfolio size].
6. Place the stop-loss at the same time as the order.
7. Do not ever, ever break these rules. *The market can stay irrational longer than you can stay solvent.*
8. If you can't find a trade, don't try to make one.

(That bit in italics is a quote from John Maynard Keynes. Whatever you think of him as an economist, he was a genius market trader.)

Your rules could be a bit different. You might be less risk-averse than I am. You might use different indicators and look for different patterns. But they shouldn't be very different - and particularly not Rule 2, Rule 6, and Rule 7. They are the gold standard for traders. They will keep you in the game.

Because the one thing the rules *will* guarantee, if you get them right, is that you can stay in the game. That you will still have money to trade. That you won't lose the lot on one throw of the dice. And that when there is a profit to be made, you'll be there, at the right time, with some money to trade.

A word on being realistic

Many trading books and particularly trading gurus who sell seminars or advice lines will use words guaranteed to get your emotions racing. "Get rich quick," "Make a million," "How I made two million on Nasdaq," "Rags to riches." A lot of people think you'll only be a success as a trader if you are up there with George Soros - multi-billions and big, big calls like the bet he made against the Pound Sterling.

Well, maybe you do want to be a millionaire. But I wrote this book so you can start with $1,000 and have a chance of making a bit more. You may then want to go on and keep growing and growing and growing. You may say, "Okay, that was good, but I want to put some money aside"; one trader I know takes 20% of the winnings off the table at the end of the month and puts them in long term investments that he doesn't need to manage actively, like real estate or investment funds.

Or you may decide that while trading is great, you want to be able to take some time and bike Route 66 on a Harley, play with your kids, renovate an old house, or finish your Ph.D. One of the things a lot of very successful traders say is that they regret not having closer relationships with their children because they were too obsessed with the market.

So if your trading strategy is about just making your financial life a little better, and not about breaking out and becoming a multi-millionaire, *that's fine*. Don't ever feel guilty about it. You need to be disciplined as a trader, but that doesn't mean it has to be the only thing in your life - or that you need to be totally obsessed by it.

Me? When I'm not trading… I actually rather enjoy throwing dart arrows on my dart board. I'm never going to win the World Championship, but it doesn't stop me from having fun trying to get just that little bit more throwing accuracy out of the board!

STOP-LOSSES

Warren Buffett was once asked what were the rules for being a successful investor. He said: "Rule One: Don't lose money. Rule Two: See Rule One."

Chapter 11 Quiz

1. Your money at risk in a single trade is
   a) However much capital you invested
   b) The difference between potential profit and your stop-loss
   c) The difference between your money invested and your stop-loss.

2. Trading profit overall is created by
   a) Your win rate times your profit/loss per trade
   b) Your win rate times the amount you invest in each trade
   c) Being right 100% of the time

3. Who is responsible for making your trading rules?
   a) The Securities and Exchange Commission
   b) The writer of this book
   c) You

4. Which of these things should *not* affect the size of your trades?
   a) Your recent performance
   b) The fact that you really, really like this particular opportunity
   c) The amount of capital you have available

5. Which of these should you know before you execute a trade?
   a. The expected profit
   b. The stop-loss
   c. Both the expected profit and the stop-loss

6. Will you leave a review on Amazon?
   a) Yes, of course!
   b) Yes, I was thinking of doing it now!
   c) I'll think about it after I've finished reading.

Leave a 1-Click Review!

I would be incredible thankful if you could take just 60 seconds to write a brief review on Amazon, even if it's just a few sentences!

Customer reviews

⭐⭐⭐⭐⭐ 5 out of 5

4 global ratings

5 star		100%
4 star		0%
3 star		0%
2 star		0%
1 star		0%

˅ How are ratings calculated?

Amazon.com readers
http://www.amazon.com/review/
create-review?&asin=B0C1J7PB9Q

Amazon.co.uk readers
http://www.amazon.co.uk/review/
create-review?&asin=B0C1J7PB9Q

Conclusion

In this book, I've given you all the basics of good technical analysis. How to look at charts and spot patterns; how to draw trendlines, support and resistance lines; candlestick patterns; and how to use indicators like volume, stochastics and RSI.

The patterns are not always easy to see, but I hope I have given you enough examples both of the schematic way the patterns *ought* to look, and of real-world situations, that you have a good idea of what you're looking for. And while mathematical indicators like stochastics aren't all that easy to understand, once you start using them alongside other indicators and chart patterns, you'll soon see how they fit in.

But the most important chapters, I think, are those where I talk about psychology and about setting up your system. A good system will almost always beat a good trader without a system. And a system that you've created for yourself, that you understand and that suits your personality as a trader, will always beat anything that you can buy in the market.

I have to emphasize that even though turning $1,000 into $10,000 is a big ask; *you can do it*. Most traders fail for a number of reasons;

- They jump in before they're ready. They don't paper trade first.

- They don't understand how to evaluate the risk and reward ratio of the positions they take.

- They take positions that are far too large. If you do that, it only takes three or four bad trades to wipe you out. If you take limited risks, then even 20 or 40 losing trades will still leave you enough capital to stay in the game.

- They double down on losing positions. With technical trading, if a position is going the wrong way, it's very unlikely that it will reverse direction just to make you money. Instead, you need to concentrate on getting out of the trade as soon as it starts to go wrong, limiting your losses.

- They take tiny profits. If you're not winning a lot more than you're risking, then you only need a couple of losing trades and you're back in the red.

- They don't have a system. They chase reversal patterns one day, and they're following the moving averages the next, then they try Ichimoku, then they try candlesticks, then they try something else. Take time to find out the kind of signals that make sense to you, the patterns that you spot time and time again, and stick to the trades you know how to win.
- They let their emotions rather than their common sense drive their trading.
- After a couple of losing trades, they get despondent and give up.
- They think they don't have to put any work into the job.

These are all things you can do something about. Maybe you've read the book and you said to yourself, "That sounds really great ... but I can't see myself doing it."

Why not? Do you think you're not smart enough? Or do you not know how to work hard? Probably at the back of your head is a little voice saying 'You don't deserve to make money'. (I wonder where that comes from. A schoolteacher who thought you were dumb? Some kid in your class who wanted to rile you? An ex- boss you never got on with? It probably comes from way, way back - and you ought to stop listening to it!)

That's where the psychology comes in. You have to believe in yourself
- you also have to be willing to say, "okay, I got this trade wrong". You have to treat your mind as one of the big assets of your trading business. If you run a big server farm, you'd want to make sure you maintain your equipment, keep the data servers cooled, and protect them from malware and viruses and intrusions. Treat your mind like that - keep it cool and calm, protect yourself from distractions and negative beliefs, and maintain your asset by occasionally reading a new investment book or looking up some new ways to trade.

The 90% of amateur traders who don't make money, or who don't make much money, are the ones who don't treat their brains as an asset. Don't fall into that trap.

Even if you looked at some of the psychology chapter and thought, "whoah, this is all a bit New Age", believe me - you don't need dreamcatchers and sacred crystals, but you do, absolutely, need to have a way of keeping your mind focused and calm.

You'll hear some people say that *no one* makes money out of trading. That is simply not true. You *can* trade using technical analysis and do well. Many traders use these techniques and make good money. You don't hear about all of them; some of them live a quiet life, don't get any publicity, don't want any publicity, but have a nice lifestyle and a good big pension fund thanks to their trading. Some blog or go on Reddit to boast about their best trades - and occasionally whine about their worst ones; you can take what they say with a pinch of salt!

One thing that's changed over the past 20 or 30 years has been the increasing use of computers in trading. Program trading shifts millions or even billions of dollars a day. But guess what? They're often using exactly the same kinds of mathematical patterns that we've looked at through charts and indicators. So if you're trading a breakout, you may well be trading a breakout along with a whole load of Goldman Sachs money or Morgan Stanley money - or hedge fund money.

And through sites like StockCharts, you can get access to huge amounts of data - just the same data that they have.

Add to that the fact that brokers like Robinhood offer free trading on stocks. You used to have to pay out minimum commissions of $40-50 a trade - and that together with the spread means there was significant 'slippage' in your deal. You needed to make over $100 just to cover these costs. Now, if you use an online broker, your costs are absolutely tiny - the spread on big stocks like Amazon is less than a third of 1% and in some cases, even less.

On some sites, like eToro, you can do 'social trading' - following traders with a recent good record. Some people do this in a lazy way, just replicating their trades.

I suggest you take a good look at their trades, as it's a great way to learn. You may learn that one style is definitely the best for you, or that there are some situations you don't feel very happy with, or you may see how not having the right stop-loss loses you stupid amounts of money - but if you go in with the right mindset, you'll learn.

You won't, of course, be starting with a huge amount of capital. But having a lot of capital is no guarantee of success; one joke going around Wall Street apparently is, "How do you make $2m from technical trading? Start with $30m in your hedge fund and just keep going." On the other hand, you'll be managing your risk, as I've shown you - my trading is a good deal more conservative than some hedge fund managers, as I don't use leverage (debt), I don't make big trades, and I have really, really tight stop-losses.

So get yourself started. If you have $1,000 as in our example, put that in as your initial capital. Keep it separate from your other money, and make sure it's money you could afford to lose. If you only have $500, start out with that. You could start with more... but to be honest, start small. When you feel more confident, you can add more capital to the business.

Paper trade for a while. If certain trades don't work out, go back to the relevant chapter and re-read it. Perhaps you misidentified a descending triangle which was actually a symmetrical triangle. Perhaps you didn't look for a confirmation from one of the momentum indicators. Work out why your trade didn't work (and remember that sometimes, they just don't).

Keep a tally of how each kind of trade performs for you - your win rate and your return on the trade. Trade the ones that do well for you and forget the other ones.

And when you're ready - make that first real trade with confidence and optimism.

May all your trades be good ones!

HOW TO GET THE MOST OUT OF THIS BOOK

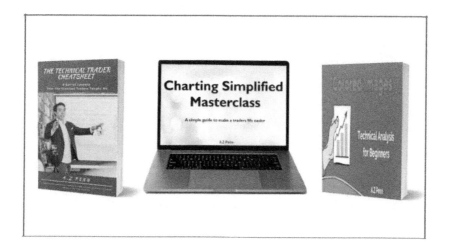

To help you along your trading journey, for this book in particular, I've created a free bonus companion masterclass which includes video analysis of real life stock examples to expand on some of the key topics discussed in this book. I also provide additional resources that will help you get the best possible result.

I highly recommend you sign up now to get the most out of this book. You can do that by visiting the link or scanning the QR code below:

www.az-penn.com

Free bonus #1: **Charting Simplified Masterclass ($67 value)**

In this 5 part video masterclass you'll be discovering various simple and easy to use strategies on making profitable trades. By showing you real life stock examples of a few charting indicators - you will be able to determine whether a stock is worth trading or not.

Free bonus #2: **The Technical Trader Cheatsheet ($12 value)**

In this cheatsheet you will be learning the 9 secret lessons that the greatest technical traders taught me. Believe me, when I started out, I thought I had everything set up to make a million on the stock market; but I was definitely in for a surprise.

Free bonus #3: **Colored Images - Technical Analysis for Beginners**

To keep our books at a reasonable price for you, we print in black & white. But here are all the images in full color.

All of these bonuses are 100% free, with no strings attached. You don't need to provide any personal details except your email address.

To get your bonuses, go to the link or QR code:

www.az-penn.com

Glossary

AI / machine learning - artificial intelligence and machine learning is giving a computer the ability to reprogram itself in the light of the information it has handled - basically, to learn. Computers can be taught to 'recognize' chart patterns and will then refine their definition of the pattern by the results.

Algorithm - an algorithm is a mathematical process, or set of rules to be followed in a calculation. Algorithmic trading uses a computer program that places trades according to the rules that have been set.

AMA - adaptive moving average: different types include KAMA, JAMA and HMA, after their inventors Kaufman, Jurik and Hull. For technical analysis, they work in a similar way to the normal moving averages and EMA.

Ascending Triangle - a formation where the highs and lows form a triangle with the point on the top edge. The price is expected to break out in an upwards direction.

ATR - Average True Range: average trading range, including the averaging out of all gaps.

Backtesting - running a test of a chart pattern against historical data to see how often a given trade rule would have been successful.

Bar - shows the open, high, low, and closing price (OHLC) of a stock for a given period in the form of a bar (high/low) with two 'tabs' showing the open and close.

Bear - someone who thinks the market or a stock will go down. They are 'bearish'; that word also describes a chart formation which is likely to lead to a downwards price move.

Behavioral economics - looking at economics as the sum total of individual actions, and bringing psychology to bear on why participants in an economic market behave the way they do.

Bollinger bands - bands that are placed one standard deviation above and below the moving average. They're useful because they show the volatility of the price - how much it's likely to swing.

Bond - a kind of security which pays a 'coupon' at a given rate of interest, issued by a government or corporate to raise debt funding.

Breakaway gap - a movement through support or resistance which is so strong that the stock 'gaps' through the line - that is, opening a trading session above resistance, or below support, leaving a 'gap' in the price chart.

Breakout - when a price breaks through a support or resistance line, or out of a chart pattern.

Bull - someone who thinks the stock market or a particular stock will go up. 'Bullish' might describe such a person, or a chart formation that suggests the price will go up.

Bull/bear ratio - a market indicator published each week that shows the number of advisors who are bullish against the number who are bearish.

Candlestick - an alternative to the bar, the candlestick draws a box between the opening and closing prices, with a 'wick' or 'shadow' to show the high and low of the trading session. It is colored white/green if the price went up, black/red if the price went down.

CBOE - Chicago Board Options Exchange, the largest US options exchange.

Chande momentum indicator - a technical indicator that uses momentum to identify relative strength or weakness in a market. Similar to the Stochastic indicator.

Channel - the band within which a stock is trading. In a typical chart, if the stock is trading in a horizontal range, you can draw one line joining all the 'tops' and one line joining all the 'bottoms', and this defines the channel.

Chart - a graphical representation of a stock's price movement.

Close - the closing price of a trading session.

Confirmation bias - when we believe more strongly things that happen to coincide with our existing beliefs.

Congestion - when a stock trades within a very narrow range of prices, showing that buyers and sellers are evenly balanced. It often happens after a major move in the share price.

Consolidation - a stock or security that is neither continuing nor reversing a larger price trend.

Continuation - when a chart pattern shows the share price should break out in the same direction as the existing trend.

Correction - when a share price falls because it has become overbought, but the overall uptrend is not broken.

Crossover line - when the price and an indicator (e.g., a moving average) or two indicators (e.g., two moving averages) cross each other.

Dead cat bounce - a sharp bounce within a major downtrend. Often, a market crash has a dead cat bounce that can look like a recovery but very quickly fails.

Death cross - when the 50-day moving average crosses below the 200-day MA. A bearish indicator.

Derivative - any security whose price depends on that of another security (e.g., an option, whose price depends on the underlying share).

Descending Triangle - a formation where the highs and lows form a triangle with the point at the bottom. The price is expected to break out in a downwards direction.

Dividend - some shares make a cash payment to their shareholders every quarter (usual in the USA), half-year (in UK), or sometimes, monthly. This is paid out of the company's profits and is called the dividend. Calculate the dividend as a percentage of the share price and you have the dividend *yield*, which you can compare with the bank interest rate - it's the money you will be paid on your investment. But of course, in the case of shares, the price can also move up or down, whereas the cash in your bank account, if you put $100 in, stays $100 - it's not going to turn into $50 or $125.

Donchian rule - buying when a stock reaches a four-week high and selling when it reaches a four -week low. The Donchian rule relies on momentum - the idea that if the stock has reached a four-week high it has established an uptrend which ought to continue.

Double bottom - a chart formation where the stock in a downtrend hits a support line twice and bounces off it both times; a breakout into an uptrend is likely.

Elliott Wave - the Elliott Wave principle attempts to identify long term 'waves' based on investor behavior, sometimes using the Fibonacci series.

EMA - Exponential Moving Average. This attempts to refine the ordinary Moving Average by giving more weight to more recent price moves.

ETF - An exchange traded fund, also known as a 'tracker', is a fund which replicates an index like the S&P500, Russell 1000 or Dow Jones Industrial Average. It's bought and sold like a normal stock, through a broker, and the big ETFs have tight spreads and low costs so they're a good way to trade the market.

Exhaustion gap - when a stock that has been rising fast gaps down. This shows that the price is no longer being driven by buyers - they are 'exhausted'.

False breakout / fake-out - when a share price crosses a resistance or support line, but then after a very small movement reverses the move. It's easy to fall into a trap here so make sure your stop-losses are good.

False signal - when a chart appears to be giving a signal, but in fact it's just 'noise'. You can help avoid false signals by checking the signal with a second indicator.

Flag - a short term rectangular trading channel running in the opposite direction to the main trend. You are looking for a signal when the price breaks out of the flag.

FTSE - the FTSE group runs a number of indexes, of which the best known is the FTSE 100, the UK stock market's biggest 100 stocks.

Fundamentals - the business realities behind the share, such as its earnings, assets, brand names, and operations.

Gap - when a share opens a trading session above or below the previous session's closing price, and leaves a gap visible on the chart. This can be a strong signal.

Golden cross - 50-day moving average crossing above the 200-day MA. This is a bullish signal.

Guerrilla trading - very short-term trading which aims for a low profit on each trade but making multiple trades within a trading session, often closing trades within just a few minutes.

Head and shoulders - a chart formation which forms three 'peaks' with the largest in the middle. It is generally completed by a breakdown from the third peak, signaled by the price closing below the 'neckline' joining the lowest prices in the series.

Heiken Ashi bar - Heiken Ashi takes candlesticks and uses an averaging formula to attempt to remove 'noise' from the chart, minimizing false signals.

HFT - high frequency trading, using computerized orders based on algorithms; can trade many times a second.

High - the highest price reached by a share during any particular formation. Also, 52 -week highs, which are reported on financial news pages and websites.

Ichimoku indicators - this is a relatively new technique we have not covered, which attempts to forecast potential price ranges as 'clouds'. It's based on candlestick charting, but tries to extrapolate it forwards.

Index - a 'bundle' of shares created by mathematical means (e.g., the S&P 500). The index reflects the aggregate performance of all the component shares.

Indicator - an indicator is based on an arithmetic manipulation of the raw price data. Examples would be a moving average, RSI, stochastic or Price By Volume.

Island reversal - a candlestick pattern in which the stock price creates an 'island' top or bottom separated by gaps from the 'mainland' trends.

Kondratieff wave - Kondratieff waves are very, very long term waves. Personally, I am not willing to wait 40-60 years to see if my trades work out. Many academic economists don't believe in these waves, either.

Limit order - an order where you state a limit above which you are unwilling to buy, or below which you are unwilling to sell, a stock.

Linear regression line - the 'line of best fit' which allows all data points to be equally distributed around the line.

Liquidity - the ease with which a given security can be traded. More generally, the volume of trading in the stock market.

Long - to 'go long' is to buy and hold shares.

Low - the low point in any given price pattern or formation. 52-week lows can be informative and are found on financial websites alongside other basic price information.

MACD - Moving Average Convergence Divergence indicator. It shows the relationship between two moving averages, and can show changes in the momentum of the stock price.

Margin - if you trade on margin, you are borrowing money from your broker to buy the stock. I do not advise you do this. It is an easy way to ruin yourself.

Market indicators - these are used to forecast trends for the market as a whole, such as the market breadth index (the ratio between stocks which closed up, and stocks which closed down).

Market order - an order to buy stock 'at market', that is, at the best price your broker can get.

Market timing - trying to buy the market at the bottom and sell at the top. An impossible dream. Good traders are happy with getting 80% of the price action.

Maximum adverse excursion - the largest loss a single trade can suffer while it is open.

MBar or momentum bar (Constant Range Bar) - these charts, unlike conventional share price charts, do not show time. A bar is created for each move of a given amount, e.g., 10 cents. Some traders like these because they cut out a lot of 'noise'.

Mean reversion - the statistical likelihood that eventually extreme values will revert to the mean.

Momentum - the rate of change in prices.

NASDAQ - the second US stock exchange. It is all- electronic trading and has a higher percentage of tech stocks than the New York Stock Exchange.

Noise to signal - 'signal' is what we are looking for, something that tells us a stock is going to go up or down. 'Noise' is all the other stuff. It's like listening to old vinyl - the music is signal, the crackle and scratches are 'noise'.

NYSE - the New York Stock Exchange.

OBV - On Balance Volume, an indicator that shows up volume and down volume, giving a feel for how much of the trading volume relates to purchasers/bullish action and how much to sellers/bearish action.

Open - the share price at the opening of a trading session.

Option - a derivative that gives you the right to buy a share at a given price before a given date. It could simply be a private agreement, but most options are standardized and traded. Options are potentially useful because (1) they give you leverage, going up or down more than the share price, and (2) put options enable you to trade downtrends and breakdowns.

Oscillator - an indicator that shows values oscillating in a band between two extreme values, e.g., price acceleration between 0 and 100. RSI, Chaikin and ROC are all types of Oscillators.

Overbought / oversold - when a stock is 'overbought', all the buyers who are interested have already bought it, and it is exposed if any of them decide to sell. Indicators such as RSI and OBV attempt to show when stocks are overbought or oversold.

Pennant - a short term triangular formation within a defined up or downtrend. It is a continuation pattern, meaning that you'd expect to see the price break out in the same direction as the main trend.

Point-and- figure chart - these charts don't take account of the passage of time but create columns of price rises of a certain magnitude, reversing direction when the price direction changes. So if a stock price went up $10 every day for a week, and you had a $10 unit, you would end up with a column of five X's (or O's if the price were to go down) . They are not much used these days, but the MBar is a more modern version of the same idea.

Put/call ratio - the proportion between put and call options purchased on a given day. It's a good way to measure whether the market is bearish (more puts) or bullish (more calls).

Pyramiding - involves adding to a winning position as the price moves in the desired direction. It can be a good way to make more profit from a really strong breakout, but the stop-loss for the whole position needs to be reassessed to take account of the higher average purchase price.

Quant - basically any individual in the investment community who bases their work on mathematics rather than gut feel, fundamentals, philosophy, or hype.

Range contraction - when the range within which the share price varies becomes smaller.

Range expansion - when the range within which the share price varies becomes larger.

Range trading - identifying the range within which the share price trades, and aiming to buy towards the bottom of the range and sell towards the top of it, again, and again, and again.

Resistance - the concept that a stock will have a certain price level that it has touched several times but never exceeded, and that this forms a 'resistance' to a move upwards. Drawing a resistance line is often a useful way of showing this.

Retracement - the amount that a stock 'gives back' from a rise (or fall) in the share price before the uptrend (or downtrend) resumes.

Reversal - a change in the overall share price trend.

Risk appetite / risk aversion - a trader's desire to take on more risk, or desire to avoid risk. Risk is a spectrum, and not all traders have the same appetite for risk.

Risk reward ratio - the ratio between the risk you run and the reward you expect. For an individual trade, the ratio between the profit target and the stop-loss.

RSI - Relative Strength Index. An oscillator that displays bullish and bearish price momentum.

Runaway gap - a gap in the direction of the trend, usually associated with high volume. A bullish indicator.

Security - any form of negotiable instrument representing financial value (e.g., a stock, bond, or option).

Share - a security entitling the holder to a share in the earnings and assets of a business.

Short - to 'go short' is to sell shares you do not own. You will consequently profit if the share price goes down, as you can 'cover your short' by buying the shares at a lower price.

Slippage - when your order is executed for a worse price than you expected.

SMA - Simple Moving Average. The average of the share price over the last x time periods.

Spike - a sudden and large move in the share price.

Spread - when you buy stocks you pay a higher price than you'd get if you sold - the difference is the 'spread' and its how market makers and specialists make their money. Spread is one of the costs you need to allow for as a trader.

Standard deviation - a measure of how far values differ from the mean. For instance, a class of ten-year-olds probably have a low standard deviation in height; they will all be roughly as tall as each other. SD is one way to measure the volatility of a share price.

Standard error channel - parallel lines drawn equidistant from the linear regression trend line to form a channel.

Stochastic Oscillator - an indicator which shows momentum based on the price history of the asset.

Stop-limit order - An order which specifies a price at which the order becomes valid, *and* a price limit after which it is no longer valid, e.g., "Sell 100 IBM *if* the stock price falls below 90 but *not* if it goes below 95." It's a good way of entering a breakout or breakdown trade.

Stop-loss - the price at which you will close a trade if it goes in the wrong direction. You should always set a stop-loss at the same time as you make your original trade.

Support - a line which the share price repeatedly hits and then bounces. If a stock falls, it will usually stop at the support line, either temporarily, or before returning to higher levels. If a stock falls through the support line, it may well fall all the way to the next support line.

Swing trader - traders are aiming to make gains by trading a stock and holding it just a few days. They almost always use technical analysis.

Technical analysis - reading patterns in the movement of the share price to ascertain the probability of the share price behaving in a particular way in future.

Tick bars - tick bars show price movement only if there has been a minimum number of trades.

Tracker - a fund that represents an index, that is automatically created and traded on a stock exchange in the same way as a share.

Trailing stop - a stop-loss that is increased as the price of the share goes up, so that you can't lose all your gains.

Trend - the general movement in a share price, either upwards, downwards, or sideways.

Trendline - a line that can be drawn to show the trend.

Triple top - where the share price forms three peaks all hitting the same resistance level. The third time, it is likely to break downwards.

VIX index - an index which measures share price volatility.

Volatility - the amount of change in a share price. A share price that tends to move 1% a day is much less volatile than one that swings by 5-10% some days.

Volume - the amount of shares traded on a single day.

Wedge - a chart formation in which the share price forms a wedge that is pointing up or down in the opposite direction to the trend. The price should break out in the direction of the trend.

Whipsaw - a sudden change in the direction of the share price. Sometimes a whipsaw happens before a real breakout, which can be deceptive.

WMA - weighted moving average.

References

There are a lot of books covering specific aspects of technical analysis if you want to go further.

If you're interested in candlesticks, Steve Nison has written several books on the subject which go into a lot more depth than I could here. He seems to know what he's doing, though personally, I find his mustache rather Ron Burgundy.

Jack Schrager's series of 'Market Wizards' books will not teach you technical analysis or trading - but they *will* give you a really good idea of how successful traders run their businesses. And they are very easy to read. What I particularly like is that Schrager does the interview, but then he sums up the learning points afterwards. My copies are well-thumbed because I'll always go back and read one of the chapters if I have some spare time.

John Murphy - Technical Analysis of the Financial Markets. If you want one big encyclopedic book with everything in it, this is as near as you'll get... apart from Tom Bulkowski's Encyclopaedia of Chart Patterns. One of the things I really like about Bulkowski is that he tells you the probability of each pattern making a successful trade - he's backtested all the patterns so his statistics are genuine. I can tell you I've made money out of this or that trade - but he has the math to prove it. He also shows loads and loads of examples (as does Steve Nison) so that you learn how to read a chart, and points out where common patterns sometimes *don't* work out so you know how to spot the signs if they're going wrong.

Curtis Faith's The Way of the Turtle is a great book particularly if you are undisciplined, a scatterbrain, or trade on 'gut feel'. He talks about learning to trade a system and learning to be cool with the results. I learned a lot from the book, not so much about technical analysis but about where I was going wrong not setting the right stop-losses, or picking and choosing my trades.

Martin Pring's Technical Analysis Explained is a lot of traders' basic book, and it's very comprehensive, but it was written in 1980 and to me, it does feel a bit like it.

Websites that are useful to anyone starting off technical trading include Investopedia (www.investopedia.com/terms/t/technicalanalysis.asp), Slope of Hope (slopeofhope.com) which has good community functions so you can learn from other traders, and StockCharts' Chart School. And don't forget that if you trade with eToro (etoro.com) you have access to 'copy portfolio' and social trading features, so you can identify people who are performing well right now and follow them to work out what they're doing right. That's practically as good as the education you would have gotten sitting in an office with the old guy penciling those lines on the chart paper!

Quiz Answers

Chapter 1:
1. b
2. c
3. b
4. a
5. a & b

Chapter 2:
1. a
2. b
3. a
4. a
5. a

Chapter 3:
1. a
2. b
3. a
4. a
5. a

Chapter 4:
1. a
2. c
3. b
4. a
5. a

Chapter 5:
1. a
2. b
3. b
4. a
5. c

Chapter 6:
1. b
2. c
3. a
4. a
5. b

Chapter 7:
1. b
2. a
3. c
4. b
5. a

Chapter 8:
1. d
2. d
3. c
4. a
5. b

Chapter 11:
1. c
2. a
3. c
4. b
5. c
6. a & b

Fundamental Analysis for beginners

Grow Your Investment Portfolio Like A Pro Using Financial Statements and Ratios of Any Business with Zero Investing Experience Required

A.Z Penn

HOW TO GET THE MOST OUT OF THIS BOOK

To help you along your investing journey, I've created two free bonus companion masterclasses, one which includes walking you through an investors mindset on how to find potential companies to invest in. There's also a free companion DCF model spreadsheet of Amazon which I created specifically to simplify your learning of this valuation model. I also provide an additional colored images resource that will help you get the best possible result.

I highly recommend you sign up now to get the most out of this book. You can do that by visiting the link or scanning the QR code below:

www.az-penn.com

Free bonus #1: **Company Valuation Simplified Masterclass ($97 value)**

In this video masterclass, I will be walking you through an investors mindset on how to find potential companies to invest in, which includes what to look out for and major red flags to keep in mind. This class will help you decide whether a company is worth investing in or whether you should move on.

Free bonus #2: **Charting Simplified Masterclass ($67 value)**

In this 5 part video masterclass you'll be discovering various simple and easy to use strategies on making profitable trades. By showing you real life stock examples of a few charting indicators - you will be able to determine whether a stock is worth trading or not.

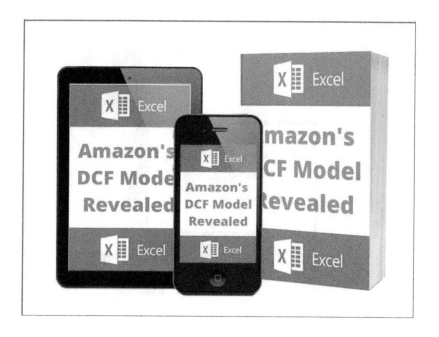

Free bonus #3: Amazons DCF Model Revealed ($37 value)

This Excel spreadsheet will be a great companion for you whilst reading this book. It will reveal the complete DCF model calculations I've presented in the book for Amazon. With this insightful spreadsheet, you will find it easier to duplicate my DCF model example on any company you're researching.

Free bonus #4: **Colored Images – Fundamental Analysis for Beginners**

To keep our books at a reasonable price for you, we print in black & white. But here are all the images in full color.

All of these bonuses are 100% free, with no strings attached. You don't need to provide any personal details except your email address.

To get your bonuses, go to the link or QR code:

<u>www.az-penn.com</u>

Introduction

You might think investing in the stock market isn't for you. Or maybe you got started on Robinhood or another trading platform, and you started losing money. That can leave a nasty taste.

But you know something? Investing in the stock market is for everyone!

First of all, if you don't invest in stocks, you're losing out. Over the years, stocks have almost always beaten 'safer' investments like bonds. They give greater annual returns, and over time, the effect of compounding will make a stock based (investment) portfolio vastly outperform a cash and bonds (savings) portfolio. So even if you invest via mutual funds or through ETFs (exchange-traded fund), it's worth investing in the stock market.

For some investors, ETFs are all they want - a relatively trouble -free way to invest. They give you a broad exposure at a low cost. But you'll only do as well as the market as a whole. If the market goes up, the ETF will follow. If it goes down... you get the message. Over time, if you 'buy and hold' forever, you should make a reasonable return (the S&P 500 made an annual return of 10.5% from when it started in 1957, to 2021).

Other investors prefer to pick mutual funds that are more actively managed (a pool of money managed by a professional fund manager). But of course, there's a cost for that management, which will be taken out of your returns. And you don't have a guarantee of beating the market, though some funds have better success than others.

Would you like to improve your return even more? Then direct investment could be the way forward. But if you're going to make it work, you'll need to learn the basic skills of fundamental analysis (which can be more fun than it sounds).

With this, you can ensure that you are investing:

- in companies that have a good, strong business,
- in companies that don't have financial problems waiting to trip them up, and
- in stocks that aren't so highly valued you'll never make money out of them.

Remember that the broader stock market, and consequently the ETFs, come with the rough as well as the smooth. The S&P 500 included the fraudulent, and eventually bankrupted company, Enron - but if you'd looked at Enron's annual report, you'd probably have seen a few issues which might have kept you from investing in the shares in the first place.

So, what is fundamental analysis? In general, it's about understanding each company's business, finance, and value, just as if you were buying the business and not the stock. Fundamental analysis says that the value of a stock is based on what the company actually does, earns, and possesses - and that whatever the market does is just noise. The market goes up and down, but if you've made the right investment at the right price, that shouldn't matter. It can be a worry, but in the long term you should win out.

One big part of fundamental analysis is understanding how the business operates in 'the real world'. For instance, if you're investing in a retail business, you'll need to get a feel for how many stores it's opening, what its footprint is, and what people think about the retailer and its product. But of course, as stock market investors, we're interested in how that comes through to the bottom line - and that's where the numbers come in.

If you read some analyst research, it's easy to think that this is too hard to do or that you need to be a CFA (chartered financial analyst). Remember, professional analysts write for fund managers and other specialists, so they don't have to try to make their reports readable for a non-specialist. They'll even fight battles over the best ratios to use and how to calculate them - but then they're paid for that.

You can use some really basic ratios to assess the strength and health of a company, and it doesn't take a lot of time to learn. In fact, it's not calculating the ratios but understanding the answers that are the most important factor in making good investments.

So, if you didn't excel at math, think accountancy is boring, or don't have 'a head for numbers', it doesn't matter - as long as you can use a spreadsheet and calculate percentages, you can learn to invest wisely and productively. And that's what I'm going to teach you here.

I've traded the stock markets for a while and learned my lessons the hard way. I've made a few mistakes and learned from each one, working out where I had gone wrong. Quite often, I found I had overlooked a warning sign I should have seen in a company's Annual Report, or not noticed that the trends in the company's business were changing. That led me to some very dry reading such as Security Analysis by Graham & Dodd. But the knowledge I gained helped me improve my investment returns significantly.

I still think the books I read were great, but I can't call them user-friendly. That's why I've written *Fundamental Analysis for Beginners*. I want you to learn fundamental analysis easily, without being bored, and with some good real-world examples. If you've made a few mistakes of your own, maybe you'll see where you went wrong and how you can avoid making the same mistake twice. And I hope that by the end of the book, you'll feel confident in your ability to choose the right investments, click your broker's 'buy' button, and start making your money work a bit harder for you than sitting around in a bank account.

Let's get started!

1

Chapter 1: What is Fundamental Analysis?

What Fundamental Analysis Isn't

"My friend gave me this great tip" is not fundamental analysis.

"It's trending on Reddit" is not fundamental analysis.

"Warren Buffett bought it" is not fundamental analysis.

"Goldman Sachs' analyst recommended it" is not fundamental analysis.

"I saw it on CNBC" is not fundamental analysis.

"I'm buying because the price is going up" is not fundamental analysis.

"I bought it because it had dipped 10% in an uptrend" is not fundamental analysis.

"It's growing really fast" is not fundamental analysis.

"It's a game-changing technology, and it will control the whole market" is not fundamental analysis.

"I like their burgers/jeans/tacos/smartphones" is not fundamental analysis.

Okay smart guy, what is it then?

Fundamental analysis is an attempt to establish the *intrinsic* valuation of a business, using what you know about a company's business and the financial figures it publishes to show what the business should be worth.

Only then do you look at the share price. Obviously, you wouldn't want to buy the stock if it's higher than the intrinsic valuation. But, if it's the same, or mainly if it's lower, you might.

So, if you just buy a company because you like the product, that's not fundamental analysis. You don't know that the product makes money, how much it makes, or how the share price relates to that. (But if you like the product, research the company and its market, and *then* buy the stock, that's fundamental analysis. That's how famed fund manager Peter Lynch funded many of his best ideas.)

Suppose you buy a 'story stock' like Tesla, Internet stocks in 1999, or solar energy stocks. In that case, if you haven't done the numbers, again, that's not fundamental analysis. But if you come up with an idea of the numbers, then yes, it is.

Suppose you buy a stock by looking at what the share price has done in the past. In that case, that's not fundamental analysis (though it can still be a helpful tool for refining your timing, and we'll talk about that later).

And if you just buy what your friends tell you to, that not only isn't fundamental analysis, but it's a quick way to lose a lot of money.

So, to recap, if you're doing fundamental analysis, then you need to cover three factors:

- How good is the underlying business?
- How much should that business be worth?
- And is the value reflected in the share price?

Or to reduce the whole of fundamental analysis to a single question: "What is this business really worth?"

Why you need to understand Fundamental Analysis

You don't absolutely need to understand fundamental analysis. If you really find it too hard to do or don't have enough time, you can invest via ETFs for the long term. You will get (within a small margin of error) the same performance as the market that your ETF tracks. You can even buy ETFs that will pay you regular dividends.

But if you want to beat the market, as a long -term investor, you need to invest directly in stocks for at least part of your portfolio. And you'll need to understand fundamental analysis to do it well.

- You get a tip from a friend? You'll need to understand fundamental analysis to check it out and ensure the stock is worthwhile. (Often, it won't be.)
- You hear Warren Buffett is buying something? Even Warren Buffett gets it wrong sometimes (he's human, after all). You'll need fundamental analysis to ensure you agree with him about the stock.
- You like the burgers? First of all, you need to find out if the company is making money. Then, you need to work out what it's worth. That's fundamental analysis.

- There's a great story, like solar power? First, you need to check out the risks. How do solar energy suppliers set their prices? Could government action damage their business models? Are too many companies chasing the same business? Fundamental analysis will find out (and you should find the answers you're looking for in the company's annual report).
- If you're looking for fast growth, fundamental analysis will let you find stocks where earnings are likely to grow fast and the company has sufficient financial resources to cope with a fast-expanding business (some don't).
- If you're looking for the most profitable companies, you need to understand fundamental analysis to look for the right ratios.
- Fundamental analysis will let you look under the hood and check whether a company is as great as it says it is.
- Fundamental analysis will also let you check out whether management is telling the whole truth or hiding a few problem areas.
- And fundamental analysis can show you when a company is running out of cash.
- If you're looking for the cheapest companies, only fundamental analysis can deliver what you need.

Really, suppose you try to be a successful long-term investor without understanding fundamental analysis. In that case, you will rely a lot on your luck. But if you understand fundamental analysis, you will increase your percentage of good calls - and you should manage to reduce the unpleasant surprises very significantly.

The Origins of Fundamental Analysis

Even in the seventeenth century, when the Amsterdam and London Stock Exchanges led the world, merchants had worked out some way of analyzing the businesses they invested in. They didn't always get it right, as you'll know if you've heard about the South Sea Bubble (1720).

But the discipline of fundamental analysis as we know it today started in 1934 when Benjamin Graham published his first book, *Security Analysis*. Indeed, he's sometimes known as the father of fundamental analysis.

Graham was the first to formulate a complete methodological structure for the valuation of companies and stocks. At the same time, he preached *value investing*, which aims to look for stocks trading at 20% or more below what the analyst considers their intrinsic or fair value. He believed that this gave a good margin of error, which helps when dealing with the multiple uncertainties of forecasting company growth, economic growth, and stock markets.

However, you don't have to be a value investor to use fundamental analysis. Even if you prefer to invest in growth companies, fundamental analysis can help you avoid the companies that are at the highest risk, whether that's because their underlying business isn't very profitable, their debts are too high, or because they have management that is always too optimistic and never quite manages to do what they say they'll do.

The Pros and Cons of Fundamental Analysis

Like any technique, fundamental analysis has its advantages and disadvantages, and let's quickly sum them up.

Advantages:

- Value - Fundamental analysis allows you to find stocks priced at less than their actual value. It's letting you into the stock market's bargain basement.

- Risk avoidance - Fundamental analysis allows you to spot major risks such as an unsustainable level of debt, companies that are 'buying' sales (for instance, by giving customers extended credit terms), or enormous valuations.

- Lie detection - Doing fundamental analysis properly will ensure that you know exactly what you are buying. If you think you're buying a growth company, but you're actually buying a cash-burning business, it will tell you. If all the good stuff is in related companies, or the directors are doing dodgy deals, it will give you the best chance of finding out.

- Helps reduce churn - Churn, turning over your portfolio too rapidly has all sorts of costs, even if you use a zero-commission broker. It may create tax liabilities you don't want. By knowing all about the stocks you buy and weeding out the ones that don't qualify, you won't need to trade so often or watch your portfolio every day.

- Factual - Many of us let our emotions take a big part in investment decisions, even if we don't realize it. Fundamental analysis helps by focusing on factual data. For 'story stocks,' you can get beneath the glamorous story and test whether the engine is working.

Disadvantages:

- Time-consuming - Fundamental analysis takes time. It takes time to learn how to do it, and it takes time to do it. To analyze a single company properly could take a couple of evenings or a good part of your weekend.
- It can be dull. I hate to admit this, but even finance nerds find page 101 of the footnotes to the annual report tough going. There is no glamour in fundamental analysis. (Masters of the Universe probably don't bother with it.)
- It tells you **what** to buy, **not when** - I always love a clip of Peter Lynch talking about 'buying the dip'. He was a big buyer of Kaiser Corp at $26. then at $16. then at $14. Then at $10. Then at $3... the payoff? He did make money in the end because the stock split off all the different businesses and the payout added up to about $50 a share! Fundamental analysis will tell you *what* to buy, but it's not at all useful in telling you the right time to buy (That's where technical analysis comes in).
- It tends to look back rather than forwards. Looking at past years' financial reports will not necessarily help you if there's a significant disruption in the industry now. Even quarterly results come out several weeks after the end of the quarter.
- GIGO - As the nerds say, 'garbage in, garbage out'. If there's a fraud going on and the figures have been faked, analyzing them won't always be able to detect that - though sometimes you will get an inkling that things don't quite add up.

A little bit of philosophy

I should be honest here and tell you that many academics have questioned whether fundamental analysis works in achieving better performance than an asset allocation approach or a monkey picking stocks' names out of a hat. According to the *Efficient Market Theory,* stock markets are incredibly efficient at absorbing and interpreting new information, so at any given time, the share price reflects everything known about the company. If that's true, you can't know more than anyone else.

It's a nice theory. However, we live in the real world, and things aren't quite so simple.

First of all, the stock market is not driven by purely rational actors. It's often driven by emotions, of which the two most prominent are *fear and greed.* Those emotions can change overnight - as they did in the tech stock crash. One moment the market was saying, "The internet is growing really fast; these stocks will rocket," and the very next day, investors were saying, "None of these companies will ever make any money; we'd better look for the exit".

Secondly, while the Efficient Market Theory may work quite well for many of the biggest stocks, if you are interested in buying smaller, high-growth companies, you may find that the press or analysts do not cover them well. So, the assumption that the market knows all the facts probably doesn't work out in practice for these stocks.

If you're the only person to read all the way through the annual report, it is just possible you've come across something the market missed, or only a few people have noticed.

And thirdly, Ben Graham made money for his clients. Warren Buffett, who takes a fundamental analysis approach, has made himself a billionaire, as has his long-time business partner Charlie Munger. Peter Lynch, who ran Fidelity's Magellan Fund for many years, used fundamental analysis to become a consistent top performer among fund managers.

That suggests fundamental analysis can work rather well. I'm also pleased with the results it's delivered for my investments too.

Some examples of the Fundamental Analysis Toolbox

Let me give a few examples of the tools you might use in fundamental analysis. We'll talk about them in more detail in later chapters.

- Liquidity and debt ratios give you a way to pry open the company's bank accounts and find out whether it has too much debt, whether it can pay its interest expense, and whether it has the financial resources to cope with a cash crunch.
- Valuation ratios let you assess what you're paying for each dollar of earnings, or what dividend yield you'll get on your money invested. They also let you compare the stock you're interested in with others in the same line of business to find out if it's a good bargain or not.
- Closely reading the footnotes to the accounts shows you where the bodies are buried. All kinds of interesting wickedness goes on page 98 or so, and it's up to you to find it!
- Profitability ratios show you whether the company is as profitable as it should be, and whether it's becoming more or less profitable over time.
- Competitor analysis techniques help you decide whether the business you're buying has an advantage over its competitors - Warren Buffett calls this a 'moat' - and whether (and how) it's likely to grow.
- Return ratios help you see whether the company is making a return on its money invested that's above or below average - in other words, how successful it is at investing in its own business.

Chapter 1 Quiz

Just to check your understanding, every chapter in this book will have a short multiple-choice quiz at the end. Don't worry; no one's keeping the score, and you'll probably find that you do pretty well in most chapters. If you don't, all that's telling you is to re-read the chapter, maybe after a couple of days, and see if it makes better sense. The quiz answers are on page 523.

1. Fundamental analysis is
   a) A way of trading shares
   b) A form of psychotherapy
   c) Predicting how share prices will move
   d) Valuing the underlying business in which you buy shares

2. Who is the 'father of fundamental analysis'?
   a) Benjamin Franklin
   b) Cracker Graham
   c) Benjamin Graham
   d) Franklin Templeton

3. Which of these is *not* an advantage of using fundamental analysis?
   a) You can buy shares that are priced at less than fair value
   b) You might spot a problem with the business before the market does
   c) It's quick to do and requires no effort
   d) You can check whether management is telling the whole truth

4. Which of these is part of the fundamental analysis toolbox?
   a) Profitability ratio
   b) BMI
   c) Oscillator
   d) Graphological analysis of the CEO's signature

5. Which of these things won't fundamental analysis tell you?
   a) The company is running out of cash
   b) The shares are too highly priced
   c) The shares are going to go down tomorrow morning
   d) The company is growing fast

2

Chapter 2: Finding Fundamental Data

Things have really changed in the last 20 years or so. I'm certainly not ready to retire yet, but when I started trading, some of the older analysts were still working out their ratios with calculators and writing the results down in a notebook. One big change is this one:

- The old days: asking nicely for a report to be posted. One company wanted $3.50 for the report and postage - to be sent by check in the mail, as you would expect.
- Nowadays: the internet. Data on finance websites, the company's investor relations site, and the SEC site. And when you're done, don't ring your broker, just click the button on your broker's trading app to buy the shares.

So, finding the basic financial data is easy. That's the same for foreign stocks; for instance, stocks quoted on the London Stock Exchange have to file with the Regulatory News Service (RNS), and you can check their filings at www.londonstockexchange.com.

The same goes for French stocks, but the filings will be in French. If you don't speak French, the largest French stocks often have an ADR (basically, it's a way for U.S shareholders to buy the stock) listed on the New York Stock Exchange (NYSE), where you can find the filings. That's true, for instance, of French pharma stocks Sanofi and Valneva. The same is true for other foreign stocks, such as Japan's Toyota and Honda, China's biggest e-commerce stock Alibaba, India's IT stock Wipro, and many more.

If you have the filings, you have all the basic information to analyze a company. However, additional information may give you a richer and deeper appreciation of the business. Many companies produce a presentation for analysts that gives strategic long term predictions, information on the industry, and breakdowns of the business or its KPIs (key performance indicators) in addition to what's shown in the annual report.

Often, you can find industry-specific data here. The table on the next page has a few of these so you can see how specific some of them are. If you use these ratios, you're really getting to the heart of what makes that kind of business profitable.

Industry	KPIs
Airlines	ASK (available seat kilometers) = seats x distance Flown RPK (revenue passenger kilometers) = ASK that were paid for
Retail	Sales per square foot Same-store sales
Media and Telecoms	Customer acquisition cost Revenue per subscriber
Insurance	Persistency ratio (customer renewals) Solvency ratio (capital compared to claims) Incurred claims ratio (ratio of claims paid out in the year to the premium collected) Commission expense ratio
Hospitality	Occupancy ratio ADR = Average Daily Rate RevPAR = Revenue per available room
Services Businesses	Revenue per employee Cost per employee

You'll also find a much more user-friendly graphical representation of business trends than you typically get in the annual report. So, it's worth seeing if these presentations are on the company's website, under 'Investor Relations'.

Why companies have to publish data

Private companies can get away with publishing very limited data. However, if a company wants to list its shares on the Stock Exchange, in return, it has to accept several commitments. One is publishing annual and quarterly reports up to a high standard. In some markets, such as the UK, bi- annual reporting (occurring twice a year) is more normal, but the same rules apply.

There are also rules about when companies need to issue other reports. For instance, if the company has information that will have a material effect on its results and share price, such as the cancellation of a major contract, or a downgrade in expectations for the year based on current performance, it needs to release a statement. Acquisitions also require a statement to be issued if they are above a certain size; Starbucks acquires a single coffee bar would not need to issue a statement, but if it wanted to acquire Dunkin' Donuts, it certainly would need to.

Imagine a stock market in which companies didn't need to publish this kind of data. Individual shareholders might not know that the CEO had just quadrupled his pay check, that the company was buying a competitor twice its size, and that it was so heavily in debt it would be lucky to survive the next 12 months. An analyst who knew the company and met its executives personally would know all these things.

Who do you think would have sold the shares before the company hit the skids? And who would be left with the worthless paper?

That's why these rules exist. They level the playing field and make sure everyone in the market knows what's going on, and have equally good information on which to base their investment decisions. In the U.S, they're policed by the SEC (Securities and Exchange Commission): financial regulators or the stock exchange in other countries.

You may have heard of the 'Pink Sheets' - an over-the-counter market that doesn't comply with these strict regulations. That's why a lot of smart people will tell you not to bother with the Pink Sheets; you have no way of checking that a company is achieving its objectives.

The Pink Sheets now tiers its stocks; 'International Premier QX' are pretty good (foreign shares which meet NYSE standards), but the bottom tier is named 'Caveat Emptor' (In Latin in means: 'Buyer, beware!') and has skull and crossbones as its symbol. That tells you all you need to know!

The financial data that have to be published are quite specific. There are also rules about other features that need to be included in the reports, particularly in the annual report, such as the management discussion and analysis of operations (MD&A), disclosures of executive compensation, and names of major shareholders, together with management shareholdings.

Why you should always read back to front

The front, or the top, of any earnings announcement or annual report is where management brag their stuff. It's where they feature the figures they are most pleased with (or least ashamed of), where they polish their image; it's publicity.

The footnotes are where they hide the things they don't want you to see. The footnotes are also where all the detailed information like sector breakdowns, debt maturities, and cash flow details are hidden. They put the spin first and the facts second.

That's why it's the footnotes you should read first. Always read back to front! (Okay, probably you should just have a quick look at the front page first, but then start looking at the footnotes.)

By the time you get to the front page, you'll be able to judge whether the summary gives you a fair picture of the company, or whether it's hopelessly over-optimistic.

What data companies have to publish

First of all, companies are required to publish their financial accounts, with a full income report (profit and loss account), balance sheet, and statement of cash flow. They're required to do that in the annual report, and they have to give some of this information in the quarterly reports (or in some markets, bi-annual reports). In the annual report, the results must have been audited by an accountancy firm, and come with extensive footnotes, some of which are mandatory, such as showing a breakdown of debts, while others are optional, such as sector breakdowns.

Companies are also required to publish the agenda for the annual stockholder meeting (or any other big meetings needed, for instance, to decide on a major share issue or an acquisition). In the U.S, this is called the proxy statement, and the SEC calls it by the catchy name of Form DEF 14A. Shareholders are entitled to vote on the proposals.

Let's look at the different forms that need to be submitted to the SEC. You'll notice that the SEC is not imaginative when it comes to names.

- 8K – Companies required to announce any unscheduled events (such as acquisitions or the need to write off an investment) or corporate changes within four days of the event. Companies also often issue an 8k as a preliminary report or trading statement just after the end of a quarter, talking about how things have gone but without giving a full financial breakdown.

- 10Q - This form shows the firm's business and financial performance each quarter, and it's not audited. (In the last quarter, the 10K takes its place).
- 10K - the comprehensive annual report, including an overview of the business, risk factors, financial data, MD&A, and audit report.
- Schedule 13D - This report must be produced whenever an owner acquires more than 5% of the shares in the company.
- Forms 3, 4 and 5 show if insiders are buying or selling stock in the company.
- Form 144 shows proposed sales of restricted stock.
- DEF 14A - Proxy statement, which we already talked about.

Most companies also produce an annual report for shareholders that is prettier than the 10K and has pictures and some supplementary information. But it will still have the 10K included in the back (often on cheaper, non-glossy paper). The corporate glossy report is good for understanding how the company wants to present itself, but most of the real information is in the boring-looking 10K.

All these forms can be accessed through the SEC's Electronic Data Gathering, Analysis, and Retrieval system. For once, the SEC has a catchy name for something - EDGAR! You'll find this fantastic source of information at:

www.sec.gov/edgar/searchedgar/companysearch.html

If you're a bit of a geek, you may want to download statements in XBRL, an XML standard that tags financial reporting data so that you can easily process them in a spreadsheet or database.

The rules are similar for companies quoted on the Euronext exchanges in London and Tokyo, though they differ in detail. For instance, London stocks only have to issue two statements a year (not quarterly), accounting details are different, some of the names of accounts differ (e.g. statement of comprehensive income vs profit and loss account), and the exact format of releases differs. But they all have to release detailed accounting data and a discussion of operations at regular intervals.

Why proxy statements and Forms 3,4, & 5 and 144 are useful

Proxy statements can be dry as dust. They are a document the SEC requires companies to provide shareholders that includes information needed to make decisions at shareholder meetings. Very often, they are business-as-usual. They simply ask stockholders to reappoint some of the directors, reappoint the auditors, and approve the accounts. That's it. The same motions and even the same words as last year. This kind of proxy statement you can usually ignore.

But sometimes, a proxy statement shows that storms are brewing. For instance, an activist shareholder such as Carl Icahn or Nelson Peltz might want to appoint a director of their own choice to the board. They may even want to overthrow the entire management or stop the company from making what they think will be a disastrous or risky acquisition. So, proxy statements are well worth reading because they show the fault lines in the company.

Proxy statements also have to detail related party transactions. An example might be where a company lends money to one of its customers, and that customer uses the money to buy or lease the company's product. I've seen that happen several times, and every time I've spotted it in a company I covered, that company ended up losing money for shareholders. (If you imagine going to a bar where the landlord lent everyone money to pay for their drinks... it wouldn't keep going long, so you'd want to enjoy it while you could!) Or the company might employ a consultancy in which the CEO holds a significant stake. Would you think the company is getting good value for money? Or would you guess the CEO is making more out of it than the company is getting in benefit?

In the proxy statement, you'll also get a rundown of who the executives are and what they get paid.

As for insider buying and selling, it's often an indication of the amount (or lack of) confidence management have in the company. Even though they're not allowed to trade based on inside information - such as selling the shares just before bad results come out - insiders generally have a good feeling for the general direction in which the company's going.

Watch out, particularly for Form 144. Companies often issue restricted stock to executives and employees during their IPOs. These stocks can't be sold during a lock-in period (the period during which investors are not allowed to redeem or sell their investments), say six months or a year. But at the end of that time, you may see large amounts of stock coming on to the market as insiders sell out.

That's not always a sign that they are negative about the company's future. If let's say, you're just a marketing assistant at HotStartup.com, but you end up with shares worth $10m, then it's easy to understand why you might want to sell some of that and pay off your home loan. But if a large number of shares come on the market, it will still probably depress the share price. (I mean, there may be a good reason for a large number of shares coming on the market. It's not necessarily a sign that management is selling out because the company is hitting the skids. But that's still going to hurt the market because firstly, there's more supply, and secondly, traders will see the sale of shares and jump to negative conclusions, and sell their shares too which would depress the share price.)

The earnings season

Most companies will have a December year-end. That means their results will all come out at roughly the same time, with annual results coming out in late February or early March. Similarly, most quarterly reports will cluster around dates around three weeks to a month after the end of the quarter. (The SEC's official deadline is 40 days.)

In the retail sector, a December year-end would bring way too much pressure because of the clustering of sales around Black Friday, Thanksgiving, and Christmas. Many retail companies draw up their accounts at the end of January instead.

This is the busiest time of year for analysts and should also be the busiest time of year for investors. Some days, several companies you look at will report at once. However, you don't need to feel that you have to read the whole 10K within a few minutes of its publication. Usually, traders read the headline, journalists read the front page, and only analysts read the whole report (one thing you learn quickly as an analyst is that traders can't read more than three lines of text before their attention span ends). Often, the direction a stock took after the results can reverse on the next day of trading; that's because the analysts have found something interesting buried on page 10, or they've done a bit more work and don't like what they've found out.

One of the most important things to understand when you're looking at how share prices behave in the earnings season is that the stock market is driven by expectations. Analysts will already have made their forecasts for the quarter. Earnings tend to be assessed by whether they meet, exceed, or fall short of that forecast. We say, for instance, that a company "missed its earnings" or delivered "a positive earnings surprise".

So always make a practice, *before* the earnings are due out, to use a service like Yahoo Finance or Zacks and look up what the analyst expectation is for the quarter. Then you'll be able to make the same immediate assessment of the figures as anyone in the stock market.

By the way, those sites will also give you a financial calendar, as well as MarketWatch - and each individual company's investor relations website. That lets you be sure nothing gets under your radar!

Where else to get useful data

Wall Street and City analysts usually benefit from the chance of a phone call or Zoom meeting with management on the day of the results. That used to be a huge advantage for the professional analyst over the retail investor, but now it's become common for companies to open up the call to retail investors, or to record the meeting and have a recording plus a transcript available on the company's website. You can also find analyst calls on fool.com and other finance websites.

These are definitely worth listening to. You're not going to get any insider information, as executives know they're not allowed to give out non- public information that could affect the share price. But there are other advantages to listening to the analysts' call. First of all, the participants will often go into more detail about operational aspects of the business than you might have found in the report.

There's also usually a PowerPoint presentation which will often contain plenty more detail. As I mentioned, they often have neat charts too. Make sure if you're going to listen to a transcript that you print out the presentation, or download it to your laptop first.

Make a particular note of any other companies or new technologies or products that the company talks about. You can look them up later and find out more.

But of course, a company will usually only talk about itself and its own products. If you want a different view, find its competitors and look up what they have to say. Reading one company's report is like going to the top of a mountain; you get a wonderful view, but you can't see everything in the landscape because you can't see into dips or past the nearest hills. Climb another mountain a few miles away and while it's the same landscape, you'll be able to see a few things you couldn't see from the other peak. You've also got a chance to check whether that hill over there looks as high as it did from the other peak - to triangulate your observations and confirm them.

That's why you want to pull up data on companies that compete with the one you're analyzing and listen to their calls too.

Analysts' reports

If you get a chance, you should definitely look at analysts' reports on the company. There are two good reasons to do so:

- In the case of regular 'information' reports, you get the earnings forecasts. You need to see the latest forecasts to know what the market expects for the next results season. However, you can also get the consensus forecasts from finance websites.
- Larger reports, initiating coverage or looking at major events, will include a detailed breakdown of the business and its prospects. These reports are really worth looking at as you can see how a professional analyst looks at the business, what kind of ratios they're using and what comparisons they think are most useful. Industry reports are particularly worth reading, as they cover numerous companies and often have insights into the direction of the industry as a whole.

Many analysts publish a 'year in focus' report. Saxo Bank also makes a series of 'Outrageous Predictions' at the start of a new year (just Google 'Saxo bank outrageous predictions'). I love these because they really make you think. In fact, some of them are not so outrageous after all!

Additionally, sometimes analysts will explore the different bases of valuation that might be applied. This can occasionally be the best part of the report. For instance, moving from valuing a railroad company as a transportation stock to looking at it as a potential source of real estate values might make a huge difference to the valuation.

These reports are usually directed to institutional investors such as pension funds and mutual fund managers. However, some services allow you to access them for a fee, while some large brokers offer access as part of client perks - Merrill Edge, for instance, gives you access to Merrill's analyst reports as well as Morningstar.

You might also want to look at what the credit analysts are saying. The major credit rating agencies - Fitch, S&P and Moody's - are paid to rate every bond issued by a company. Their clients are banks and bond investors, and their objective differs from equity analysts. In brief, you could say that equity analysts want to make their clients money, while credit analysts want to stop their clients from losing it. Equity analysts are quite bullish by nature and default to 'hold' as their worst recommendation, while credit analysts are naturally pessimistic and will tend to err on the downside.

Credit reports are a great reality check. If you're looking at a company with fast growth in revenues, and a good story to tell, but the credit report tells you all the financial trends are getting worse and the bonds are rated as junk, you may just have saved yourself a lot of money.

As with annual reports, I prefer to read analyst reports back to front. Ignore the recommendation; look at the numbers first, and the assumptions the analyst used in forecasting them. Then read the body of the text. Finally, look at the front page. (The way recommendations are reported in news media is completely useless to a fundamental analyst. It doesn't matter that Goldman Sachs has changed a hold to a buy recommendation; what matters is *why*, and they rarely tell you that!)

The only time a recommendation has ever been interesting was when a UK media analyst called Derek Terrington was looking at Mirror Group Newspapers - a group run by Bob Maxwell, a larger-than-life character who ended up floating in the sea, after which it was discovered he was effectively bankrupt. Terrington had his suspicions and decided that although he wasn't allowed to make a 'sell' recommendation, he would give good advice. His recommendation was original: "Cannot Recommend A Purchase."

You might like to go back and look at the capital letters of those 4 last words...

The bond markets

Many large companies have a number of bonds in issue. The bond markets work rather differently from the equity markets, but you can find out how bonds are trading through FINRA Trace, which reports bond prices.

You can then work out the current yield on the bond. For example, a 5% bond issued at par, at $100, and that's now trading at $50, would currently yield 10%. (So basically the 5% bond at $100 par = $5 payment. And then the $5 payment on the new $50 trading price = 10% current yield.)

Of course, if the bond price has doubled to $200, the yield has halved to 2.5%. ($5 payment / $200 bond x 100 = 2.5% new yield).

The $5 payment is set by the company on the issue price. So, it will remain the same, whatever happens to the market price. It's like having a fixed rate mortgage.

Bond traders will tell you that calculation is simplistic, but it's good enough for us.

Now you just have to compare the yield with the rest of the market. The difference is called the *spread*. If, let's say, Bankrupt Corp bonds are trading at 8% while 10-year Treasuries are trading at 1%, that tells you something important about the bond market's view of Bankrupt Corp. It can be particularly useful to see if the spread is getting wider or narrower. A pronounced widening trend would tell you that the market is getting increasingly worried about the company's ability to pay, so it wants to be paid a higher and higher coupon for the risk.

On the other hand, a company that starts to get its balance sheet in shape and starts to make a profit again will usually see the spread narrowing, as investors realize they aren't running such a high risk and can accept a lower return.

Other information

Finally, let's not forget other sources of information which won't necessarily tell you directly about the company, but will help you understand the industry sector and also give you some useful comparisons to see just how well the company that you're analyzing is performing. Briefly, you might look at:

- Industry journals, such as AdAge (advertising), Aviation Week, Women's Wear Daily, Packaging World, or sites like HotelBusiness.com. They often have articles that look at trends_in the sector on a broad scale, which can be very helpful when you're learning about an industry. They also cover what the biggest private operators in the sector are doing - information that you won't find on the stock exchange.
- Actually, 'kicking the tires'. That's easy to do with consumer businesses, for instance, go and stay in hotels, eat in restaurants, buy the clothes (or ask friends and colleagues what they think of them). But you can also visit show homes for residential developments, for instance. One analyst employed someone who lived opposite a factory to count the number of trucks coming in and going out, to see how much business the firm was doing!
- Many major accounting and consulting firms have sector reviews on their websites. These can sometimes be rather theoretical, but other times they're quite interesting in talking about factors such as factory automation, demographic change, regulation and government action, and venture capital funding coming into the sector. Usually, you'll know by reading the abstract whether it's worth reading the whole report.
- Trade shows and exhibitions can be a good place to head if you want to see what's happening in the industry. However, remember not to be distracted - you're there to find out what's happening and how products are emerging, not to collect corporate ballpoint pens. Be honest and introduce yourself as an individual investor, and find the people who can tell you how things work, not the people who have been hired in to front the stands. If you find good contacts, keep them forever.

- Some people like using LinkedIn to find contacts in the sectors they cover. I must admit that it doesn't work well for me, but, as they say, "Your Mileage May Vary".

Make sure you understand the business model

Before you start crunching numbers, make sure you know the business model. For instance, do Chipotle and McDonald's have the same business model?

No, they don't! Chipotle owns and manages the vast majority of its own restaurants. McDonald's, on the other hand, operates through a franchise model. Though from the street they look like similar businesses, when you look at the business model and the cash flows, they work differently. Chipotle is a typical retailer, taking what you pay for your meal in revenue and then paying staff costs, rent and the cost of ingredients. McDonald's, on the other hand gets someone else to run each individual business, pay the rent, pay the staff, and take the money, and McDonald's takes a franchise fee when they start up, plus a share of their income every year.

So, what are McDonald's costs? They're all what you might call 'head office costs' - running finances, setting up the operating procedures, developing new recipes and offers, marketing, and training their franchisees.

Where do you think Aéroports de Paris (Paris Airports) makes its money? Think hard before you answer that question.

In the third quarter of 2021, it made more than half its income from retailing and real estate. Aviation fees made up less than half. And nearly a fifth of its revenue came from international airports. In fact, the biggest growth came from Amman, in Jordan, and Almaty, in Kazakhstan - Paris was virtually flat.

Don't ever trust a company name to tell you how it makes its money or where it makes its money; "what it says on the tin" can be highly misleading!

Chapter 2 Quiz

1. Which of these is not an SEC filing?
   a. 10K
   b. 10Q
   c. C3PO
   d. Form 144

2. Which way should you read the annual report?
   a. Back to front
   b. Upside down
   c. Only odd numbered page
   d. In one sitting

3. What is the big problem with Pink Sheet stocks?
   a. They are small
   b. They are only in risky industries
   c. They are pink
   d. They don't have to publish information

4. What is MD&A?
   a. Mergers Disposals & Acquisitions
   b. A dangerous drug
   c. Management's Discussion & Analysis of operations
   d. Marketing, Differentiation & Advertising

5. What is the 10K?
   a. A running race
   b. The annual report SEC filing
   c. An addendum to the quarterly report
   d. A footnote to the accounts

3

Chapter 3: Beat the Street

You may believe that the odds are stacked against you. Surely, big banks and brokers with their highly paid teams of analysts, huge trading teams, expertise and information... Surely, they are going to beat you hands down every time?

Well, that's not exactly true! And there are quite a number of reasons why.

Professional constraints vs single-minded motivation

For a start, consider motivation. What's yours? To make money.

But that's not what motivates analysts or fund managers. Fund managers are under pressure to ensure they don't underperform the market. They also have regulatory pressures - for instance, they may not be allowed to invest in smaller stocks. And because one of fund management companies' big concerns is AUM (assets under management), they'll launch funds in whatever is today's flavor in order to get more customers - whether that's tech, 'green' investing, high income, whatever.

In fact, cynics often say you can tell when a bubble is about to crash by the number of new funds being launched!

Other funds are 'benchmarked'. That means the fund manager has to reflect the relevant index, for instance, the S&P 500. That could mean they are forced to invest in the biggest stocks in the market; they can decide to have, for example, less Tesla and more Alphabet, less Coca-Cola and more PepsiCo, but they can't make any really big bets. An index fund is a fund which is created to match the performance of a given stock market index, such as the S&P 500 or the FTSE 100. (On the other hand, a benchmarked fund measures its performance against the index, but the fund manager can overweight or underweight stocks or sectors to try to achieve better performance. Of course, sometimes fund managers don't do better; they do worse.)

Analysts are driven by the need to create a 'story'; sometimes one analyst will break cover with a big sell story, and they may be right (it's always worth looking at these standout recommendations), but they're motivated mainly because if they get it right, they will have made their name. But analysts are also driven by the agenda of the bank they work for; they may be told to 'go gently' with a stock because it's a corporate finance customer, for instance.

Analysts also have to worry about their competition. Can they get to the number one spot in the Institutional Investor research rankings? Whereas you don't care at all about that kind of thing - you just want to make money in the long term.

You also don't have to worry about quarterly performance. You don't have a boss who will fire you if a stock sits out for a while - you can afford to take a long term view. You don't have to track the market. You make your own decisions, for your own benefit.

And that's why you can beat the market.

Fund managers' constraints: why size is important

Many mutual funds are massive in size. In the UK, for instance, Fundsmith Equity Fund has a total market capitalization of £24.8bn - there are only 11 companies in the FTSE 100 index that it wouldn't have enough money to buy! But that's chicken feed compared to the USA's biggest mutual fund, Vanguard Total Stock Market Index Fund Admiral Shares, which has assets under management of $921bn, way ahead of its next rival, the Fidelity 500 Index Fund, which manages a tiny sum of $274bn.

Of course, these funds are by far the biggest, and the fund universe goes all the way down to boutique funds with just a few million dollars invested, often niche funds investing in a single country (like Vietnam) or a single subsector (like nanotechnology or REITs - Real Estate Investment Trust). But there are a lot of large funds, and their sheer size means they have to choose a large minimum size of investment - too big for many smaller companies.

Add to this the fact that most funds have strict limits on the percentage of a company that they can purchase, and you end up with many smaller and even mid-sized companies which just aren't possible candidates for the biggest funds.

For instance, the Fidelity Magellan Fund, with $32bn under management at the end of 2021, had a mathematical average holding size of nearly $500m (with 69 total holdings).

Suppose we find a small cap company - that means all its shares, at the current share price, would be worth below $2bn. Even if the company is right at the top of the range, Magellan's average holding would represent 25% of the company's total stock (if it took its average holding of $500m - that's 25% of $2bn). So, it's unlikely that any fund of that size would be interested in researching a small cap stock.

Table below shows the capitalization of different sizes of stock

Stock size	Market capitalization
Big cap	$10bn plus
Mid cap	$2-10bn
Small cap	Below $2bn
Micro-cap	$50-300m
Nano-cap	Below $50m

There's also an issue for funds that don't have their own dedicated research team, if they buy stocks that are not covered by a good number of analysts. Without in-depth research coverage, the fund could be accused of having been unprofessional or even negligent in its investment strategy if the investment goes wrong. So, such funds tend to stick to the larger and well-researched stocks, which are covered by numerous analysts and on which a lot of research reports are available.

You, on the other hand, can choose whatever size of company you like. If you do your research properly, and you don't pick obvious choices that have got popular on social trading or Reddit, you can bet that very few people outside the small boutique funds are doing so. That means, to go back to the Efficient Market Theory, you're taking maximum advantage of the market inefficiencies in the small cap market. But it also means you need to do your research properly!

Oh, another small thing. Because an analyst of an investment bank is publishing their research, they have to get absolutely *everything* calculated and forecast, even if it's not material (technical definition: won't account for more than 5% of costs, revenue or profits). You don't. If you've satisfied yourself, for instance, that stock-based compensation isn't important with the company you're looking at, or that the 'other' item isn't worth forecasting and never has been, just leave them out! That is, if these items are really small and aren't going to impact the earnings figures, you can just not bother looking at them or putting them in the spreadsheet - analysts have to show everything, but an investor can do a back-of-envelope calculation.

Taking the emotion out of investment

You'd think the professionals are cold-blooded, wouldn't you? But actually - and I speak from experience - being too close to the market can mess around with your mind. For a start, every sell-side analyst (working for a broker, not a fund) is close to a trading desk, and when the trading desk is roaring away, it's easy to get caught up in the excitement. And, of course, that trading desk will watch the stock price every second. If the stock falls 2% in early trading, someone will phone the analyst to find out why. You don't get much peace in that job.

Any financial trading center is also quite self-contained, which helps groupthink take hold. Since it's a little world of its own, it's easy for a consensus to be created which doesn't actually reflect reality, and it can be difficult to go against it. It's difficult to ignore the current narratives and come up with an independent view.

While analysts may be quite honest in setting their target values for stocks, it can be difficult to be the only person with a very different view from the market.

Besides, getting things wrong carries major penalties, whether you're an analyst or a fund manager. It can affect your career and even lead to your termination, which can involve public shame. 'Maverick' fund managers who have taken a minority view often don't survive the first six months of underperformance before their strategy starts to pay off - they're attacked in the press, and their employer lets them go. No wonder most analysts and fund managers want to follow the crowd, or at least not be so far out of step with the market that they run any significant risks.

You have an easy way to take emotion out of your investments. Simply don't look at the share prices. Don't look at finance TV shows. Don't log on to your broker every day. Just ignore all this noise and the emotions connected with them.

As a fundamental analyst, you can afford to do that because:

- you're looking for long term investment ideas, perhaps with a 5-10 year horizon or even longer;
- you've probably bought stocks at 10-20% less than they're worth;
- you care about the intrinsic value of the stock, not the market value.

Having your own target price

When you're in the market, you're always looking at the latest move up or down. It's easy to forget about the intrinsic value of the stock.

You, on the other hand, have worked out what the business is actually worth. If a stock that you thought was too expensive falls a little, it might end up at your buy price. Assuming that the fundamentals haven't changed, you are happy buying - because you named your own price.

What you've done is exactly the same as saying, "That new Ford pickup is too expensive at $30,000. I'm gonna wait a few months and see if the price comes down." If you've been waiting for a new model to be reduced in the dealerships, when at last it's discounted, you don't say, "Oh, but that proves it's not a good pickup at all," do you? No, you snap it up!

You'd be surprised how often people look at a share price falling and think it's time to sell. (Very occasionally, when a share price plummets for no good reason - and I mean plummets, like 20% or 30% in a couple of days - you should take notice; someone, somewhere, knows something.) In fact, 'buy on the dips' is great - as long as you have the patience to wait for the stock to start performing again, and enough left in the bank to buy even more if it keeps heading downwards for a while.

Well, Peter Lynch got away with it, but most fund managers would be facing some very awkward questions from their employers - and possibly also from investors in their funds!

Specialist knowledge

Maybe you think you need specialized knowledge to find the right stocks. For some stocks, you certainly will. For instance, if you have never even managed to find your way onto Facebook and think Twitter is for the birds, you probably should give social media stocks a miss. And it's difficult to value pharmaceutical stocks unless you have at least some basic knowledge about how both drugs and the health system work.

That's why you should ensure before buying a stock that you fully understand its products and business model.

However, you may actually have some specialist knowledge that you haven't given yourself credit for. For instance, if you work in retail, you probably have a very good idea of evaluating other retail businesses in terms of their stores' size, attraction, and siting, and how well their products play to their intended market. As I write this, Meta (the renamed Facebook) has lost $230bn off its market capitalization in a massive single-day plunge. But the first signs of problems were already there - not only was Facebook getting into regulatory trouble, but when I asked my friends' kids if they used Facebook, they looked at me as if I was crazy. They're all TikTokers now. Having teenage kids, apparently, makes you a good social media analyst!

And, of course, if you're a doctor, you probably have an edge on the rest of us if you invest in pharmaceutical stocks. You know what you're doing. At least, we hope so!

This is also somewhere your friends can help. Don't listen to stock tips from your friends - but do listen to what they're telling you about their jobs and about products they buy and use.

- "My firm's given up using that software because it's fallen behind in functionality over the past few years."
- "You're not serious? No one shops at Gap anymore!"

- "Seriously, I know everyone thinks that town is stuck in the mud, but new stores are opening all the time, and there's a huge amount of construction happening."
- "The store where we get building supplies just put up the price of plumbing copper pipe by nearly half!"
- "They don't have any second-hand cars left in inventory at the dealers, we're going to have to buy new."

These kinds of comments can give you valuable insights into the market. It was actually the prices of second-hand cars that made Peter Lynch think about one of his best investments in the auto industry, just when everyone had decided that the car makers were all going bankrupt. He realized there was more demand for potential buyers than the car makers could supply - and the market was about to turn.

By the way, you can also leverage this kind of specialized knowledge by joining an investment club. If you enjoy working with other people rather than on your own, it will be worth your while anyway - you'll be happier with a social background for your investment journey. www.betterinvesting.org is your hub for contacting local investment clubs and finding out more.

Chapter 3 Quiz

1. Analysts' recommendations can be affected by all except one of these factors.
    a. Other relationships between the bank they work for and the company they analyze,
    b. Not wanting to go too far from the consensus,
    c. Something they ate the night before,
    d. Wanting to make their name by a bold recommendation.

2. What's the definition of a mid cap stock?
    a. A stock with $2-10bn market capitalization,
    b. A stock with less than $500m capitalization,
    c. One of the ten biggest stocks on the exchange,
    d. A stock with a skull and crossbones symbol.

3. Which of these is not a retail investor advantage?
    a. Being unconstrained in investment choice,
    b. Having a long term investment horizon,
    c. Having more time to devote to the market,
    d. Not having to hit quarterly targets.

4. Your friends can help you by
    a. Giving you stock tips,
    b. Lending you money to invest,
    c. Giving you the benefit of their specialist knowledge,
    d. Giving you insider information.

5. Why should you be investing in stocks?
    a. To achieve above average performance,
    b. To make money,
    c. To impress people,
    d. To track the market.

4

Chapter 4: The three types of statements you need to know, and where to find them

In this chapter, I'm going to show you the three financial statements you need to know to analyze a company. I'll also talk about how much each one of them can tell you about the health of a company - and where to find them in the annual report and other filings.

The three statements are:
- the income statement – what profit the company is making,
- the balance sheet - what the company owns and owes, and
- the cash flow statement - what actually went through the bank account (and I'll explain why that's *not* the same as the profit the company made).

You'll find all the statements under Item 8 of the 10K filing, 'Financial statements and supplementary data'. To make life much easier than it use to be, SEC filings now come with internal hyperlinks to each section - the days of having to scroll through pages and pages of text are gone forever!

What I'm going to do here is to base our work on a single company's annual report, so that you get used to hopping around it and seeing how the different parts relate to the whole. It's Amazon's annual report for 2020, available on the company's investor relations website. Simply type in "Amazon investor relation" on your browser, then on the left side of the website, click "Annual reports, proxies and shareholder letters". You can find it by clicking "2021", and then "2020 Annual Report". You might want to download it, or even print it off. Here's the link for you anyway;

https://ir.aboutamazon.com/annual-reports-proxies-and-shareholder-letters/default.aspx

It's stated according to GAAP - Generally Accepted Accounting Principles. Rather than a set of rules, it's more a framework of standards for accounting, so it does allow quite a lot of caution to accountants and auditors.

I'm going to take you through each of the three main statements of accounts separately. But I'd like to warn you never to look at any one of the statements in isolation from the others. All three are interconnected.

By the way, in my free bonus #1 - Company Valuation Simplified Masterclass, I walk you through some of the financial statements discussed in this chapter and share my real-time analysis on a company called Vesta. It would be practical for you to watch this masterclass to gain a better idea on how to think like an analyst. Please visit www.az-penn.com to watch the class.

A.Z Penn

Income Statement

The income statement is referred to as the 'consolidated statement of operations'. 'Consolidated' because if the company owns smaller subsidiaries, those are all included in the accounts.

And below is what one looks like. It's on page 39 of Amazon's 10k for the Consolidated Statement of Operations in 2020.

AMAZON.COM, INC.
CONSOLIDATED STATEMENTS OF OPERATIONS
(in millions, except per share data)

	Year Ended December 31.		
	2018	2019	2020
Net product sales	$ 141,915	$ 160,408	$ 215,915
Net service sales	90,972	120,114	170,149
Total net sales	232,887	280,522	386,064
Operating expenses:			
Cost of sales	139,156	165,536	233,307
Fulfillment	34,027	40,232	58,517
Technology and content	28,837	35,931	42,740
Marketing	13,814	18,878	22,008
General and administrative	4,336	5,203	6,668
Other operating expense (income), net	296	201	(75)
Total operating expenses	220,466	265,981	363,165
Operating income	12,421	14,541	22,899
Interest income	440	832	555
Interest expense	(1,417)	(1,600)	(1,647)
Other income (expense), net	(183)	203	2,371
Total non-operating income (expense)	(1,160)	(565)	1,279
Income before income taxes	11,261	13,976	24,178
Provision for income taxes	(1,197)	(2,374)	(2,863)
Equity-method investment activity, net of tax	9	(14)	16
Net income	$ 10,073	$ 11,588	$ 21,331
Basic earnings per share	$ 20.68	$ 23.46	$ 42.64
Diluted earnings per share	$ 20.14	$ 23.01	$ 41.83
Weighted-average shares used in computation of earnings per share:			
Basic	487	494	500
Diluted	500	504	510

The first thing you may notice is that it gives you three years of data - for 2018, 2019 and 2020. That's really useful as it lets you look at trends rather than just having two data points. I always like to see if I can get a five - year run of figures - if I got the 2018 report, I'd have 2017 and 2016 figures too, which would really give me confidence in whatever trends I have noted.

- If I only had two years of data, for instance, if sales went up between 2019 and 2020, that might just be because 2019 had been a particularly bad year. In fact, 2020 sales might still be below 2018 levels for all I'd know.
- If I had three years of data, I'd see whether there was a steady trend. So, if in 2019 sales were up 20% and in 2020, they were up 15%, yes, there's an upwards trend. But I might not have a good feeling for whether it was slowing down or whether that's just a normal variance.
- Suppose I get the additional two years of data of 2016 and 2017, and I see that previously, sales have risen by 15% and 18%, then I could see that 2020 is perfectly normal. On the other hand, if I saw that sales had risen by 70% in 2017, then 35% in 2018, then 20%, then 15%, I know the trend is slowing down.

As Oscar Wilde might have said, "To have one bad quarter might be regarded as a misfortune; to have two looks like carelessness."

You might also want to calculate CAGR - the Compound Annual Growth Rate. This averages out growth over, say, a three or five year period, ironing out all the intermediate ups and downs.

The formula is the difference between the final figure and the figure at the beginning, to the power of 1/number of years, minus 1. See below:

$$\text{CAGR} = \left(\frac{V_{\text{final}}}{V_{\text{begin}}} \right)^{1/t} - 1$$

But never mind all that, there are loads of CAGR calculators on the internet, and a function in most spreadsheet packages. (CAGR is particularly interesting if you want to get a long term growth rate you can use in forecasting.)

In the screenshot below, I have a CAGR calculator using cagrcalculator.net to work out the sales CAGR from the Amazon 2020 income statement.

CAGR (Compound Annual Growth Rate)	15.01 %
Starting value (Initial Investment Value)	141915
Ending value (Ending Investment Value)	215915
No. of periods (Months/Years)	3
Calculate	
CAGR (Compound Annual Growth Rate)	15.01 %

Over the course of **3** years/months your investment grew from **141915.0** to **215915.0**. Its compound annual growth rate (CAGR) is **15.01** %.

I used the sales figures for 2018 and 2020, and the time period was three years (2018, 2019 and 2020). It gives us a 15.01% CAGR. It's as simple as that to calculate!

Okay, so now I'm going to look at Amazon's Consolidation of Operations, from the top to show you how the income statement works. Basically, it's all about subtraction. We start at the top with sales (or revenues); it's nice to see that they are growing steadily. (Let's not worry about the split between product and service sales for the moment - we'll look at that in the next chapter. For now, focus on the *total net sales*). So this is all the company's sale, everything coming into the company, and as we go down the statement, we'll be subtracting various costs till at the bottom we get the profit, or *net income* for the year. (In some instances, there may be a few additions instead of subtractions, for example, if the company has money in the bank, it might have *interest income*, which would need to be added rather than subtracted.)

Sales/revenues is "the top line".

Next comes the *operating expenses*. These are the regular expenses the business incurs, such as cost of sales, payroll, head office, marketing, etc. Here they are split in a rather different way.

- *Cost of sales* relates to the direct costs of business. For instance, with a retailer like Walmart, cost of sales is what Walmart pays for its supplies - in that case, I always like to work out *gross profit*, which is revenue deduct cost of sales. That shows whether Walmart is managing to keep its mark-up stable over time (the money it makes on each item before it starts paying for the store's and the business's cost).
- *Fulfillment covers* costs of Amazon's logistics network - sending stuff out to customers.
- *Technology and content* includes all the tech costs. If you do a bit of research on Amazon's business model, you'll find that the tech doesn't just cover the cost of Amazon's e-commerce site, but also Amazon Cloud services (AWS) which it provides to third parties.
- *Marketing* includes all the costs of promoting the company's products and services. It's worth keeping an eye on - some businesses cut marketing costs to push up short-term profits, but then they see their revenues have no growth. That's happened to Kraft Heinz and brewer Anheuser-Busch, for instance.
- *General and administrative* are all the other costs of the business. Watch this line - sometimes you can see how a company is getting bloated and wasteful. If this line expands more than all the others, either a growing company has taken a step up (a new headquarters, new accounting system, new and more experienced board), or the executives are not keeping an eye on costs.
- *Other operating expenses* is the amount which generally does not depend on sales or production quantities. Go to page 29 on their annual report and you'll find out what this figure represents.

Take away all of these *operating expenses* from the *net sales*, and you have *operating income* - the basic profitability of the business, before we start thinking about debt service or taxation. This is a good level at which to compare businesses. (However, as you'll see in the next chapter, accounting treatments can make a difference at this level and we might want to make a few adjustments.)

Next comes finance - *interest income* and *interest expense*. Most companies have both cash in the bank, on which they collect interest, and debt, on which they pay out interest. That's the case here; in fact, Amazon pays more interest than it collects. Take a look at the interest paid of $1,647m and operating income of $22,899m, and you can see that Amazon isn't in trouble here - it makes enough profit to service its debt several times over (13.9 times over, that's $22,899m/$1,647m).

Also included at this level is *other income*. This usually isn't very significant, but look at Amazon's 2020 result - it's a nice little slug of extra income. I might want to take a look at the footnotes, or the MD&A, to find out what that represents. But it's probably a currency adjustment or a revaluation of warrants, something like that.

Once the financial and other costs are removed from operating income (or in 2020, financial and other income is added to it as *total non-operating income*), you have *Income before income tax*. Take a look at that line and you can see it's growing strongly - it made a really big jump in 2020. I wonder why? (Let's find out in the next chapter when we look at ratios.)

After that comes a *provision for income taxes*. This isn't the same as tax paid. It means Amazon's accountants have sat down and worked out what they need to pay the IRS when they file. Then they have made an allowance for that. So, this isn't cash that has actually gone out of the business, it's what's *expected* to be paid.

If you think that's a bit odd, let me introduce you to the *accrual system* of accounting (which I will discuss in more detail in the next section).

The income statement is about what the company made in the period, but it's not about cash coming in and out - and that's why, later in this chapter, I'm going to take you through the *cash flow statement*.

There's also a very small item called *equity-method investment activity*. Sometimes, a company decides to take a share in a business partnership instead of running the entire business itself. What's reported here is only the amount Amazon is entitled to, and it's not particularly significant.

Subtract the *tax* and *equity-method investment* from the operating profit, and you have *net income* or profit. And, this is "the bottom line".

But as a shareholder, you haven't quite got everything you need from the income statement yet. You may want to know how much of this net income your handful of Amazon shares entitles you to. For instance, if Amazon had doubled the number of shares in the year, then although net income as a whole has gone up, you'd actually get a smaller share- out. So, you need to work out net earnings per share. (Actually, you don't, because Amazon has done it for you.)

But there are two kinds of earnings per share! *Basic earnings per share* is calculated on the average shares in issue during the period. So, for instance, if a share was issued at the beginning of October, it would only get one quarter's earnings (from when it was issued in October, to the end of the year in December). That's reflected by *weighing* that share as a quarter (1/4) of a share when calculating the basic earnings per share.

But many companies also issue stock options to their executives and to other staff, or might issue shares to pay for acquisitions, with a second slice payable after a year. So, you have shares overhanging - they'll be issued some time, but they haven't been issued yet. Those shares are taken into account with the *diluted earnings per share*. That's the number we really want to look at.

Suppose a company doubled its revenues and profits by purchasing another company, and it did so in return for a small payment, but with the promise of a payment of shares after a year. (To make things easy, I'm also going to assume the company isn't growing.) Suppose that this would actually double the number of shares. If you looked at basic income, it would double this year and then halve next year. It would double this year because all the extra income is being divided between the same number of shares, and then it would halve next year as the new shares were issued.

Diluted earnings per share this year, on the other hand, would adjust for the new share issue. So, you would see earnings exactly the same next year.

It's not a realistic example, but it shows you how these things work!

(By the way, if a company splits its stock, by giving everyone five shares for every one, for instance, all the historic figures are restated. Stock splits often happen when the shares have gotten too expensive, so that instead of a stock being worth $5,000, shareholders get ten shares at $500 instead. A stock split happens when a company increases the number of its shares to boost the stock's liquidity.)

Example: Accrual system of accounting

The income statement isn't about cash going in and out. To explain how accruals work, it might be best to take a simple business example of two kids deciding to set up a lemonade stall.

They both take $10 each out of their piggy banks, and borrow the same amount of $10 interest- free from their parents. That's the starting capital - $20 equity, and $20 debt.

Then they buy a table and tablecloth for $20 and lemonade for $20.

They sell all the lemonade for $45 cash. How much money have they made this week?

Assuming they'll carry on with this lucrative business as long as the sun keeps shining, the table and tablecloth are a capital expense (that is, an investment in the business for the long term). Maybe they expect them to be useful for the whole 10 weeks of the season. This week, they'll only pay for 1/10 of the kit - $2 (that is, $20 / 10 weeks).

On the other hand, the lemonade has all been used up this week, so the full cost of that is taken.

That makes the profit $45 sales, less $20 cost of sales, less a $2 a week charge for the kit (which is called *depreciation*) - a grand total of $23 profit.

If you look at cash flow, though, they've paid out $40, and got back $45. Cash flow generated was just $5.

That, in a nutshell, is the accrual system - spreading sales and costs over the period that they cover - in this case for 10 weeks.

Balance Sheet

This is the next statement to look at. It shows what Amazon owns and owes, and it's on page 41 of the annual report. Here, we've only got two years of figures, not three.

While the income statement shows what Amazon earned over the whole period of the year, the balance sheet is a snapshot taken on 31st December. It's a single moment of the company's assets (things it owns) and liabilities (amounts that it owes) frozen in time. That's why, when I start talking about balance sheet ratios, you'll see that many of them use *averages* for the balance sheet numbers.

Take a look at the Amazon Consolidated Balance Sheet in 2020 example on the next page.

AMAZON.COM, INC.
CONSOLIDATED BALANCE SHEETS
(in millions, except per share data)

		December 31,	
		2019	2020
ASSETS			
Current assets:			
Cash and cash equivalents	$	36,092	$ 42,122
Marketable securities		18,929	42,274
Inventories		20,497	23,795
Accounts receivable, net and other		20,816	24,542
Total current assets		96,334	132,733
Property and equipment, net		72,705	113,114
Operating leases		25,141	37,553
Goodwill		14,754	15,017
Other assets		16,314	22,778
Total assets	$	225,248	$ 321,195
LIABILITIES AND STOCKHOLDERS' EQUITY			
Current liabilities:			
Accounts payable	$	47,183	$ 72,539
Accrued expenses and other		32,439	44,138
Unearned revenue		8,190	9,708
Total current liabilities		87,812	126,385
Long-term lease liabilities		39,791	52,573
Long-term debt		23,414	31,816
Other long-term liabilities		12,171	17,017
Commitments and contingencies (Note 7)			
Stockholders' equity:			
Preferred stock, $0.01 par value:			
Authorized shares — 500			
Issued and outstanding shares — none		—	—
Common stock, $0.01 par value:			
Authorized shares — 5,000			
Issued shares — 521 and 527			
Outstanding shares — 498 and 503		5	5
Treasury stock, at cost		(1,837)	(1,837)
Additional paid-in capital		33,658	42,865
Accumulated other comprehensive income (loss)		(986)	(180)
Retained earnings		31,220	52,551
Total stockholders' equity		62,060	93,404
Total liabilities and stockholders' equity	$	225,248	$ 321,195

Look for the figures that have <u>double underlines</u>.

There are two of them; one represents *total assets*, and the other is *total liabilities and stockholders' equity*. What do you notice about the figures?

Yup, they're the same, and they balance, which is why this is called a **balance sheet**.

It might be easier if you imagine the assets on one page and the liabilities on the facing page, instead of one on top of the other. They would then balance.

Let's go back to the lemonade stall and work out how balance sheets operate.

At the beginning of the week, the two kids have $20 of their own money (stockholders' equity) and $20 borrowed from the Bank of mum and dad (long-term debt). That's the *liability and stockholders' equity* side.

And at the beginning of the week, it sits opposite $40 of cash in the *asset* side.

At the end of the week, they have a table and tablecloth worth $20, less the $2 depreciation charge for the week.

They have sold out of lemonade, and they have $23 in profit, and $45 in the cash box (what they got from selling all the lemonade).

This is how the balance sheet changes;

- On the *asset* side, they now have equipment worth $18 ($20 – $2) and $45 in cash - that's $63.
- And as *liabilities and equity*, they still have the original $20 stock and $20 loans, but they have added another item, retained profit of $23. Which is also $63; hence it balances.

They have grown the total value of the business. But who benefits - them, or Mum and Dad? They do, because if we split down the liabilities and equity, the retained profit is part of the equity. They can either keep it on the balance sheet, or they can decide to pay themselves a dividend out of it. I would like to think these kids are smart enough to reinvest the money and sell even more lemonade next week!

Now with that out of the way, let's tackle the Amazon balance sheet, which, as you might imagine, is quite a bit more complex than the lemonade example above.

The assets start with *current assets* - that is, assets that are expected to be used up in less than 12 months. These are also assets that are liquid. That is, Amazon could get money for them in a short amount of time.

Cash and cash equivalents are fairly obvious.

Marketable securities include any investments such as a bond or stock, but not cash - basically anything that can be sold on the stock market.

Inventories would be items that are fairly easy to sell and probably turn over several times a year. So, if you're a retailer, you buy stock, and you expect to sell it pretty easily and quickly. For instance, if you're a fashion retailer, you expect to sell all your winter clothes, then your summer collection, then the fall collection... you get through three or four loads of different stock a year.

And *accounts receivable* represent sums other people owe Amazon and presumably will be repaid in the short term. (If you send goods by post with an invoice, and your year end comes before the money comes in, you have a receivable. That is because the customer would have to pay for the goods in the next accounting period. If the money comes in before the year end, you have cash.)

Current assets account for a little over a third of Amazon's assets. (That is $131,733m current assets in 2020, in comparison to total assets of $321,195m in 2020.) The rest are long-term assets.

The big item here is *property and equipment*. That includes all types of assets that support the business in the long term; warehouses, office buildings, computers, vehicles, conveyor belts, robotic systems, etc. I'm just looking at property and equipment here, and I think Amazon must have made relatively large investments in 2020. That's a thought we might remember for later when we look at the cash flow account. Remember that this number is a historic number. When Amazon buys a property, it's recorded in the balance sheet at what was paid for it, *less* depreciation, so it gets smaller over time.

Of course, in the real world, real estate generally increases in value. With most companies, it's not a big deal, but with older companies, you may sometimes find that there are significant assets that are worth more than is shown. For instance, a company may have an old factory site that is now in a residentially zoned area and worth far more to a residential developer than the value shown in the books. How do you find out? You have to read the notes *very* carefully - there's a note that tells you where the largest properties are.

Operating leases represent assets that the company leases rather than owns and probably cover similar types of assets.

Next is *goodwill*. This is a little bit more difficult to explain, but let me try. If you have a business and sell it, some of the money you get will pay for the assets in the business. But probably, you'll get paid more than just the liquidation value (net value of a company's physical assets if it were to go out of business and the assets sold) - you'll get paid for the business as a profit-generating enterprise. *So basically, the difference between the actual value of the assets and the price paid for the business is goodwill.* For example, if company A purchased company B for $5m, but the actual value of company B was $4.5m. In this case, company A has paid $500k as a Goodwill. Does that make sense?

Add in the *other asset*, and that's the total of the first side of the balance - *total assets*.

On the other side of the balance sheet, we have the liabilities and stockholders' equity.

In the *current liabilities*, again, the balance sheet starts out with the short-term stuff (i.e. within 12 months).

Accounts payable are amounts that Amazon owes to its suppliers. You might want to just note how they relate to inventories and accounts receivable. These three items together are called *working capital,* and they're quite important because they show how healthy the company's short term cash cycle is. Particularly with growing companies, you want to know that the working capital is being well controlled. I'll show you the ratios for checking that in the next chapter.

Next comes *accrued expenses.* These are expenses that you need to pay but haven't paid yet - such as unpaid vacation pay, utilities used but not paid for, and so on. They may also include tax for which the company has already incurred the liability but which will not need to be paid till sometime in the future - a deferred tax liability.

Unearned revenue is the other way round. If you have a subscription service, and the customer has paid you for 12 months but only used six, you have six months of unearned revenue. You have to carry on providing the service for the next six months.

All of these items make up *total current liabilities.*

But if you want to see how the company's long term funding is structured, you want to look at the long term liabilities. Basically, these split into two:

- equity, which is what the shareholders own, and
- debt, which is what the banks are owed.

You can treat long-term lease liabilities as debt because the company can't get out of them without repaying the amount it borrowed, and it has to pay interest on what's outstanding.

Long-term debt could be borrowings from banks or from the bond markets, which aren 't repayable within 12 months, and on which the company has to pay interest.

Then we get to *stockholders' equity*.

The way it's displayed here is a bit over-complex for my needs; all I'm interested in is how much is 'original' capital, what stockholders paid the company for new stock, and how much is retained earnings. Basically, I want to see that the company has been adding a significant amount of retained income to what shareholders originally forked out. And yes, it has $52,551m retained earnings out of $93,404m total equity means well over half the equity has been added by the company and not subscribed by shareholders.

That's pretty much all you need to know about the balance sheet, but let's just think about different ways of balancing it. What you've got here is:

ASSETS = LIABILITIES + EQUITY

but you could also balance it differently, as:

ASSETS - LIABILITIES = EQUITY.

Don't trust me on this - do the sums, and check it out!

Cash Flow

People often talk about the cash flow statement as the third of the statements, but in the Amazon annual report it comes first, on page 38. It reconciles the numbers in the income statement with those in the balance sheet - so once you know your way around the math, you can always check that everything adds up. It also shows how much actual cash the company is generating. To do that, it strips out the accrual basis and only shows the movement of cash.

I particularly like the cash flow statement because the chances are, if a company tries to 'fix' its income statement by using aggressive accounting policies, it will show up in the cash flow. It will also show if a company is 'buying' its profits (that is, profits are growing, but the company is increasingly getting into debt).

The screenshot on the next page is from the Amazon Consolidated Statement of Cash Flows in 2020.

AMAZON.COM, INC.
CONSOLIDATED STATEMENTS OF CASH FLOWS
(in millions)

	Year Ended December 31,		
	2018	2019	2020
CASH, CASH EQUIVALENTS, AND RESTRICTED CASH, BEGINNING OF PERIOD	$ 21,856	$ 32,173	$ 36,410
OPERATING ACTIVITIES:			
Net income	10,073	11,588	21,331
Adjustments to reconcile net income to net cash from operating activities:			
Depreciation and amortization of property and equipment and capitalized content costs, operating lease assets, and other	15,341	21,789	25,251
Stock-based compensation	5,418	6,864	9,208
Other operating expense (income), net	274	164	(71)
Other expense (income), net	219	(249)	(2,582)
Deferred income taxes	441	796	(554)
Changes in operating assets and liabilities:			
Inventories	(1,314)	(3,278)	(2,849)
Accounts receivable, net and other	(4,615)	(7,681)	(8,169)
Accounts payable	3,263	8,193	17,480
Accrued expenses and other	472	(1,383)	5,754
Unearned revenue	1,151	1,711	1,265
Net cash provided by (used in) operating activities	30,723	38,514	66,064
INVESTING ACTIVITIES:			
Purchases of property and equipment	(13,427)	(16,861)	(40,140)
Proceeds from property and equipment sales and incentives	2,104	4,172	5,096
Acquisitions, net of cash acquired, and other	(2,186)	(2,461)	(2,325)
Sales and maturities of marketable securities	8,240	22,681	50,237
Purchases of marketable securities	(7,100)	(31,812)	(72,479)
Net cash provided by (used in) investing activities	(12,369)	(24,281)	(59,611)
FINANCING ACTIVITIES:			
Proceeds from short-term debt, and other	886	1,402	6,796
Repayments of short-term debt, and other	(813)	(1,518)	(6,177)
Proceeds from long-term debt	182	871	10,525
Repayments of long-term debt	(155)	(1,166)	(1,553)
Principal repayments of finance leases	(7,449)	(9,628)	(10,642)
Principal repayments of financing obligations	(337)	(27)	(53)
Net cash provided by (used in) financing activities	(7,686)	(10,066)	(1,104)
Foreign currency effect on cash, cash equivalents, and restricted cash	(351)	70	618
Net increase (decrease) in cash, cash equivalents, and restricted cash	10,317	4,237	5,967
CASH, CASH EQUIVALENTS, AND RESTRICTED CASH, END OF PERIOD	$ 32,173	$ 36,410	$ 42,377

The first line shows *cash at the beginning* of the year. That's from the balance sheet, and what this account does is it shows the way cash came into and went out of the business during the year, which are all adjustments to the income statement. And then we'll finish up with the *cash at the end of the year*, the figure that goes in the balance sheet.

The balance sheet and cash flow figures for total cash don't quite agree. That's because the balance sheet excludes what's called restricted cash, for instance where it's needed as security. The cash flow account includes it. There's a note explaining that in the accounts. But frankly, it's a small number here, so we don't need to worry too much about it. (The cash in cash flow is $36,410m, and cash in balance sheet is $36,092m.)

So, the *operating activities* starts with *net income* - the bottom line of the income statement.

Then the cash flow statement adjusts it for all the accruals, which is shown under *Adjustments to reconcile net income to net cash from operating activities.*

The biggest item is almost always *depreciation and amortization*. If you remember, we depreciated the table in the lemonade stand example by $2 each week to spread the cost out over the 10 week summer season. In the Amazon accounts, depreciation is quite a bit more than net income. (By the way, amortization is the same thing as depreciation, only when intangible assets like software are involved.)

The *other expenses* are less significant, though *stock-based compensation* is worth keeping an eye on. Sometimes companies ramp it up, and it can involve heavy shareholder dilution. So here, it's not an issue, but just make sure you spot it happening if it starts becoming one.

Then you see *changes in operating assets and liabilities*, which is a non-user-friendly way of saying 'Changes in working capital'. When you build up your inventories, or when you give a customer credit, you are tying up your cash, so any increase in inventories or accounts receivable has to be subtracted from net income to get to the cash flow (you are paying out of your own pocket basically).

On the other hand, *accrued expenses* and *accounts payable* can be added back in. We add back accrued expenses because we haven't actually handed over cash for them yet, and accounts payable because we haven't paid them yet. (Wow, what happened to accounts payable in 2020?)

When all these adjustments have been made, you get the net operating cash flow or *net cash provided by operating activities* (no one ever calls it that).

Amazon has generated three times more in cash than it makes in net income, and its cash flow has been growing fast (that is the net operating cash flow of $66,064m over net income of $21,331m).

But now you need to look at how much Amazon had to invest in getting there. So, the cash flow adjusts for *investing activities*.

These figures should explain the movement in long term assets on the balance sheet; *purchases of property and equipment*, for instance. Just as a quick check, $40,140m of cash was spent on property and equipment, and in the balance sheet, the difference between 2019 and 2020 property and equipment items is $40,409m. Near enough!

Amazon has sold a few bits and pieces too, but not much. It also spent $2,325m on *acquisitions*.

But look at the figures for 2020 of *sales and maturities of marketable securities* and *purchases of marketable securities* - they're fairly chunky. In fact, when I looked up what was happening, it seems Amazon has been managing its treasury operations by buying a lot of short term government debt and other bonds, which is really cash management, not investment. Treasury operations are managing the company's cash and debt effectively - it's quite a niche element of head office finance.

So, for instance, a company will try to make sure its debt is secured for as long as possible at as low an interest rate as possible, and if it has cash on hand, it will invest it in short term bonds rather than leaving it in the bank, to make that little bit extra in interest. But if Amazon was buying stakes in other companies, that would probably have been for other reasons, like it wanted to support a small company that had technology useful to Amazon's operations or it wanted to lay the foundations for an eventual takeover.

At the bottom, you can see how much Amazon has invested each year under *net cash provided by investing activities*. It's a negative item, but it's still less than Amazon is generating from operating activities. However, the two lines of *net operating activities* and *net investing activities* have been getting closer together. So, I am going to want to find out what that big splurge of spending on capital and equipment was in 2020 and see what happens next.

Sometimes, companies invest much more in one year than they generate in cash. That's often the case with start-ups, and it can happen with companies that want to make a step -change. For instance, when software companies decided to switch from selling software licenses to selling Software As A Service, they often had to make huge investments in plant and equipment to support their cloud services. They then collect the benefits over the next several years. It can also happen with cyclical companies like automakers and chemical companies; they have to invest in big chunks.

But is that the case here? Or is Amazon spending too much? That's another thing I'm going to make a note of, to take a good look at.

The last set of cash flow items is cash flow from *financing activities*.

You can see here whether Amazon is borrowing more money or repaying debt; you'd also see here if it has issued any new shares. I'd be worried if I saw big numbers of new loans coming in. As it is, Amazon seems to be repaying its finance leases and has been repaying debt most years. That's a pretty solid performance, and if 2020 looks different, it's still not a huge change.

As you can see, before we start working out any of the ratios, I've already identified a few things I want to think about.

By the way, one number that's not shown here but that many analysts like to use is EBITDA (earnings before interest, tax, depreciation and amortization). It adjusts operating profit, or EBIT (earnings before interest and tax), but adds back *depreciation and amortization* - the big non-cash item, to get what you could call 'cash operating earnings'. It's a quick and dirty addition that you can do very easily, and it will come in useful later when we come to do valuations.

Normalizing earnings

With some companies, though not with Amazon, you may find that there's a big spanner in the works. For instance, a company might have discontinued a loss-making line of business, which - with the closure of businesses, write-off of obsolete stock, and write-off of all the equipment used in the business - creating a huge negative item. Or a company might have sold its old headquarters building to a real estate developer, making a huge profit, but obviously, not one that you'd expect to happen ever again.

Whatever the treatment of such sums by the accountants, as a fundamental analyst, you'll want to put a barrier on them and try to work out what are the underlying earnings. Most analysts do this, but it can create problems when looking at an adjusted figure from the analyst and an un-adjusted number from the company.

The most important thing is that you understand the impacts on the numbers and can detect the underlying trend.

You might want to adjust some other figures, too. For instance, if the company has a huge pension liability, it won't show that on the balance sheet, but you might decide that the value of the company should be shown adjusted for the pension's black hole. So, you would take the balance sheet total and subtract the pension liability, and then you would restate book value per share to take account of the liability.

You're restating book value per share so that you can see what the company's assets are worth if it has to pay the pensions liability first. That's being pessimistic. In the same way, if a company had a big lawsuit hanging over it, you might restate its net worth as if it had lost the lawsuit, and that gives you a bottom dollar figure for what it's worth - if the share price is less than that, it's safe to buy.

If you'd done that, you wouldn't have bought General Motors (GM) in the early years of the century; it had a negative net worth when restated. You also wouldn't have been surprised when GM filed for bankruptcy in 2005.

But that's not all!

While any analysis of a company and its stock will start with these three statements, you'll need to look further to make sense of the numbers. For instance, in Part I of the Annual Report, you'll find a description of the business and risk factors that could affect it. There's also a pretty brief recap of financial data for the past five years, which shows just headline figures, but gives you a good feel for the medium term performance of the company.

Looking at the notes in that table gives you two useful tidbits of information; first, that Amazon acquired Whole Foods in mid-2017, and secondly, that the account presentation of operating leases was changed in 2019. So, you might want to follow those up and see what difference those facts made to the numbers.

There's also a note on "Effects of COVID-19". You'll probably have guessed that lockdowns and customers' desire to avoid crowded shops led to increased buying from Amazon. But it also had costs, and Amazon strips them out here; $11.5bn in 2020, $4bn in the last quarter. Now, if you remember, I wondered why Amazon had so much capital spending in 2020, and this is part of the answer, I would guess. It's also why Amazon may not have repaid debt as much as it usually does.

On page 25, there's a breakdown of net sales, continuing with a breakdown of operating income on page 26. Amazon breaks down its business into three parts: North America, International, and AWS - the Cloud business. It also shows you the growth rates and percentages, so you don't have to work them out for yourself.

AWS only accounted for 12% of total sales. However, it made up more than half the operating profit! Because of those extra COVID costs, Amazon's retail business didn't improve its profitability very much. In contrast, AWS shot up from $9,201m to $13,531m. If you thought you were buying a retail operation, you might want to think about what that means for your assessment of the company.

I hope you're now beginning to get an idea of how the numbers in the accounts can provoke questions that may (or may not) be answered by the management's discussion of operations or the notes to the accounts. That's really key to being a good analyst, being able to join the two up - and it's something you will gradually learn by experience.

The footnotes - the best bit!

Reading the footnotes is always enlightening. I won't go through the whole report line by line because that would be really boring, but here are a few interesting items.

- When vendors use the Fulfilled By Amazon service, they send their goods to an Amazon warehouse, but they retain ownership. This stock *doesn't* appear on Amazon's balance sheet. That means its inventory might appear quite a bit lower than for conventional retailers with the same level of sales.
- The notes on accounts receivable and inventory tell you what Amazon had to write off or provide against possible bad debt. Those notes, for some companies, will be the first sign that their product is getting behind the times or they're giving too much credit to low quality customers. But there doesn't seem to be a problem here.

- Software development costs are capitalized, that is, they're put on the balance sheet (as if they were a piece of equipment that had been bought) - but the number wasn't significant. Sometimes, companies capitalize on very large amounts of software development costs or even customer acquisition costs; in some cases, that makes them look profitable when in fact, they're not. Well, that's not a problem here.

- Amazon tells you its depreciation policies. For instance, servers are written off over four years, and heavy equipment over ten years. Again, sometimes companies use depreciation to pad their income statement - everything seems in line here, though Amazon has possibly benefited a little by extending the life of servers from three to four years from the start of 2020 (they'll incur less depreciation annually).

- Note 3, on property and equipment, shows that Amazon has a huge leap of $15,228m of construction in progress. That gives me a feeling that there's a good chunk of spending to come next year.

- Note 6, debt, shows the maturities of Amazon's debt - that is, when it has to repay the loans. There's a small amount that has to be repaid by 2022, but the average life of the remaining debt is more than 11 years, so there's no big repayment coming up (with other companies, sometimes this note makes very uncomfortable reading).

- Note 7 is interesting: commitments. It shows all the finance leases, rent agreements, and debt payments that need to be made over the next five years. Check with the balance sheet to see if Amazon has enough cash to pay, and check with the income statement to see if it's making enough profit. Do you see any problem? I don't.

- One thing I'm delighted to see is that under 'suppliers,' the company says "no vendor accounted for 10% or more of our purchases." It's not good news when a company is dependent on a single big supplier.

- 'Legal proceedings' is always an interesting note. There's quite a lot going on here, so it's something stockholders need to keep an eye on.

- Note 10, 'segment information', gives you even more information on the breakdown of Amazon's business. It breaks down sales through online and physical stores, third-party sellers, and subscription services and also breaks out three big overseas markets - Germany, UK and Japan.

You'll also find, on pages 36-37, a letter from the auditors. It's boring, which is the way we like it. If an auditor's letter ever mentions words such as "qualified" or "going concern", it's a sign that the accountants have real worries about the way things are going. In the case of a going concern qualification, they think the business might not be able to make it through the year without refinancing. Ernst & Young seem to have no big issues other than the difficulty of calculating Amazon's tax position.

So, just going through a single year's annual report without getting out a calculator or doing any work on the ratios, we already have some interesting facts and some questions to ask.

Do you think you now know more about Amazon than you did? I bet you do. Do you think you have enough to value the shares?

Well, that may have made you think. We haven't really got to that stage yet. So, we need to do a little more work!

P.S. Before we go onto looking at the ratios, if you are finding this book useful so far - I would really appreciate if you could spare 60 seconds and write a brief review on Amazon on how this book is helping you. It would mean the world to me to hear your feedback!

Chapter 4 Quiz

1. Which of these is not an asset?
   a. Goods for resale held in inventory
   b. The headquarters building
   c. A loan note the company issued in 2009
   d. Money owed by a customer for goods sold by the company

2. Which of these is not a liability?
   a. The company's share capital
   b. Long term debt
   c. Cash
   d. Overdraft

3. Which of these is a non-cash item?
   a. Depreciation
   b. Capital expenditure
   c. Change in inventories
   d. Repayment of finance

4. What is goodwill?
   a. Amazon's chain of thrift shops
   b. What you paid for a business
   c. Anything you paid for a business more than the cost of its assets
   d. A nice feeling

5. What is 'diluted' income per share?
   a. A dividend paid to stockholders who don't drink alcohol,
   b. Income per share including all stock that is to be issued later,
   c. Income per share less tax already paid,
   d. A measure of cash flow

5

Chapter 5: Why adding two and two sometimes makes more than four

In this chapter, I'm going to take you through the kinds of ratios that you can calculate from the numbers shown in the annual report. These ratios compare one item in the accounts with another, giving us information on what's happening in the business. Think of the ratios as being like a stethoscope, ultrasound, X -rays - they can show you what's going on underneath the skin. It's a way of comparing two numbers to create additional information, such as "two and two makes five".

They also give you ways to conquer time and space. That is, ratios let you compare Amazon today with Amazon in 1997 or in 2010. And they let you compare Amazon with Alphabet, Walmart, or any other company you consider as its peer group.

Financial news items often don't contain any ratios at all. They just report numbers - IBM's profits were down, PepsiCo's shares were up.

You'll get a story that leads with "Such and such stock was up 3% today as earnings rose 5%."

But suppose you know that the company's revenues were up 20%, and the debt on its balance sheet increased from 40% to 60% of the total capitalization? Then the real story is actually this one: "The margins the company is making on its sales fell dramatically, and its debt ratio increased making it a riskier trade if interest rates rise." But you won't hear that on CNBC.

What you're doing with ratios is comparing the different numbers in the financial statement in a way that shows you how the business is performing. For instance, you might compare revenues and profits to see how well the company is turning each dollar of sales into profit; you might compare profits and interest payments to work out if the company can service its debt easily; you might look at inventory turnover to see whether it's moving its stock out of the warehouse.

If you have surprises, such as a bad quarter, or a ratio that doesn't look right, try to find an explanation elsewhere. For instance, a bad quarter might involve:

- the beginning of a downturn - if sales, gross margin, operating margin, and accounts receivable are all down;
- a lot of sales made but to customers who haven't yet paid - if accounts receivable is high; that means next quarter should be back on track;
- a big step change in a single cost (which you can see easily and which might reflect investment in a new area of business), or all the costs rising significantly (which is more likely to be a control issue and suggests management has lost its way);
- settlement of a major lawsuit (which is a non-recurring item).

Doing all the ratios properly and reading the annual report in detail will let you know which of these is the case. On the other hand, if you just look at the bare bones account in the newspapers, you won't be able to tell.

Every analyst has their favorite ratios. No single ratio on its own is going to tell you the whole story, but once you've worked out a number of them, you'll see how they relate, and you'll be able to use them just the way a detective uses clues.

Ratios can analyze current trends, the company's operations, its long-term investment in productive capacity, its financing, and its valuation. I'll show you each of these areas in turn. And again, I'll be using Amazon's 2020 financial statements.

Dear readers, if you want the full calculation breakdown of each ratio discussed in this chapter, please check the end of the chapter on page 379 as I have compiled together all the ratios and their calculations.

Trends

First of all, work out the trends in revenue, costs, and cash flow. You've probably done some of it already in the back of your head as you looked at the numbers in the last chapter. Now, calculate the percentage changes - what mathematicians call delta (Δ), but there's no great mystery in how to do it.

The table below shows Amazon's total net sales for periods 2018 – 2020.

	2018	2019	2020
Total net sales	$232,887m	$280,522m	$386,064m

So, Amazon's total net sales grew how much in 2019? And in 2020?

Simply take the difference between the 2020 and 2019 numbers; then work out the difference / 2019 number x 100, and you have the percentage.

And then do the same for 2019 and 2018 figures to get 2019's growth rate.

You should have 20.4% for the first year, and 37.6% for the second. That's a big increase!

The calculations are ($280,522m - $232,887m) / $232,887m x 100 = 20.4%, and ($386,064m - $280,522m) / $280,522m x 100 = 37.6%.

You can do the same for any of the figures in the report. And you can check trends against other trends. For instance, if sales are rising at a steady 15%, then accounts receivable should also be rising around that level, as should the Cost of Goods Sold and inventories. There might be a little difference, but there shouldn't be a major one.

Looking at trends is really interesting when you consider GameStop (GME). GameStop is a videogames and wargaming retailer. In its 10-K, it refers to this as an "intensely competitive industry" and also warns that gamers are increasingly downloading games direct rather than going to buy a DVD from a shop. Let's see how this plays out in the trends, using the selected financial info from the 10-K.

The table below shows GameStop's sales and growth rate for periods 2016 – 2020

	2016	2017	2018	2019	2020
Sales	$7,965m	$8,547m	$8,285m	$6,466m	$5,090m
Growth		7.3%	-3.1%	-21.2%	-21.3%

Okay, 2020 was affected by the pandemic. But 2019 was already looking bad. This company has been ex-growth for a while. Now let's look at the net income trend for GameStop in 2016 - 2020.

	2016	2017	2018	2019	2020
Net income	$305m	$230m	$-795m	$-464m	$-214m
Growth		-24%	n/a	-42%	-54%

I'm not getting a clear picture other than that this company has had either declining or negative profitability for five years. True, losses are declining. At the current rate, you'd feel the business will lose about $100m in 2021, half what it lost in 2020. (The 2021 results weren't out when I wrote this, but the consensus is that part way through 2022 it's just on the verge of breakeven.)

Also, 2018 growth is n/a because you can't work out a % change with one negative and one positive number.

I'm going to look at two other trends for GameStop. Let's put them both in the same table: dividends, and a statistic that's important for all retailers, same-store sales. (GameStop has recently been closing stores at quite a pace, so you'd expect same-store sales might go up if it closed the worst stores, which would be a reasonable expectation.)

Again, these stats are straight out of the 10-K, so you can go check them in their SEC Filings if you like.

The table below shows GameStop's dividend growth and same store sales for periods 2016 – 2020.

	2016	2017	2018	2019	2020
Dividend	1.48	1.52	1.52	0.38	0
Same store sales	-11%	+5.8%	-0.3%	-19.4%	-9.5%

What you see with the dividend is the first 3 years show the kind of progress you'd expect of a company in a mature industry sector with a stable business that's not growing fast. Then suddenly, the dividend gets cut to almost nothing, and then it's gone. That says management doesn't believe the problems are over. It's no longer trying to maintain the dividend, as it did in 2018 despite the poor results. It's in trouble, and it knows it.

And same store sales? Falling all the time since 2017.

Seeing this, there's no way I would have joined the Reddit WallStreetBets group in buying the stock. No way at all. They put on a classic short squeeze - hurting the hedge funds who had sold the stock short (selling without owning the stock) - and saw the price soar from below $20 to over $300. It's still sitting over $90 as I write this.

The underlying business hasn't changed, but GameStop's management are smart. They issued shares to take advantage of the high share price, so they now have $1.5bn more cash - they cleaned up the balance sheet nicely and that cash now accounts for about $13.6 a share.

So, to help you understand how I calculated the $13.6 per share, I looked through the financial report, on the company's website to find;

The cash in Q1 2022 was $1,035m.

Shares in issue 75.9m.

So, $1,035m / 75.9m = $13.6 cash per share.

I still don't think the rest of the business is worth the remaining $76.40.

A philosophical note: you could say I'm dumb, and I missed a fantastic opportunity to make money. However, what about the guys who got in a little late and bought GameStop at over $300? They've lost two-thirds of what they put in. Fundamental analysis will sometimes mean you don't benefit from a big stock market movement - but it will stop you from buying trash that glitters but isn't gold.

Operations

These ratios are going to tell you how well the company is working on a day-to-day basis in running the business and serving the needs of its customers. The first set of ratios you'll want to look at comes from the income statement: different types of **margins**.

First of all, I want to calculate Amazon's *gross margin*. This is sales *less* cost of sales. For retailers, it's one of the most important ratios. Some retailers tell you exactly what it is, but Amazon doesn't. You have to calculate the gross profit first. So, looking at 2020, the total net sales is $386,064m *minus* cost of sales which is $233,307m, and that gives us $152,757m gross profit.

Gross margin is gross profit as a percentage of sales. That's $152,757m / $386,064m x 100 = 39.57%$. You can calculate 2019 and 2021 yourself if you like. They don't look very different.

The next level of margin you want to look at is *operating margin*. This is a bit easier because Amazon gives you the operating income line; you don't have to calculate it. This comes in at $22,899m / $386,064m x 100 = 5.93%$. That's actually higher than in either of the previous two years, so Amazon appears to be controlling costs well.

Remember that you need to have a feeling for the business behind the numbers. For instance, if you see a fall in margins, it could reflect a number of different factors, and your decision on whether to buy a company or not might be different, depending on the factors involved.

- Margins could have fallen because a company acquired a business that has lower margins, such as a distributor - a change in the *mix* of profits.
- Margins could have fallen because the product mix has changed. For instance, if consumers are buying more expensive meals as they feel more wealthy, a restaurant might see its margins increase markedly.
- Margins could have fallen because a company took over a lower-margin business that had been badly managed. In this case, you might expect better management to increase the margins over the next few years.
- Margins could have fallen because a company has decided to grab as much market share as possible from its competitors and is reducing prices to do so.
- Or margins might have fallen because management hasn't been controlling costs very well.

You won't know which of these explanations is right unless you read the words as well as the numbers!

Another figure I find quite helpful is tax as a percentage of profit before taxes. Here, it's 11.84% in 2020, against 16.98% in 2019 and 10.62% in 2018. That's all over the place. So that's something I would want to talk about with the company because I don't get a good feeling about what's normal and what tax rate is likely in the future. Remember, this figure is a provision - it's the tax that Amazon expects to pay, but it hasn't actually paid it yet.

In case you're wondering how I calculated tax rate of 11.84% in 2020...

Income before income taxes was $24,178m.

The provision for income taxes was $2,863m.

Tax rate = provision for income taxes / income before income taxes.

*Tax rate = $2,863m / $24,178m x 100 = **11.84%**.*

Another set of useful ratios are the *working capital turnover* ratios. These can show you how well the company is managing its current assets. Let's look first at *inventory turnover*. You can calculate the ratio quite simply, as inventory / cost of sales, for instance, but you can also calculate it in days - just multiply the number by 365. If a company has 30 days' inventory, that's not bad; if it has nearly a year's worth of inventory, that could be a problem.

Think about what this means. 30 days' inventory means I've sold all my stock in a month - if I was a store owner, I'd be pretty happy with that. But if I only trade my stock over once a year, I have all that money sitting in inventory in my store, and it's not selling.

Why do I use cost of sales, not sales? Because inventory will be in the books at what the company paid for it, not what it's sold for. Make sense?

Inventory turnover slowing down might mean the company has issues with outdated products. It might just mean management hadn't focused on inventory. Or it might involve a single bad decision; for instance, UK publisher Dorling Kindersley (DK) made a very bad decision on promoting the Star Wars franchise in 2000, pushing it to a £25m loss. (In fact, DK had other problems with its inventory; two months after it announced its results, it was bought out by Penguin books.)

The formulas for accounts receivable and accounts payable are similar. They both show you the amount of working capital in terms of the number of days of business that it supports.

Accounts receivable, the amount of credit given to customers, is calculated compared to revenues; it's sometimes called Days Sales Outstanding (DSO). Business to business (B2B) companies usually extend credit to their customers and DSO shows how good they are at getting paid on time.

Now, I'm going to introduce a little refinement here, because as you remember from the last chapter, the balance sheets show you snapshots at the beginning and the end of the period, while the income statement covers the whole year in between. So, you take the average value of accounts receivable over the year, rather than starting or ending balance. (That's simple to do - just add the starting and closing balance amounts together, then divide by two.)

So, can you do those ratios for Amazon? If you're struggling, check page 379.

As for accounts payable, this represents the amount of credit the company can get from its suppliers. You may think it's good that a business can get its suppliers to pay for its goods. Tour operators don't have to pay hotels till after their vacationers stay in the hotel, even though the customer has already paid for the vacation. That can give the operator significant amounts of credit from suppliers. However, not all businesses are like this. Sometimes, lengthening accounts payable can show the company has problems.

UK bookseller Pentos was a case in point - this is going way back to the 1990s before Amazon started challenging the bricks -and-mortar bookshops. Pentos bought many bookshops, including the famous Foyles on Charing Cross Road in London. It looked good on paper.

However, if you analyzed the annual reports, you would have seen its accounts payable increasing every year, way ahead of its sales. That meant it was getting its suppliers to pay for its business.

My friend's father knew someone who was working in a publishing house at the time, and he was getting a bit worried about Pentos not paying his bills when he sent them books. Fortunately, his dad mentioned it to his accountant. And his accountant said, "Look at the accounts payable. What's happening there?".

Well, his dad took a look at the annual report and saw what was happening to accounts payable. And then he phoned his friend who worked at the publishing house and explained what he'd found. And his friend decided not to do business with Pentos anymore.

6 months later, Pentos went bust. That was a good call!

Of course, you wouldn't normally want to buy or sell a share based purely on the accounts receivable ratio. But the story goes to show that spending quality time with a set of accounts can sometimes pay off in a surprisingly big way.

The ratios for Amazon's 2020 inventory turnover, accounts receivable and accounts payable are presented below.

Inventory turnover

Total inventory was $23,795m.

Cost of sales was $233,307m.

Inventory turnover = total inventory / cost of sales x 365 days

Inventory turnover = $23,795m / $233,307m x 365 = 37 days.

This means Amazon turns over its inventory in a little more than a month.

Accounts receivable / Days Sales Outstanding

Accounts receivable were $24,542m.

You already have the net sales figure of $386,064m.

Day Sales Outstanding = account receivables / total net sales x 365 days.

Day Sales Outstanding = $24,542m / $386,064m x 365 = 23 days.

Amazon gets paid in less than a month.

Accounts payable turnover

Accounts payable were $72,539m.

You already have the cost of sales figure of $233,307m.

Accounts payable turnover = accounts payable / cost of sales x 365 days.

Accounts payable turnover = $72,539m / $233,307m x 365 = 113 days.

Amazon gets four times more credit from its suppliers than it gives to its customers, which is 113 days in comparison to 23 days.

Long term investments

These ratios compare the income the company is generating to the assets it uses to create that income. It's a way of seeing whether the company has invested well in its business and is getting value out of its property and equipment.

Again, I prefer to use average values for the balance sheet data. But if for whatever reason the prior year's balance sheet is not available, then use what you have in the current year.

All of these ratios are slightly different in their exact significance. But don't sweat the small stuff here. All of them will give you good information.

Return on Invested Capital (ROIC) is calculated as *net operating profit after tax (NOPAT) / invested capital,* or you might like to work it out as *(net profit + dividends) / (debt + equity).* This tells you how efficiently the company is investing its capital to generate positive returns.

If ROIC is less than the interest rate, or less than the company's cost of capital (WACC), then the company isn't getting a good enough return on its funds. On the other hand, a high ROIC suggests the company is successful in using its finance to generate returns, and might justify the company being re-rated (given a higher price/earnings ratio to reward its performance).

Return on Capital Employed (ROCE) is a slightly different look at efficiency, because it takes income before interest and tax (EBIT), and compares this to *total assets less current liabilities.* It gives us pretty much the same information as ROIC, just at a different level.

Return on Assets (ROA) looks instead at the return it makes on its total asset base. It is calculated as *net income / average total assets.*

These ratios work out the profitability of the company as a whole. But of course, if the company has long term debt, some of the returns will go to paying banks and bond interest. You want to know as a stockholder how good the returns are for you specifically. The ratio to find this out is **Return on Equity,** calculated as *net income / shareholders' equity.*

Okay, now let's calculate the ratios for Amazon!

ROIC

Total net income was $21,331m.

Invested capital is made up of equity $93,404m, long term debt $31,816m, and long term lease liabilities of $52,573m, which added together is $177,793m.

ROIC = total net income / invested capital

ROIC = $21,331m / $177,793m x 100 = 12%.

ROCE

EBIT was $22,899m

Total assets were $321,195m, while current liabilities were $126,385m.

That gives us total assets *less* current liabilities of $194,810m.

ROCE = EBIT / (total assets - total liabilities).

ROCE = $22,899m / $194,810m x 100 = 11.75%.

ROA

Total net income was $21,331m.

Average total assets is calculated by adding the total asset figure at the beginning of the year (i.e. the end of 2019) and the end of the year (the 2020 figure), then dividing by two.

Total assets were $225,248m at the start of the year. And $321,195m at the end.

$321,195m + $225,248m / 2 = $273,221m.

ROA = total net income / average total assets

ROA = $21,331m / $273,221m x 100 = 7.8%.

ROE

Total net income was $21,331m and shareholders' equity $93,404m.

ROE = total net income / shareholders' equity

ROE = $21,331m / $93,404m x 100 = 22.84%.

Now, how can you use those ratios? First of all, you can compare companies with other similar companies and see which are doing better than the others. For instance, if you compared food processing companies, retailers, or video games publishers, you'd find that most of them had ratios that looked fairly similar across the sector, though they might be very different from other sectors like mining or energy. You can also see if a company has managed to improve the return on assets. For example, if a company is relatively new and has been spending money to develop a new product, that might have held returns back for a few years, but you'll see it improve as the new product gains success.

You should also consider what the company pays for its finance - **WACC**, the Weighted Average Cost of Capital. Although it's easy to think of equity as 'free', the company has to generate a certain amount of profit to keep stockholders from selling out, so there's a rate of return it needs to make for this purpose. It's usually calculated, and this gets complex, using the Beta (β), a measure of the share's volatility compared to the market (that is, whether it moves in step with the market, ranges much more widely, or moves less).

The formula is: *Risk-free rate + (Beta x [market rate of return - risk-free rate])*.

Or if you're a mathematical genius, you would be familiar with expressing it as:

$$E(R_i) = R_f + \beta_i(E(R_m) - R_f)$$

If an economist ever mentions CAPM (Capital Asset Pricing Model), that's the formula they mean! Basically, it's the same formula as WACC, but seen from another aspect. The required rate of return for it to be worth investing, given the risks.

You don't really need to know how to do this, as you can find WACC for most companies on the internet, but it's a good idea to understand it.

Taking it apart a piece at a time: the risk- free rate is usually the return on short term Treasury bills - the safest thing you can buy, or some people use 10 Year Treasuries. Short term Treasuries are safe because (1) they have U.S government backing, and (2) since they are short duration, there is not a big risk to the price if interest rates change, compared with longer term bonds.

Market return is the return for the whole stock market, so that's around 9%, according to global investment bank Goldman Sachs. If the stock is quite volatile, it might have a beta of 1.3 (according to Bloomberg).

So, I looked up the 10-year Treasuries today and got **1.92%** as the risk-free rate.

So, if we plot in the formula, we'd get 1.92 + (1.3 x [9 - 1.92]).

In simpler terms that's *1.92 + (1.3 x 7.08), or 1.92 + 9.204 = 11.12%.*

I hope that makes sense, but wow! That's a lot higher than you probably thought, am I right?

Most people think cost of capital is around the level of mortgage rates (2-3%), because they don't understand how much equity costs.

So, then you need to *weight* the cost of capital. That means looking at the mix of debt on the balance sheet and its average cost.

That's one reason the note on debt in the Amazon accounts shows so much detail - as well as the cost of equity.

So, then you work out:

- *debt / total liabilities as a percentage, multiplied by the cost of debt*
- *and equity / total liabilities as a percentage, multiplied by the cost of equity.*

Add the two together, and there you have the WACC.

Amazon's Debt/equity calculation

Total liabilities aren't shown as a figure on the balance sheet, so you need to add together the current liabilities of $126,385m, long term lease liabilities of $52,573m, long term debt of $31,816m, and other long term liabilities of $17,017m. That adds up to $227,791m. Equity is $93,404m, so you should get:

$227,791m / $93,404m = 2.43 (or 243% if you prefer to calculate the percentage).

But you could probably, as a shortcut, miss the beta part of the calculation to make life easier. It's not methodologically correct, but it's *good enough.*

Remember that one of the advantages you have over a stock market analyst is that you can take shortcuts if you need to...

I once looked at a company that some analysts highly rated only to find its return on capital was lower than keeping money in the bank. That didn't look like it was going to change in the medium term. What would you have done?

Well, I walked away. I decided my money would be better off staying in the bank till I found a better investment.

Financing

The next set of ratios tells us how well the company is managing its finances and its financial strength. Sometimes, this set of ratios warns me when a company's business isn't really sustainable, even though it looks quite good in terms of operational ratios.

These ratios involve the balance sheet. First of all, there's a very simple ratio that just looks at the liabilities side of the balance sheet and that's the **debt to equity ratio**.

The easiest way to calculate it is to take the total liabilities that aren't equity, and divide it by the equity; *Total Liability / Equity*.

It's a useful number, but you have to compare it to other companies in the sector, as the kind of ratio that a company can carry depends on its business model. For instance, REITs and subscription service companies can manage a high debt to equity ratio because their revenues are highly stable. The debt / equity ratio in the real estate sector is 352%. For food producers, it's just 79%.

One of the things the debt / equity ratio makes very clear is how many suppliers and lenders are in the queue ahead of you as a shareholder.

But I find the debt/equity ratio a bit unconvincing. Those liabilities include some things like deferred tax, which you wouldn't normally call 'debt'.

Also, companies sometimes have large amounts of cash, which I think needs to be set off against their debt. So, I prefer to calculate debt by taking the *cash, current debt, and long term debt*. And then I prefer to look at that compared to the balance sheet total as a whole. This is the **gearing** ratio - another percentage. It's a bit more difficult to calculate, as sometimes I need to delve into the notes to the accounts to get the right numbers.

Suppose the gearing ratio is over 100%. In that case, it tells me that the bankers are ahead of the stockholders in the queue for payment if anything goes wrong. Remember that the banks get paid first, so if debt is growing and equity isn't, that means the banks are more likely to get paid than you are.

By the way, remember when you're looking at stockholders' equity on the balance sheet that it doesn't relate to the price of the shares or how they trade in the secondary market. If I sell my shares in Amazon to you or a broker, that will not be reflected in the accounts. What's shown in the accounts is what Amazon received for new shares that they issued, most notably in the IPO.

Even if a company is well funded, life can get difficult if it doesn't manage its working capital well. If they don't manage to get customers to pay them on time but have to pay suppliers and banks in the meantime, things can get awkward. It's the corporate equivalent of realizing you have five more days till payday but you need to fill the tank with petrol and pay your home loan before then, and there's not enough money in the account. That happens, even if you're earning good money. And it can happen with companies, too.

The ratios for Amazon's debt/equity and gearing are presented below.

Debt/equity

Total liabilities isn't shown as a figure on the balance sheet, so you need to add together the current liabilities of $126,385m, long term lease liabilities of $52,573m, long term debt of $31,816m, and other long term liabilities of $17,017m. (Or you could simply deduct shareholder's equity from the liabilities and equity total.) That adds up to $227,791m.

Equity is $93,404m.

Debt/equity = Total debt / equity

Debt/equity = $227,791m / $93,404m = 2.43 (or 243% in percentages).

Gearing

Here again, you need to calculate a figure that's not shown on the balance sheet by taking the long term debt of $31,816m and subtracting the cash of $42,122m.

Oh, Amazon actually has more cash than debt!

Otherwise, you'd need to calculate long term debt / $93.404m equity.

Fortunately, you can work out a ratio that tells you if the company is likely to get caught with its pants down, so to speak. This is the **current ratio.** It's easy to calculate: *current assets divided by current liabilities (CA/CL).*

The higher the ratio, the better; the lower, the trickier. If a company has current assets several times its current liabilities, it should be able to find the money to pay its bills by selling off some inventory or getting a few customers to settle their bills.

Suppose it has lower current assets than current liabilities. In that case, it will not be able to cover its bills if it has to do so suddenly. It generally needs to be compared within a company's sector as different businesses have different cash flow characteristics, but if it is lower than the sector average without a good explanation, you might worry.

For Amazon in 2020, current assets are shown on the balance sheet as $132,733m, and current liabilities as $126,385m.

Current ratio = current assets / current liabilities

Current ratio = $132,733m / $126,385m = 1.05.

Retailers are between 1 and 1.5, so Amazon is towards the lower end. It's still above 1, but it might be worrying if it was below 1.

Some analysts also like to use the **quick ratio**. Instead of using current assets as a whole, it picks out just the following: *cash + cash equivalents + short term investments + accounts receivable.*

The argument for the quick ratio is that inventories might not be liquid. That is, the company couldn't easily turn them into cash in short order. This is usually the same as the **acid test** - *cash and accounts receivable divided by current liabilities.*

But suppose you were looking at a company where accounts receivable could take a long time to receive, for instance, in construction or in aerospace. In that case, you might also miss out on the accounts receivable.

If the quick ratio is less than 1, the company doesn't have enough liquid assets to meet its liabilities. That can be a problem. However, you need to consider the type of business. Retailers, for instance, get through inventory very fast, so their inventory is pretty close to cash - particularly with grocers, less so with white goods or fashion retailers. A retailer's acid test could look poor, but it's probably not a major problem if the current ratio is good.

Again, for Amazon in 2020, this is very similar to the current ratio, but we take out the inventories, which might not be sellable in time.

So liquid current assets are $132,733m less $23,795m, which is $108,938m.

Current liabilities are the same $126,385m.

Quick ratio = (current assets - inventories) / current liabilities

Quick ratio = $108,938m / $126,385m = 0.86.

Those ratios above just look at the balance sheet, but you can also look at whether paying debt services puts pressure on the company in terms of its income statement.

You might look at either **EBIT / interest payable** . Or you can look at **EBITDA / interest payable** (which removes depreciation and amortization).

For the EBIT version, 1.5 is a good healthy ratio; anything below that puts the company at risk of being unable to pay its debt servicing.

For Amazon in 2020, EBIT was $22,899m.

Net interest is made up of $1,647m interest expense, deducting $555m interest income, making a total of $1,092m net interest payable.

Interest cover = EBIT / net interest.

Interest cover = $22,899m / $1,092m = 20.9 times.

Amazon is unlikely to have problems paying its debt servicing, as its EBIT can cover it 20x times over.

A digression - catching out the creative accountants

It won't surprise you to know that companies are keen to push their earnings up as high as they can. Sometimes, the accountants decide to give reality a little help.

That can go all the way from adding a little sparkly eyeshadow to a beautiful set of accounts, to full-scale lipstick on a pig - except that you will need sharp eyes to spot the latter!

For instance, sometimes, sales can be artificially created. If you're desperate for revenue, you could pad out your accounts by making sales;

- to partners or affiliates - related party transactions,
- by bartering or promising to offset the cost against future sales,
- by offering large discounts for early booking.

So how can you catch the bad guys? For a start, if there are sales to partners or affiliates, the notes to the accounts will have to show *related party transactions* under the relevant note. I checked; there were many entries under this heading in the 2000 Enron report. Whether they would have been enough to put me off buying the stock, I don't know.

Secondly, if the company indulges in 'channel stuffing' to bring forward sales that would otherwise have fallen next quarter, you'll likely be able to tell because accounts receivable will be swollen. It's like that picture of when a python has eaten an elephant - the company hasn't got around to 'digesting' those extra sales. The ratios will help you here.

Companies can sometimes report artificially high profits for a long time by using aggressive accounting policies. For instance, start-ups sometimes capitalize a lot of their expenses, meaning they don't have to take their costs as an expense on the income statement. They sweep them under the carpet by putting them on the balance sheet and calling them "development" assets. You can check this by looking at the accounting policies and the long term assets for intangible assets; *look at the footnote and find out what they are.*

Amortizing assets too slowly is another way to boost profits. Again, look at the summary of accounting policies or the footnote on fixed assets.

If, for instance, Amazon had decided to amortize its real estate over 120 years instead of 40, it would have shrunk that cost by 1/3. That would be outrageous!

As you do your research, you'll get a feeling for each industry's norms on depreciation. A big paper-making machine will probably last 10-20 years; a server farm, because of the fast progress in technology, probably won't last so long.

Valuation ratios

When you calculate the ratios for Amazon, use the share price when the 2020 results came out: $3,292. That means you'll be seeing the ratios the way they actually were at the time, regardless of when you are reading this.

It might be interesting to think about the fairy tale of the Golden Goose in terms of valuation. The goose can lay 1 golden egg a day.

- As a bird for eating, she's worth about $12.
- A golden egg is worth about $2,500 (for one and a half ounces). So even if you just put off the roast goose till tomorrow, you've made a much bigger return.
- So that's $912,500 a year ($2,500, x 365 days). We're not looking at any growth here, though, just 365 eggs yearly.
- A domestic goose can live 20 years.
- So, the question is, how many years' worth of egg income do you want to pay for the bird? 20? She'll make the money back - but not anymore. And there's always the possibility of a revenue loss, for instance, if someone steals your goose.
- In any case, she *can't* be worth more than $18.25m (20 years x $912,500 a year).
- So now the question is, how much do you need to discount future years' cash flows back?

Perhaps the market values the goose at 12 years' revenue, that is, $10.95m ($912,500 x 12 years).

On the other hand, one analyst has seen the real money-making opportunity. If the chicks of the goose that lays the golden eggs can also lay golden eggs, you could have exponential growth... what would she be worth if you could breed her offspring and have 365 geese all laying golden eggs by the end of the year?

That was a bit of fun, but I hope it's made you think. It's also introduced you to the idea of valuation ratios.

The gold standard of valuation ratios that everyone uses is the Price/Earnings Ratio (or P/E ratio for short). It's really simple to calculate - *Price divided by earnings.*

So, a company with a share price of $528, and income per share of $30... you work it out!

... is selling on a P/E ratio of 17.6.

If you like to think of it this way, if you buy the shares, you are paying 17.6 years' earnings, so that's how long it will take for the company to earn its share price. Of course, you'd normally expect earnings to grow so that the payback would accelerate in future years.

As I write, the S&P 500 is trading at 25.78 times earnings, so 17.6 would be quite cheap compared to the market. But you would also want to compare the stock with other stocks in its sector, as valuations for different sectors can vary widely.

Amazon shows diluted net income per share of $41.83 at the bottom of their income statement for 2020.

If you used the $3,292 share price from the end of January 2021 when the report came out, you should have got:

P/E ratio = $3,292 / $41.83 = 78.6.

That's a very high valuation!

The table below shows you some of the highest and lowest valued sectors - software looks way high. The figure for air transport, though, is affected by the fact that the pandemic has depressed earnings, and no one really knows when the airlines will recover.

Sector	P/E ratio	Expected growth (next five years)
Banks	21.4	13%
Software	107.62	22%
Wireless telecom	76.82	19.5%
Air transport	7.4	45.6%
Building materials	34.82	17.9%

Source: Aswath Damodaran http://pages.stern.nyu.edu/~adamodar

By the way, do you remember we looked at the trends in GameStop's revenues, profits and dividends? Now, let's take a look at their valuation.

Analysts currently forecast that sales will continue to fall, but the company will make a profit in 2023 with a net income per share of $0.15.

Talking today's share price of $92.69, that gives us a price/earnings ratio of 617 ($92.69 / $0.15).

At the top of the boom, GameStop was trading on a two-years-in-the-future P/E ratio of 2,166.

Amazon is trading about 40 times year two forecasts.

And Amazon is one of the retailers that's taking shares away from GameStop. Which would you rather have in your portfolio?

Another option for a valuation ratio that was very popular in the tech boom is **price/EBITDA**. It's still a useful ratio, but I prefer to use it as a secondary ratio, putting the P/E ratio first.

The problem is that if you only concentrate on pre-interest and pre-tax earnings, you run the risk that once the bank has taken their cuts, there's nothing left for you as a shareholder. It can still give you some insights when you are comparing companies to each other.

For Amazon in 2020, EBITDA is calculating by operating income of $22,899m, together with the $25,251m of depreciation and amortization, which is shown on the cash flow statement. That's a total of $48,150m.

For price, you need to take the market capitalization of the company rather than the share price, so multiply the share price of $3,292 x 510 million shares, the amount shown at the bottom of the income statement. That gives you $1,678,920m.

Price / EBITDA = $1,678,920m / $48,150m = 34.8 times.

Obviously, it's less than the P/E ratio because EBITDA is more than net income - it's before a lot of costs get taken out like interest, taxation, depreciation and amortization.

Something I like to do with the P/E ratio is to turn it back to front and express it as **earnings yield**. (The mathematical term for a ratio turned back to front is the *inverse*.) The formula for that is simply *earnings per share / stock price x 100.*

For Amazon in 2020, diluted net income per share of $41.83 was shown in the income statements. And their share price was $3,292.

Therefore, earning yields is calculated as *$41.83 / $3,292 x 100 = 1.27%.*

I like earnings yield as a ratio. The price/earnings ratio doesn't easily compare with other investments. But you can directly compare the earnings yield as a percentage with returns on other investments, like interest rates on bonds or rental yields on real estate.

However, if you want to compare the dividend return on a stock to the return if you put the money in the bank, you'll want to look at **dividend yield**.

Amazon doesn't pay a dividend, so you don't need to calculate it.

However, if you were to buy REITs, real estate trusts which by law have to pay out a certain percentage of their rents in dividends, the yield would be one of the more important valuation ratios you'd want to know.

Let's look at Omega Healthcare Investors, ticker OHI. It's a REIT that owns elder care establishments and lets them out to assisted living operators.

The shares are trading at $27.62, and it pays a $2.68 dividend. The yield is *$2.68 / $27.62 x 100 = 9.7%*.

That's high, even for the REIT sector, which has an average yield around the 3.5% mark.

There are some concerns that OHI isn't well positioned - some of its major tenants are in financial trouble, and the elder care sector has done very badly in the pandemic, with occupancy levels declining markedly. OHI missed its Q4 forecasts, too. The dividend *might* be cut, but the company appears to have prioritized keeping investors on board so far. So, it's a higher risk, but potentially higher return investment than Realty Income (ticker O), one of the largest and best known REITs, which yields about 4%.

By the way, even if you're not a dividend investor, it's worth noting that dividends historically have accounted for more than a third of total equity returns.

How can you get a better idea of whether the OHI dividend is going to be paid? You can look at **dividend cover**. It's calculated as *net income per share / dividend per share*.

In the third quarter of 2020, for instance, OHI had $0.81 a share available for distribution and paid a dividend of $0.67, so the cover was 1.2 - safe, but only just. (This means the company is distributing the vast majority of its profits. If profits were to fall, it might have to cut the dividend. A company with higher dividend cover would be less likely to consider a dividend cut.)

REITs are a special case, by the way. They have a special tax break, in return for which they are legally bound to distribute a set percentage of their income. For other companies, dividends are entirely at management's discretion. Many, like Amazon, don't pay a dividend at all.

Price to book used to be a ratio that analysts loved. If you read any investment book written before about 1980, there will be a lot about the price to book in it. It's less important nowadays, and the technological revolution, along with the shift in the economy away from manufacturing and towards services, is a big reason.

Price to book can be very simply calculated - *market capitalization* (which is all the shares in the company at today's share price, usually shown on the summary page of financial websites) *divided by total stockholders' equity.*

So, for Amazon, as I write this the market cap is $1,678bn, and equity at the end of 2020 was $93.4bn. It's trading at 17.9 times its book value.

But there are two ways to calculate this.

You could either calculate shareholder's equity per share as $93,404m / 510m shares = $183, and compare that to the share price of $3,292:

$3,292 / $183 = 17.9 times.

Or you could calculate market capitalization to the total shareholders' equity of $93,404m: it's just the same (or should be if you've got it right).

510m x $3,292 = $1,678,920m (you already did that calculation once for market capitalization, remember?)

So, $1,678,920m / $93,404m = 17.9 times.

If you look up the works of great value investors of preceding generations, they liked to buy stocks at less than book value if they could. But they were buying railroads, aluminum smelters, and big auto factories - the kind of businesses with huge amounts tied up in plant and equipment. Even with its big logistics side, Amazon's business is far more biased towards the skills economy - creating its own software, algorithms, and marketing strategies. So, to conclude, price to book is not really such an important ratio these days.

Which earnings and which P/E ratio to use?

You may already have spotted an issue with the P/E ratio. If I use last year's earnings, they're already out of date; but if I use next year's forecast earnings, how good is the forecast?

Usually, I look at TTM - the 'trailing twelve-month' P/E ratio. This adds together the quarterly income per share for the last four quarters. Hence, it is only ever one quarter in arrears, not a whole year. Yahoo Finance and most other websites show it - though it's easy to calculate yourself, as long as you have the last four quarterly reports.

For fast growth companies, though, it's useful to forecast earnings and to look where the P/E ratio will be in two years' time. I'm just going to show you on the next page an example of a fast growth company against a mature company and how the P/E ratios work out.

	Last year	Year 1 forecast	Year 2 forecast
Mature company share price	$150	$150	$150
Earnings	$10	$11	$12
P/E ratio	15	13.6	12.5
Growth company share price	$300	$300	$300
Earnings	$10	$20	$30
P/E ratio	30	15	10

Although, right now, the growth company looks twice as expensive as mature company. If our year two forecasts are right, it will end up selling on a lower P/E ratio in two years' time.

Now, the keywords here are "if our year two forecasts are right".

During the tech boom, the forecasts ran away with themselves. And you can imagine, if a growth company disappoints and ends up just earning $12 instead of $30 in year 2, it will still be outrageously highly valued - or else, the share price will take a dive.

There is no 'right answer' here. But you have lots of tools for assessing both companies. The growth company might be a steal, or not.

There are two other tools can help you when you're thinking about P/E ratios. One is the long term average P/E ratio, for the market or for a stock. This takes past earnings and the share price when those earnings were announced. It's a bit of a hassle to calculate. Fortunately, for the S&P 500, you can get the long term average. I use a site called Macrotrends which lets me see it as a chart, but you can hover over any data point to see the value...

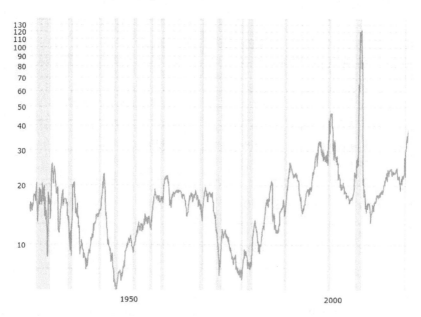

Wow! P/E ratios hit 120 in May 2009! On the other hand, in around 1980, you could have picked up the S&P 500 selling at just 7.5 times earnings, at the end of the decline that began with the early 1970s crash.

The second tool helps address the problem of whether a P/E ratio for a growth company is worth paying. It's called the **PEG ratio**, or *price earnings to growth,* and it tells you how much you're paying for each dollar of growth.

It's straightforward calculate too; *price earnings ratio / growth rate.*

Let's look at high- PE, high-growth stock Tesla (TSLA). It's on a P/E ratio of 188. And it's expected to more than double its earnings this year - 108% growth - and then to grow by 25% next year.

So, depending on which year we want to look at, the PEG could be 188 / 108 = 1.74 this year, or 188 / 25 = 7.52 next year.

I will quote Peter Lynch again because I think he often gets things right. He thinks that a good growth company should sell on a PEG of 1.0 - that is, the P/E ratio should be exactly the same as the expected earnings growth. If you can get it below 1.0, it's a bargain.

I have not found out what Lynch thinks about Tesla... but you can probably guess. I would think Lynch would have thought Tesla was heavily overvalued, and he might have it on a watch list in case the shares fell to where they represented fair value, though.

The numbers are never the whole story - but they are the clues. And like a good detective, if you follow up the clues, you'll find out what's really going on.

Chapter 5 Quiz

1. Which of these is *not* a reason that gross margins would increase?
   a. The company put prices up
   b. A major cost input became cheaper
   c. The company sacked half its head office team
   d. The mix of products sold changed

2. Working capital is made up of
   a. Inventories and accounts receivable
   b. Inventories and accounts payable
   c. Inventories and accounts receivable, less accounts payable
   d. Long term debt less short term assets

3. Why could return on assets increase?
   a. Profits increase on a stable asset base
   b. Interest rates go up
   c. The company launches a new product
   d. A long term loan becomes due

4. What is gearing?
   a. A measure of debt compared to equity finance
   b. The relationship of inventories to sales
   c. The Shimano ratio multiplied by the Sturmey Archer factor
   d. The speed of increase in sales

5. The earnings yield is ---- of the P/E ratio.
   a. The inverse of
   b. The opposite of
   c. Irrelevant to
   d. The same as

Answers to Amazon ratio calculations

As this is probably the first time you're going to be doing these calculations, I haven't just given the answers, but also the numbers found in the annual report for 2020, and the calculation that gives you the right number. (If Amazon's 2021, 2022, and 2023 reports have come out since this book was published, your next step is to grab those and do the same calculations till you find all of them easy to do.)

Gross margin

Total net sales were $386,064m in 2020.

Cost of sales was $233,307m.

Gross profit = net sales - cost of sales = $152,757m.

Gross margin = gross profit / total net sales x 100

Gross margin = $152,757m / $386,064m x 100 = 39.57%

Operating margin

You already have the net sales figure of $386,064m.

Operating income was $22,899m.

Operating margin = operating income / total net sales x 100

Operating margin = $22,899m / $386,064m x 100 = 5.93%

Tax rate

Income before income taxes was $24,178m.

The provision for income taxes was $2,863m.

Tax rate = provision for income taxes / income before income taxes.

Tax rate = $2,863m / $24,178m x 100 = 11.84%.

Inventory turnover

Total inventory was $23,795m.

Cost of sales was $233,307m.

Inventory turnover = total inventory / cost of sales x 365 days.

Inventory turnover = $23,795m / $233,307m x 365 = 37 days.

This means Amazon turns over its inventory in a little more than a month.

Accounts receivable / Days Sales Outstanding

Accounts receivable were $24,542m.

You already have the net sales figure of $386,064m.

Day Sales Outstanding = account receivables / total net sales x 365 days.

Day Sales Outstanding = $24,542m / $386,064m x 365 = 23 days.

Amazon gets paid in less than a month.

Accounts payable turnover

Accounts payable were $72,539m.

You already have the cost of sales figure of $233,307m.

Accounts payable turnover = accounts payable / cost of sales x 365 days.

Accounts payable turnover = $72,539m / $233,307m x 365 = 113 days.

Amazon gets four times more credit from its suppliers than it gives to its customers, which is 113 days in comparison to 23 days.

Return on Invested Capital (ROIC)

Total net income was $21,331m.

Invested capital is made up of equity $93,404m, long term debt $31,816m, and long term lease liabilities of $52,573m, which added together is $177,793m.

ROIC = total net income / invested capital.

ROIC = $21,331m / $177,793m x 100 = 12%.

Return on Capital Employed (ROCE)

EBIT was $22,899m

Total assets were $321,195m, while current liabilities were $126,385m. That gives us total assets *less* current liabilities of $194,810m.

ROCE = EBIT / (total assets - total liabilities).

ROCE = $22,899m / $194,810m x 100 = 11.75%.

Return on Assets (ROA)

Total net income was $21,331m.

Average total assets is calculated by adding the total asset figure at the beginning of the year (i.e. the end of 2019) and the end of the year (the 2020 figure), then dividing by two.

Total assets were $225,248m at the start of the year. And $321,195m at the end.

$321,195m + $225,248m / 2 = $273,221m.

ROA = total net income / average total assets.

ROA = $21,331m / $273,221m x 100 = 7.8%.

Return on Equity (ROE)

Total net income was $21,331m and shareholders' equity $93,404m.

ROE = total net income / shareholders' equity.

ROE = $21,331m / $93,404m x 100 = 22.84%.

Debt/equity

Total liabilities isn't shown as a figure on the balance sheet, so you need to add together the current liabilities of $126,385m, long term lease liabilities of $52,573m, long term debt of $31,816m, and other long term liabilities of $17,017m. (Or you could simply deduct shareholder's equity from the liabilities and equity total.) That adds up to $227,791m.

Equity is $93,404m.

Debt/equity = Total debt / equity.

Debt/equity = $227,791m / $93,404m = 2.43 (or 243% in percentages).

Gearing

Here again, you need to calculate a figure that's not shown on the balance sheet by taking the long term debt of $31,816m and subtracting the cash of $42,122m.

Oh, Amazon actually has more cash than debt!

Otherwise, you'd need to calculate long term debt / $93.404m equity.

Current ratio

Current assets are shown on the balance sheet as $132,733m, and current liabilities as $126,385m.

Current ratio = current assets / current liabilities.

Current ratio = $132,733m / $126,385m = 1.05.

Quick ratio/acid test

This is very similar to the current ratio, but we take out the inventories, which might not be saleable in time.

So liquid current assets are $132,733m less $23,795m, which is $108,938m.

Current liabilities are the same $126,385m.

Quick ratio = (current assets - inventories) / current liabilities.

Quick ratio = $108,938m / $126,385m = 0.86.

Interest cover

EBIT was $22,899m.

Net interest is made up of $1,647m interest expense, deducting $555m interest income, making a total of $1,092m net interest payable.

Interest cover = EBIT / net interest.

Interest cover = $22,899m / $1,092m = 20.9 times.

Amazon is unlikely to have problems paying its debt servicing, as its EBIT can cover it 20x times over.

Cash interest cover

EBITDA = operating income of $22,899m, together with the $25,251m of depreciation and amortization, which is shown on the cash flow statement. That's a total of $48,150m.

Interest payable = $1,092m.

Cash interest cover = EBITDA / interest payable.

Cash interest cover = $48,150m / $1,092m = 44 times.

Price/Earnings Ratio (P/E ratio)

Share price / earning per share.

Amazon shows diluted net income per share of $41.83 at the bottom of the income statement.

If you used the $ 3,292 share price from the end of January 2021 when the report came out, you should have got:

P/E ratio = $3,292 / $41.83 = 78.6.

That's a very high valuation.

Earnings yield

This uses the same data the other way round: *$41.83 / $3,292 x 100 = 1.27%.*

Earning per share / share price.

Price / EBITDA

EBITDA you worked out already (and if you've just been using a calculator, and not writing down your workings or using a spreadsheet, you've learned a lesson because you've got to recalculate it).

For price, you need to take the market capitalization of the company rather than the share price, so multiply the share price of $3,292 x 510 million shares, the amount shown at the bottom of the income statement. That gives you $1,678,920m.

Price / EBITDA = market capitalization / EBITDA.

Price / EBITDA = $1,678,920m / $48,150m = 34.8 times.

Obviously, it's less than the P/E ratio because EBITDA is more than net income - it's before a lot of costs get taken out like interest, taxation, depreciation and amortization.

Price to sales

Price to sales = market capitalization / total net sales.

Price to sales = $1,678,920m / $386,064m = 4.3 times.

Dividend yield

You don't really need to calculate this. As of today's date, Amazon had never paid a dividend.

But the formula is the annual dividend per year / share price.

Dividend cover

Nor does it need to be calculated here.

But the formula is: earning per share / dividend per share.

Price to book

There are two ways to calculate this.

You could either calculate shareholder's equity per share as $93,404m / 510 million shares = $183, and compare that to the share price of $3,292:

$3,292 / $183 = 17.9 times.

Or you could calculate market capitalization to the total shareholders' equity of $93,404m: it's just the same (or should be if you've got it right).

510m x $3,292 = $1,678,920m (you already did that calculation once for market capitalization, remember?)

So, $1,678,920m / $93,404m = 17.9 times.

Price/earnings-to-growth ratio (PEG ratio)

You already calculated the P/E ratio as 78.6, which was very high.

But the growth rate for 2020 was high, too.

Diluted net income per share grew from $23.01 to $41.83 - that's an 81.8% growth.

So the PEG is 78.9 / 81.8 = 0.96.

It's just below 1, which means you're paying less than a dollar for every dollar of growth.

However, what you need to know is whether that level of growth is going to continue. Was it a fluke?

6

Chapter 6: Industry fundamentals

Industry fundamentals are often overlooked by the 'pure mathematicians' in investment circles, but you can't do without understanding the industry. Numbers don't tell you anything unless you understand the business. For instance, here's a list of companies you might have thought were quite secure at one point:

- Blackberry
- Nokia
- Kodak
- Polaroid
- Blockbuster
- IBM.

Blackberry and Nokia missed a step in their markets. Blackberry is now a cybersecurity company, but its shares are currently listed at $7, way down from their $131 high; Nokia was acquired by Microsoft.

Kodak was way too late realizing what the digital revolution would do to its film sales, and filed for Chapter 11 bankruptcy in 2012.

Polaroid had already filed for bankruptcy much earlier, in 2001, facing a decline in the photography market.

Blockbuster saw video rental replaced by streaming and on- demand video services, and filed for bankruptcy in 2010: Netflix (which Blockbuster didn't think was worth acquiring!) ate its lunch and dominated.

As for IBM... it's currently reinventing itself as a power in hybrid Cloud, and despite some significant missteps on the way, it looks as if new CEO Arvind Krishna just might pull the rabbit out of the hat by surprising us all.

What all those companies have in common is that their markets were completely disrupted by new technologies. If you didn't understand the digital camera, or you didn't understand what was happening to the smartphone, or how cloud computing was changing the way enterprises structured their IT infrastructure, the numbers might have conned you into thinking things were okay.

In fact, sometimes the numbers look bad when companies are getting things right. Over the transition to SaaS (Software as a Service), companies were faced with a horrible dilemma. They would be cannibalizing their own revenues if they moved to a subscription model, selling a $100 a year subscription instead of a $600 software license.

What was good about the new model was that the quality of earnings was much better. So was cash generation. But the move from the old to the new business model was still a tough one.

Another thing you will need to know about a company is whether it has barriers to entry - what Warren Buffett calls 'moats'.

For instance, as a small landlord, I wouldn't have a big advantage over anyone else; but if I owned the biggest purpose-built student accommodation in a university town, I'd have a huge advantage over people who were just letting out a couple of rooms in a house. Companies with great moats might include:

- Amazon, naturally!
- Taiwan Semiconductor
- Baidu - "China's Google"
- PepsiCo and Coca-Cola, together, own the soft drinks business
- Novo Nordisk - leader in diabetes medication
- ADP - dominant provider of payroll services
- Slack - the network everyone uses to work, just acquired by Salesforce.

Additionally, I loved Slack's ticker - WORK.

A moat should be difficult for a competitor to fill in. It should also give the company pricing power because customers want the brand as they are locked into using the product. And it should keep ROCE/ROA higher than at companies which don't have moats (so check those ratios again).

You'll also want to understand the different cost inputs. Airline stocks got a double hit over the pandemic - first of all, they got ruined when passengers stopped flying, then they got hit all over again when oil prices rose.

You certainly want to know the company's market share in fragmented sectors like real estate because it can be difficult to ascertain. I always like to see 40-50%, but my feeling is that market share above 50% can be a mixed blessing or even a curse. A company with high market share is likely to draw the attention of the authorities - for instance, it may not have a free hand in setting its prices or may not be allowed to make what would otherwise be an attractive acquisition.

Also, in companies with high market share, sometimes the company starts to prioritize market share instead of profitability. For instance, management will decide not to raise the price of its most popular product in case it loses market share, when in fact, it is becoming less profitable all the time.

It is also worth noting that market share, by definition, can only add up to 100%. Sometimes, you'll find the top four companies in a niche all claim more than 25% of it. (In the internet boom, some companies stated growth rates that would have given them a 125% market share in five years.) Check what you think the whole market might be worth - see if there are any figures available from Gartner or one of the other IT research houses, for instance. Then see how much share that company is really likely to gain.

For some companies, such as retailers and restaurant chains, a map is a useful thing to have. You can easily see where the chain has room to grow. Moving into a different country or a different area can be risky - what works in the American Midwest doesn't always play in California but if, say, you see that the company can easily open new outlets in its existing markets without saturating them, it has room to grow without major risks.

On the other hand, it was obvious when people started complaining about two Starbucks opposite each other on the same block that there wasn't much room for growth in the U.S - where it cut a large number of branches in 2008 and 2009. (Since then, though, it has grown internationally, keeping the share price moving upwards.)

Mergers, acquisitions and disposals

The big question with any corporate deal is: "Is this a good deal?" That's not just about the price paid but about why the acquisition is being made.

For instance, a company could acquire up or down its value chain to capture more of the value in its business by buying a distributor or supplier. This can sometimes be an excellent deal, particularly where access to particular customers or cost inputs is difficult. This is a type of *backward integration* - in fact, Amazon did this organically. As a retailer, it relied on publishers to supply it with books, but it began to allow authors to self-publish and create content on Amazon as well.

A company might acquire a competitor in order to gain economies of scale, or perhaps in order to have a low-end as well as a high-end product. *Consolidation* strategies are often used in fragmented sectors. However, they don't always produce value.

Waste Management Inc made over 100 acquisitions from 1968 to 1972, but it appears to have increased the size of its problems as well as the size of the company.

Some basic checks on the business

I always like to carry out some basic checks on the business. It's not at all a bad idea if you create a template for analyzing companies with the major headings printed out and fill a copy in every time you look at a new company. Yes, we have computers, but I like to do mine by hand, as I find it concentrates the mind.

- Add up the different bits of the business - do they add up to 100%, or is there a big 'other' item that isn't accounted for? Some companies hide a lot of failed business ventures in that 'other' space, and it can be worrying when you find out just what is in there.
- Try to find out the major suppliers. Find out how concentrated the market is; for instance, airlines pretty much have a choice of either Airbus or Boeing when they're buying their airplanes, so unless they are both large and prominent, they're unlikely to get a great price. On the other hand, major grocery chains are in a huge position of power compared to many food producers.
- Who are the customers? Try to segment the consumer market - this can be useful. For instance, when you look at Meta (formerly Facebook), one of the major issues it faces now is that younger people, who were originally responsible for the growth of the company, now prefer TikTok.
- Does the company suffer from customer concentration? For instance, some REITs only have four or five large tenants; some food companies only sell through two grocery chains. If one of those major customers stops renting the space or taking the product, for whatever reason, the company is going to have a hard time replacing the business.
- Get a good sense of the cash flow. How quickly does the company turn products or services into cash? How regular or lumpy is cash flow? How much credit does the company need to offer? Does the company have significant up-front costs like pitch costs when it's bidding for contracts?

- It's also really useful to check out the credit ratings of big customers and suppliers and the health of their industries. For instance, if many of the suppliers are unprofitable and facing financial constraints, continuity of supply could become an issue. If a major customer is facing an uncertain future, you may want to think about how much pain the customer's bankruptcy would cause the company you're analyzing.

Next, you need to be clear about where growth is coming from and where profit is coming from. In the best case, the biggest business, the growth business and the most profitable business will all be the same. Whereas, in the worst case, the biggest business is the unprofitable one that's in decline, the growth business is tiny and unprofitable, and the profitable business is small and not growing.

You could look at Amazon here. Geographically, last year it was the international business that was growing fastest. Does that mean the U.S has reached its peak? Is the U.S saturated? How long do you think it will take for the international business to reach maturity? Will Amazon see diminishing returns as it accesses increasingly smaller and lower-income markets?

I don't have the answers - these are the issues that you need to think about if you're doing fundamental analysis properly!

Industry comparisons

Always compare companies with other companies that have the same business model. Amazon and Walmart may sell similar products to similar customers, but the business models are very different. You can't really compare them. Perhaps in ten years' time, when Amazon has set up more bricks-and-mortar distribution and Walmart has gone further down the e-commerce route, you'll be able to, but I think it's too early right now.

Across companies in a single industry, usually most of the ratios will look similar. Some companies will have higher margins, and you should ask yourself why.

Do they have higher priced products? Do they have lower costs? Or are they more efficiently run? The answer may sometimes be easy to find: other times, you'll have to do a bit of guesswork. Sometimes, it's interesting to track the trends - you can see where one company starts to gain success through cost cutting, for instance.

In the same way, the return on assets is usually fairly similar across an industry because everyone will be using the same kind of assets and paying roughly the same amounts for them. However, you'll find some differences.

For instance, a retailer that uses smaller sites will have different real estate costs from one that concentrates on bigger outlets; and in manufacturing, companies which have invested in making existing facilities smarter may be able to crack out extra profits from having lower setup costs, increased customization and lower waste.

When you come across really pronounced differences, that tells you something important. The same is true with trends - if everyone else is seeing margins squeezed, but one company has margins going up, it's getting something right; if most companies are seeing sales grow fast, but one or two aren't, market share is being won and lost, and you ought to ask why that's happening and look around for explanations.

Sometimes you'll find that one or two of the big players in a sector are private. They may not have a lot in the way of financial figures for you to view, but you can probably find out quite a lot about the size of the business in other ways. You may also be able to find out what their strategy is, particularly if they are owned by a private equity firm that wants to fatten them up for an IPO in a few years.

Watch the ETFs

One interesting way to get a view of the different sectors is to watch sector ETFs. For instance, iShares U.S Regional Banks ETF (IAT) gives you a good feel for how the share prices of small and medium sized U.S regional banks are performing.

Of course, ETFs don't show you the underlying fundamentals of the industry, but they do show you how the broad sector is performing on the stock exchange. Sometimes that's useful to know.

Chapter 6 Quiz

1. When Warren Buffett talks of a 'moat,' what does he mean?
   a. A water filled ditch around a building
   b. That a company has a particular advantage its rivals can't overcome
   c. Market share above 50 percent
   d. A very high return on capital

2. Which of these cost inputs is most significant for an airline?
   a. Raw materials and inventory
   b. Aviation fuel
   c. Marketing costs
   d. Software

3. What is backwards integration?
   a. A fancy way of describing a demerger
   b. Integration that doesn't work
   c. Buying a supplier
   d. Buying an unrelated business

4. High market share can be a mixed blessing. Why?
   a. The market leader is expected to have the lowest prices
   b. The authorities may be interested in anti-trust issues making life difficult for the business
   c. It makes a company an easy target for new entrants
   d. Consumers quickly get bored with the product

5. What do Blackberry, Kodak, Nokia and Blockbuster have in common?
   a. Pictures
   b. Memory chips
   c. Lost out to industry disruption
   d. Low market share

7

Chapter 7: What CEOs say - and what they mean

Analyzing a company's annual report, you may find that there's rather a difference between the breezy optimism of the glossy paper bit, and what you find in the small print financials. Part of that is simply that the two parts of the publication are intended for different audiences. But sometimes, the difference is more of a worry. Fundamental analysis is a great tool for working out whether CEOs mean what they say.

That's one reason I like to read the report back to front. If I've been worried about five or six of the key ratios, and I have some unanswered questions about last year's performance, when I turn to the front and read, "We had a record year, everything in the garden is lovely, and there's apple pie for dessert" (or words to that effect), it makes me worry even more.

On the other hand, if I turn to the front and the CEO fesses up - "We had a few challenges last year, things were tough, here's what we did, it could take 6 months to turn round" - I'm far more likely to think the CEO knows what they are doing.

So, for instance, in the risks facing a company, most of the risks will be ordinary stuff that the lawyers insisted on putting in. It always reminds me of that disclaimer on finance ads that used to tell you, "Warning: stock markets can go up as well as down." (Did I get that right? It certainly felt like that in the 2001 bear market!)

But you might also see a good roundup of what the CEO sees as the risks facing the company. I'm interested in a couple of things in section 1A, the risk statement in the Amazon report.

- "We are impacted by fraudulent or unlawful activities of sellers." Amazon doesn't provide its own products and can't police its sellers. What surprises me here is that this risk comes quite high up in the list - I suspect that means the company's lawyers are not 100% confident about Amazon being able to distance itself from responsibility.
- "We rely on a limited number of shipping companies" - this suggests there is a single weak link in Amazon's chain right here. I would want to keep an eye on what's happening to prices at USPS, DHL and FedEx, for instance.

Is there anything else in there that surprises you?

When you're reading the risk statement, you should also ask yourself if there's anything that you think is a risk, but that isn't included. For instance, I'd be worried if I read an annual report from a bricks-and-mortar retailer and the risk from online competition wasn't included.

Now let's move on and look at how this year is presented. At this point, when I'm researching companies, I like to look at last year's annual report and notes.

- What promises were made?
- What problems were noted?

Then I look at this year's report. Did they deliver on promises?

For instance, if cost cuts were promised, did they happen? Did new products appear on time? How successful were they?

Now obviously, Amazon's 2018 report wasn't going to put "hey guys, we have a pandemic coming in a year and a half" as a problem, but generally, if a business problem appears during the course of a year, it's likely management had an idea it was going to happen earlier. So, I will see if this has been a disappointing year, was there something in last year's report that noted it was going to be challenging.

I also like to test what management is saying against the ratios. If the report says that prices are strong and the market shows high demand, and yet the gross and operating margins declined, I smell a rat (in other words, dishonest behavior).

If the management gives earnings guidance, I want to check out whether they've usually had upside earnings surprises or a few misses. If a company is always missing guidance, it's usually a sign of poor financial controls or poor management - most companies aim to give guidance that they can narrowly beat "managing expectations".

I like to listen to conference calls for companies I'm invested in whenever I can. I could just read the transcript, but you don't get quite the same feedback you do with the audio. For instance:

- Does the CFO sound like they have all the numbers at their fingertips? Can top management answer questions directly without looking things up?

- Does management get rattled? I've heard a CEO getting more and more uneasy the longer the call went on. It sounded like a kid who hadn't done their homework. Sometimes you can hear from their voices that there's a particular subject they're not happy talking about. (That's different from things they *won't* talk about, generally because there's a legal issue involved.)
- Reaction to follow-on questions is particularly telling when the analyst wants more detail or doesn't feel they've got the answer they needed.
- I have, once or twice in my career, heard bullying by management. "That's a stupid question," "I don't even know what you mean by debt maturity", "Are you calling me a liar?". No matter how annoying an analyst is, if management reacts like that, it's problematic. (It's interesting that some analysts recall Enron management acting in this way very shortly before the company's collapse.)

Then on the factual level, compare what the company you're looking at has to say compared with what other companies in the sector are saying. Compare what management is saying with the financial ratios that you're looking at. Do the ratios agree with the statements? Have any questions you had about the numbers been answered in the conference call?

If you can't understand something, and the explanations don't seem convincing, you may be right; the emperor *isn't* wearing any clothes. 'Black boxes' and 'secret algorithms' are fine in the Da Vinci code, but if a CEO is trying to sell you them, and the numbers don't stack up, you're right to walk away.

By the way, while I make time for conference calls, I'd recommend you follow my example and don't bother with annual meetings. You can exercise your vote by proxy. Most of the time, annual meetings are pretty cursory administrative affairs. Only the Berkshire Hathaway meeting is, by all accounts, quite an amazing event, and you now only need to own one $300 B share, rather than one of the $400,000 A shares, to get in.

I would also recommend you keep an eye out for zero content press releases. Some companies want to tell you about their wonderful product, service, or corporate culture every week, and issue large amounts of statements with no facts at all. Managements that do this are very often involved in puffing their own stock, writing PR instead of getting on with running the business properly.

Mind you, if you look at the letter to shareholders in the front of the Amazon report, I find that full of buzzwords and jargon - but you can see that the company is a success. So, make sure you do your due diligence!

'Great management' - a warning

Many people think that assessing the management of a company is a vital part of fundamental analysis. I'm actually going to disagree.

One advantage Wall Street and City analysts have is that they're able to meet management and ask questions directly. They've probably had one-on-one meetings and phone calls a good few times, and they have a chance to size up the CEO's character and that of other executives. A retail investor like ourselves doesn't.

Worse, you're exposed to a lot of media that will tell you that this person is a 'great, hands-on', 'visionary', 'transformative', or whatever, manager. You can just ignore that. People who come across as visionaries may in fact have a far-reaching view of how their industry is going to change over the medium term, or they may just be idiots or even crooks with a few buzzwords and more charisma than they need. What's most important is actually very simple - you need management to be honest. Honest and stupid will do better for shareholders than smart and crooked.

You are best not trying to grade management but assess the way they work. For instance, a particular CEO may always have been able to turn around loss-making companies by cost cutting and by refocusing the product range. I would not necessarily back him if he took over a high growth company. Equally, a CEO who has typically worked in B2B companies (such as accounting software or payroll management) might not do as well in a consumer facing business. Another may be very good at making acquisitions, so you'd expect that if he moves into another company, he'll start doing that quite fast.

If management is visionary and talks a good fight and seems to have good ideas, but the company never makes any money, the CEO is a failure. If the CEO is stodgy, even boring, but produces ever-increasing earnings without going heavily into debt or fiddling the books, we have a success. The numbers tell you how good the management is. And if everyone says the management is brilliant, but the numbers don't bear it out - always, always **believe the numbers**.

Chapter 7 Quiz

1. Why should you read two successive years' annual reports?
   a. For variety
   b. To check management promises against the out-turn in the next year
   c. To check the number of shares hasn't changed
   d. To see whether the branding has changed

2. If the CEO blames poor earnings on high costs, which of these will tell you he's lying?
   a. Head office costs have increased
   b. The operating margin increased
   c. The return on capital declined
   d. Gross margins fell although revenues increased

3. The CEO says the industry is suffering from low demand, but competitors have seen increases in sales. Which of these is *not* an explanation for the apparently contradictory statements?
   a. Competitors are smaller and have increased their market share.
   b. Competitors have lower prices and have attracted business away from the company.
   c. Competitors have 'stuffed' their latest results by recognizing revenue before it should be booked.
   d. The company makes a higher operating profit than its rivals.

4. Why is the risk statement important?
   a. Because it can show you what the CEO thinks are the biggest risks,
   b. Because you have to read it according to investment rules,
   c. Because it contains price-sensitive information,
   d. It isn't.

5. Which of these is not a recommended way of listening to the analyst conference?
   a. Through the Motley Fool website
   b. Through the company's investor relations website
   c. Through dial up, if you're a shareholder and have been invited
   d. By bugging the boardroom

8

Chapter 8: What's the price tag?

So far, we just looked around the annual report, and then we practiced calculating different ratios. But now it's time to set a price tag on the company and the shares.

There are quite a few ways that you can do this. In this chapter, I'm going to look at the most usual ones, and then in the next chapter, I'm going to get technical and tell you about a more advanced approach. In fact, there's no single right answer. Any valuation is a matter of judgment as well as number-crunching - an art as well as a science.

First of all, let's look at the P/E ratio. If I told you a business had a P/E ratio of 28, would it be overvalued or undervalued? To know that, you need to know the comparisons.

- First of all, you should know the P/E ratio of the market in general and of larger companies versus smaller companies. But that's not necessarily enough to value a specific company.
- You need to know the *industry comparisons*. What's the average for the sector? That's your first jumping off point.
- You also need to have an idea of the growth rate for the sector. In breweries, for instance, the very mature Anheuser-Busch is valued at 25, which is a much lower P/E ratio than the smaller Boston Beer Co (BBC) at 48. Though BBC had a horrendous 2021, it's expected to grow faster than the big guys in the future. Growth companies within a sector will always be valued at a premium.
- You should also have some idea of the quality of the operations - all the stuff about moats, quality of earnings, whether management keep their promises, whether the brand is good, whether you feel the company is well managed.

However, how much of a premium, or discount, a particular company should be given is very much a matter of judgment.

I find it can sometimes help to set down the P/E ratio (and P/E-to-growth) of each company in a circle. I then compare across competitors in the sector, writing my comments down on the line that links each pair of companies. Comments might include "higher debt risk", "highly concentrated customer base", "unfashionable brands", "losing traction", "reliable dividend payer," "high organic growth", or "too many acquisitions", for instance. I can then keep that page as an easy reference for later on to see if a company is overvalued or undervalued in comparison to its competitors.

That applies to companies which are in a steady state. But sometimes, they're not. For instance, you might have a smaller company that has a one in three chance of getting a major contract which would transform its future prospects. Or you might have a company where analysts are very divided over its growth potential. In that kind of situation, I like to use *expected values* - a statistical method of creating scenarios.

For instance, with the small business and the big contract, I can forecast its earnings with and without the contract, and value the company for either case.

Then, I give the 'with contract' scenario a 33% probability, so I multiply the valuation by 0.33, and since probabilities always add up to 100% (*something* is 100% likely to happen), I multiply the 'without contract' valuation by 0.66.

The correct valuation for the company right now, accounting for both the potential of the new contract and its uncertainty, is the total of those two values.

Let me show you the workings on the next page.

	Without contract	With contract
Earnings	$100m	$300m
P/E ratio	18	18
Value of company	$1,800m	$5,400m
Probability	.66	.33
Value multiplied by probability	$1,188m	$1,782m
Expected value	$1,188m + $1,782m = $2,970m	

I used the same P/E ratio for both cases. In fact, it's possible that if the company got the contract, it might be re-rated (that is, given a higher P/E ratio, but I'm not going to bet on it).

I find expected value really useful to determine what's a fair amount to pay when you have different potential outcomes. It can also be good to look at a range of values.

For instance, you might say that you aren't 100% sure what is the right P/E multiple for a company, but it should probably be valued around the same as other companies in its sector. Rather than just looking at the average, you might consider the range between the highest and lowest P/E ratio in the sector. (Cut out any 'outliers' - for instance, the one company that has an outrageously high multiple because it's rumored to be the subject of a possible takeover bid.)

That would give you a feel for where the share price ought to lie - and how much variation there is between the high, low, and average.

As usual, this will not give you "the answer", but it will help to clarify your thinking.

The conglomerate valuation

You might also look at a company as the sum of the parts. Generally, you wouldn't split the value of a brewery from the value of its plant and property because the brewery couldn't brew beer and distribute it without its brewery and warehouses. But in some cases, either a company possesses assets that it doesn't use in the business, or has a number of different business types, or has assets that could be worth far more if they were used differently.

For instance, a company might operate a small retail business and use its own point-of-sale software. If you value it as a retail business, it might be worth a fairly low multiple of its earnings. But suppose you thought it could sell the software business to a computer firm? You could work out that if the software was sold on a subscription basis to 500 other small retailers at $5,000 a year each, revenues would be $2.5m, and with limited costs, perhaps you could see profits at $2m. Add in expected fast growth, you'd get a multiple of maybe 40 times earnings, which means you could add $80m to your valuation (*if* the sale went ahead).

In the case of a company with different businesses, it's an even simpler job to value the different parts of the business. For example, General Electric has aviation, healthcare, and an energy business. You simply value each area by comparing it with its sector.

This is the way Peter Lynch analyzed General Electric when the stock was trading for almost nothing, and he worked out that the finance business on its own was worth more than the stock market valuation for the entire company.

Looking back to the very beginnings of mobile telecoms, smart investors put money into a rather ordinary electronics company called Racal which had a military radio business. This small business developed into a cellular business and won one of the first two licenses granted to operators in the UK. The rest of Racal, at one point, had a *negative* value once the telecom side had been accounted for.

Sometimes, you'll see a company has a pile of cash. Normally, you'd assume a company has cash that it needs for its day-to-day operations. But if it has a really large amount of cash that it hasn't earmarked for investment, then you might decide to treat that as part of the valuation; work out the cash per share, and add that to the value of the business.

To be quite accurate, you'll need to take interest income out of the earnings statement, though. This is to avoid double counting. If you are taking the cash out of the share price, you should take out interest paid on that cash from the earnings.

Yield, EBITDA, Price/revenue, Price/book

While the P/E ratio is the most commonly used valuation, others are also useful. However, usually, they are secondary to the P/E ratio or used mainly in particular circumstances.

I like to use both yield and price to book as backstops. For instance, if a stock's yield is more than twice the yield on the S&P 500, then if the business is a good one, I think it's unlikely to increase much further. Or if the price to book value falls below 1, then again, I think it's unlikely to fall much further.

However, you need to look out for **dividend traps** and **value traps**.

Sometimes, for instance, a stock has a limited life - a mine that is becoming exhausted, or a technology that is becoming outdated - or it has high debts, a major lawsuit hanging over it (asbestos cases, for instance, lots of employees of companies like Manville Corporation had asbestosis as a result of their work. Manville Corporation actually declared bankruptcy as the claims against it were so large it couldn't pay them.) or some other major liability that could damage the business beyond recovery.

Or, in the case of dividend traps, the company doesn't have enough earnings to cover the dividend, or for other reasons, the dividend is about to be cut. You need to be quite careful - and however careful you are, sometimes you'll make the wrong call. That's inevitable.

EBITDA and revenue multiples are useful when you are looking at companies that don't currently make a profit. Although some investors are suspicious of these ratios, there's nothing wrong with them; you just need to be careful that you have a good understanding of how the company will get from loss making to money making and that the business model works.

The problem with the tech bubble wasn't so much that the wrong bases of valuation were being used, it was because some of the companies didn't have good business models and never ended up making a profit at all.

EBITDA multiples can also be useful for looking at companies in a sector where companies' financial positions and depreciation or amortization requirements are very different. If one company has a lot of debt and another has cash, when you look at EBIT or EBITDA you're comparing profitability at a level before interest, so their financial situations don't affect the comparison. You get a feel for the underlying business.

If one company has made a big acquisition and has large amortization expenses, and the other doesn't, again, the comparison at EBITDA level lets you see underlying performance without the difference that comes from the fact that one company bought a business and the other built it organically.

And of course, EBITDA is also useful for companies that are young and producing cash flow but not profits.

Price to revenues is also useful. I often use it when I'm looking at companies with below standard profitability to see what they would be worth if management got to grips with the operations. But I would never use it as my main valuation multiple because we're interested in revenues mainly as one of the factors that drives profits.

So really a company should be valued on profits, and revenues are only separately useful if there's some reason that a profit valuation won't work properly - like the company is in a *turnaround* situation.

Instead, I might work out what profits *should* be once the cost issues are addressed and then look at the P/E multiple on that scenario.

Analysts tend to restrict themselves to forecasts - actually, sometimes a back-of-envelope working for a 'what if?' scenario is more useful. What if gross margins were brought up to average for the sector? What if head office costs were trimmed by 10%? what if...

I promise this is the last time I'm going to talk about GameStop.

Let's put a few of these valuation methods together and have a look at GameStop. It's actually an interesting exercise because all your bargain-hunting instincts will say, "Hey, look, this share dropped from $300 to $90, it has to be cheap!".

So, let's put that to the test.

In the table below, I show GameStop's basic valuation criteria as they stood when the short squeeze was going on;

P/E ratio	617
Price/sales	1.4

GameStop can be compared in two different directions.

First of all, it's in video games, so you could compare it to video game developers like Take-Two (TTWO), Electronic Arts (EA), or Activision Blizzard (ATVI).

They are highly valued, with trailing price/earnings ratios from 23 to 57 times and a price to sales of an average of 6.18 times. That is, (7.25 + 5.6 + 5.7) / 3.

The table below shows the trailing 12 month P/E ratio and price/sales for ATVI, TTWO and EA.

	ATVI	TTWO	EA
Trailing 12 month P/E ratio	23.7	34	57
Price/sales	7.25	5.6	5.7

However, there are a couple of big differences between these businesses and GameStop. First of all, they own the content that they sell. Secondly, their financials are in much better shape than GameStop's (these 3 developers are profitable and growing their sales).

So perhaps they should be valued more highly than GameStop.

In fact, the opposite was the case in terms of the P/E ratio. GameStop was valued at 617 times earnings…

But, that's not the case anymore. Now, GameStop is back in losses, so the P/E ratio is irrelevant. And the shares are drifting.

The other companies to which you could compare GameStop are the big retailers. Who competes with it in selling video games and much more? Why not look at Walmart, Best Buy, and Amazon.

The table below shows the trailing 12 month P/E ratio and price/sales for Walmart, Best Buy and Amazon.

	Walmart	Best Buy	Amazon
Trailing 12 month P/E ratio	28	9.3	47.46
Price/sales	0.67	0.47	3.37

When you look at the Walmart and Best Buy, then GameStop is worth way, way less than you'd think. And Walmart is huge; it has a dominant market position.

It's only if you take Amazon as a comparison that you'd think GameStop is cheap as Amazon has a higher price/sales.

But again, Amazon is a dominant market player, and it has a huge growth rate, and it's on the right side of the bricks/chips retail divide (bricks = high street or shopping centre, chips = e-commerce).

I may be wrong. GameStop is apparently managing to get its sales back to growth and is on the brink of breaking even. It might justify its share price. But my feeling when I look at these valuations is that it has a long way to go.

GameStop's top team are smart, that I will admit! I'm just impressed that a company whose market valuation in 2000 was just $400m managed to utilize the WallStreetBets short squeeze to launch a $1.5 *billion* share issue.

Subtractions from value

There are a few items that need to be subtracted from the value of a company when you make a valuation. These can all be found in the notes on the annual report, and the main ones are:

- off-balance-sheet debt
- off-balance-sheet liabilities such as pension schemes
- potential losses from litigation.

Taking off the liabilities - all the things that you know the company will have to pay, or may have to pay, and are quantifiable. You're taking off the worst case.

Often, off balance sheet debt is something that the company will end up having to pay one way or another. You would subtract them only if you think they are chickens that will actually come home to roost.

For instance, in the case of a company with a huge lawsuit brought by former employees for terminal illness caused by unhealthy work conditions, I might take the view that the company is likely to lose or to have to settle at a high price. I'd then subtract that amount from the P/E ratio-based valuation of the business to arrive at the *intrinsic value*.

Chapter 8 Quiz

1. What is a dividend trap?
   a. A kind of piggy bank for investors
   b. A company that has a high yield but is financially risky
   c. Like a honey trap, a way to catch spies
   d. When a company doesn't pay dividends at all

2. An expected value is based on the valuation under different scenarios weighted according to their;
   a. Severity
   b. Profitability
   c. Probability
   d. Alphabetical order

3. Which is the 'gold standard' valuation ratio?
   a. Price to book
   b. Return on assets
   c. Price to revenues
   d. The price/earnings ratio

4. When might you want to use price/revenues or price/EBITDA?
   a. When the company isn't making a profit
   b. When the company has high debt
   c. When the other analysts use it
   d. When the price to book is below 1

5. Which of these would not affect your assessment of the right P/E ratio for a company?
   a. Several negative earnings surprises in the last two years
   b. High market share
   c. The company's growth prospects
   d. The rate of inflation

9

Chapter 9: 50 cents now or 10 bucks later?

Fundamental analysis looks for the 'intrinsic value' of a stock. However, so far, I've only talked about how to compare one stock with others. That gives you a comparative valuation, but not an absolute one. In other words, we might know that Amazon trades on a higher valuation than Microsoft or a lower valuation than Tesla, but we still don't know whether that's right. We can't set a price in dollars.

The **discounted cash flow (DCF)** model can give you an absolute answer as to how much a company is worth - if you get your assumptions right. It's a bit complex, both as a concept and in the calculation, so this may be the **toughest chapter** yet - but it's a crucial one so perhaps read it over a couple of times to fully grasp everything.

I want you to read it with a spreadsheet open if you can, and to play around with the spreadsheet, trying different discount factors, different rates of growth, and different scenarios, till you feel quite at home with the process.

To understand how the DCF model works, you need to understand that money exists in the length of time, and that its value depends on duration on the time that you have to wait till you receive it.

If I borrowed a certain sum of money and said I'd pay it back tomorrow, next month, next year, or in 10 years' time, your response might be very different depending on the length of time I wanted to borrow it. People say, "time is money", and money actually has what is called a *time value*. You could represent that by the interest rate on a loan, for instance.

Let's take that up a notch and think about it in terms of actual numbers rather than just emotionally. If I have $100 right now, it will be worth more in a year's time because I will have had *interest* paid on it. So, for instance, at 10% interest (just to make the math a bit easier), it's worth:

- $110 after a year ($100 x 10%)
- $121 after two years ($110 x 10%)
- $133 after three years ($121 x 10%)
- $146 after four years, and ($133 x 10%)
- $161 after five years. ($146 x 10%)

Got it?

Now, look at that backwards. If I promise to pay you $161 in five years' time, what is that promise worth right now?

Assuming my credit is good, it's worth $100.

Or if I promise to pay you $110 in one year, it's worth $100 now.

That, in essence, is how compound interest builds up forward (the compounding effect), and how you **discount back** a future payment.

So now let's look at a company, and we can see that it will deliver cash flow every year. It's a bit more difficult to analyze because it's not just a single payment that you have to discount back; so, you'd need to discount next year's dividend back 12 months, but the year after that, you'd need to discount back by two years, and the year after that by three years, and so on. So, there's a bit of added complexity, but the idea is the same.

In fact, I've got a couple of ways I could define the company's return to the investor.

- I could value the flow of dividends. *Theoretically*, the value of a stock is the value of all future dividend payments. But there are enough stocks that don't pay a dividend to make this less useful than it might be. It also ignores potential returns through capital growth, which make up at least a third of equity returns.
- I could value future net cash flow - the cash generated after investment has been taken care of. This is what I'd do if I was planning to acquire 100% of the company, and it's the way most analysts value companies traded on the stock market.

By the way, the math in this chapter is a bit complex when you have to express it in terms of formulas. However, most spreadsheets have a function to help you work out discounted values, so don't let that bother you. In Microsoft Excel, it's called XNPV in the 'Financial' function category and in LibreOffice you have the NPV function. There are several tutorials online that you can watch to learn how to use these functions.

Constant dividend model

Okay, I'm going to look at the **constant dividend model** first (it's also called the Gordon Growth Model). Even though it's of limited value, it's actually quite interesting because if you use this, you could start out with a bond and a stock that pays the same yield right now, and see the difference over 10 years in the returns you get.

When I started writing this chapter, I could have bought 10-year U.S Treasuries yielding at **1.94%** according to GuruFocus Yield Curve (which is a reliable source).

(By the way, you may have noticed I used 1.92% to calculate WACC in an earlier chapter which I had wrote a few days earlier. Of course, the yield changes as bond prices go up and down daily, which is why you might like to revisit your calculations from time to time, as the 10-year U.S Treasuries can change every day!)

Therefore, if I put in $10,000 in U.S Treasuries today, I would get $194 a year in yield, every year for 10 years. (That is, $10,000 x 1.94% = $194.)

Just for the sake of the example so you can see where the excess gains on equities come from, I found a stock from a stock screener on Morningstar to find dividend yields between 0 and 2%, then ranked stocks highest to lowest by yield so I could find the closest to 1.94%, which led me to come across Advance Auto Parts (AAP) stock which has a 1.94% yield.

Now let 's say I put in $10,000 in AAP. This will get me $194 this year in yield. But looking at the last five years, earnings grew by 9% a year on average, according to Yahoo Finance. (You can find it under the "Financial" tab)

Therefore, I'm going to moderate my expectations and forecast earnings growing by only **4%** in the future. That's because even though the companies have had a 9% on average in the previous five years, and are expecting 10% growth in earnings in 2022 (according to an article by The Motley Fool), at some rate, eventually, growth will slow down over the longer term. And the model we use for calculating earnings is a very *long-term model* - in fact, it assumes growth in perpetuity, which is a much longer investment time horizon, hence 4% would be a moderate expectation for us to be on the safe side.

So that would mean for AAP, you'd get $202 earnings in year two ($194 x 1.04 = $202), and $210 earnings in year three ($202 x 1.04 = $210), and so on.

There's a formula that will let us take a shortcut to find out the value. It's called the *constant dividend model,* and the formula is:

Value = Next year's dividend / (discount rate - dividend growth rate)

So, for U.S Treasuries, next year's coupon is $194, and there is no growth.

We can take the discount rate of 1.94%, as U.S Treasuries are usually considered risk-free since the U.S government isn't going to default on its bonds. And 10-year Treasuries are an appropriately long term investment to compare to equities. And there's no dividend growth rate.

So, if we plot in the formula, we get *$194 / 1.94% = $10,000,* which is, of course, what we invested. Hence there's no growth.

But for the company AAP, two things change. First of all, there's a *growth rate of 4%* (which we moderately forecasted). And secondly, because companies represent a higher risk than investing in the U.S Government Treasury Bonds, therefore, the discount rate is higher for companies.

I'm not going to go through how you calculate it, but right now, most analysts are using an equity discount rate of around **6%**. I tracked this down in various analyst pieces. It reflects over a decade of low/negative interest rates.

(It's worth noting that different analysts use different rates, very rarely do they all agree; and that using DCF properly is about understanding the way it works and being able to plug in different data or different rates to test your hypotheses, rather than expecting a "computer says yes" answer. Also, this is not chapter and verse, and it won't give you 'right' answers. But it will give you an idea of what long term value might be and what it's made up of. And you can then examine what a slowdown in the growth rate would do to your valuation, or what the need for a big chunk of capital spending would do to it.)

So, I can calculate next year's dividend of $202 and then divide it by the *discount rate of 6%*, less the *dividend growth rate of 4%* (which we had moderately forecasted).

So, *$202 / (6% - 4%)*, or simplified *($202 / 2%) = $10,100,* which is a very small amount more than we paid for the stock.

That additional *$100* from the $10,000 initial investment is the current value of that dividend growth, compared with the bonds in U.S Treasuries which have an unchanging coupon.

You may already have spotted a problem with this model, though.

You'd get a negative value if the dividend growth is higher than the discount rate (for example, if we had *4% - 6% = -2%*). And right now, many companies have dividend growth higher than the discount rate, which basically means you can't do the calculation for the constant dividend model in this that case.

So, let's move on to the second and more useful method, fully *discounted cash flow.*

Discounted cash flow

For this method, you'll need to build a spreadsheet and plug in numbers from the annual report. Remember that Wall Street analysts need to show *absolutely* everything, but we don't have to impress anyone, so we can cut a few corners in simplifying the process.

Before we start, I would definitely suggest you download my free bonus #3 on Amazon's DCF Model Revealed. It would be essential for you to understand the calculations and formulas I discuss in this section live on your computer. Please visit: www.az-penn.com *to download the spreadsheet for free.*

The first part of the table looks like this. We have the five years at the top, and the different headings on the left. I have not plotted in the figures yet, but this is the basic template to get us started.

	Years (in $m)				
	1	2	3	4	5
Net Income					
Depreciation					
Working Capital					
Other non-cash items					
	$0.00	$0.00	$0.00	$0.00	$0.00
Capital Expenditure					
Disposals					
	$0.00	$0.00	$0.00	$0.00	$0.00
Cash Flow	$0.00	$0.00	$0.00	$0.00	$0.00

So, now let's fill it in for Amazon (I 'd recommend you turn on your computer and do the following steps with me).

First of all, I'm going to Zacks (zacks.com) to look for AMZN, then under 'More Research' on the left-hand side, I'll look at the 'Full Company Report'.

In the 'Company Summary' section, I can see an estimated long term EPS growth rate of 28.4% (at the time of writing this, though the rate may differ when you're looking at it).

But, wow, isn't that high!?

I'm going to assume that probably, EBIT will grow at about the same rate. So, taking last year's report as the basis, I can calculate the growth rate for all the various heading from the table above.

Net income last year was $21,331m, so I'm going to multiply that by the growth rate of 1.28 (that is, 100% + 28% growth), and that's my first year's net income here.

So that's, $21,331m x 1.28 = *$27,304m* for year 1 net income.

For year 2, it's going to be year 1 figure of $27,304m x 1.28 = *$34,949m.*

Then I need a formula for year 3, 4 and 5 that multiplies the previous year's net income by 1.28 growth rate, and I can fill the whole line in for all five years for net income.

Now the spreadsheet looks like this for net income:

	Years (in $m)				
	1	2	3	4	5
Net Income	$27,304	$34,949	$44,734	$57,260	$73,293
Depreciation					
Working Capital					
Other non-cash items					
	$27,304	$34,949	$44,734	$57,260	$73,293
Capital Expenditure					
Disposals					
	$0	$0	$0	$0	$0
Cash Flow	$27,304	$34,949	$44,734	$57,260	$73,293

I'll admit, this is very basic. If you were doing this for real, you'd check out analysts' forecasts on Yahoo Finance to see if yours were similar or different, and think about why yours are different (if they are). It's fascinating - there's a huge difference between the low and high forecasts, with the low forecast for 2022 EPS at $25.78 and the high forecast at $75.44!

For me, forecasting is about thinking through all the fundamentals, forecasting revenues, forecasting margins, or if I know particular costs (like aviation fuel for instance) forecasting those. But for those without the modelling, using analyst estimates is a perfectly good short cut.

And you'd want to read through the annual report to see if there are any impacts from an increase in the number of shares issued (though, in this case, there aren't) or any expected chunky capital spending. If you have share issues, then you may end up diluted (that is, getting a smaller share of future earnings than you'd expected).

If there is big capital spending, there might be negative cash flow for a year or two, or the company might need to raise money, which would result in dilution.

Amazon is a company in a relatively steady state. It gets trickier when you have a company that's making a big change to its business - whether it's just de -merged a non-core business, made a big acquisition, or has a huge investment or a massive new product launch. You can build all of those into this DCF model - you just have to think through what you know.

But for now, I'm going to cheat by multiplying them by the 28% EPS growth rate. I'm going to just fill in all the other figures in the same basic way, starting from the 2020 annual report.

And now in the example below, I have five whole years of cash flow.

	Years (in $m)				
	1	2	3	4	5
Net Income	$27,304	$34,949	$44,734	$57,260	$73,293
Depreciation	$32,321	$41,371	$52,955	$67,782	$86,761
Working Capital	$17,256	$22,088	$28,272	$36,188	$46,321
Other non-cash items	$11,786	$15,086	$19,310	$24,717	$31,638
	$88,667	$113,493	$145,271	$185,948	$238,013
Capital Expenditure	-$76,302	-$97,667	-$125,013	-$160,017	-$204,822
Disposals	$0	$0	$0	$0	$0
	-$76,302	-$97,667	-$125,013	-$160,017	-$204,822
Cash Flow	$12,365	$15,827	$20,258	$25,931	$33,191

Now let's talk about discounting back. The easy way to do this is you can show the net present value (NPV) of each year's income. First of all, you need to work out the discount factor for each year.

The formula is this:

1 / (1 + discount rate) to the power of the period number.

The discount rate of 6% is expressed as 0.06.

So, *1 + 0.06 = 1.06.*

Then computing in the formula for the first year, it's simply: *1 / (1 + 0.06) = 0.94* for the discount factor.

For the second year, you need 1.06 to the power of 2. Or, you can do 1.06 squared, which you can calculate easily as 1.06 x 1.06.

But if you carry on doing that every year, it's long-winded, it takes forever, so use the POWER function in the spreadsheet instead: you get a formula =POWER(1.06,2) for year 2, =POWER(1.06,3) for year 3, =POWER(1.06,4) for year 4, and finally =POWER(1.06,5) for year 5.

Example below shows you how the =POWER formula should be computed in Microsoft Excel for year 2.

	f_x	=POWER(1.06,2)
C	D	E	F
	1.124		

The table below shows all 5 years after using the =POWER formula in Excel.

1	1.06
2	1.124
3	1.191
4	1.262
5	1.338

Once you've done that for all five years, all you need is to calculate one divided by each result, and you have the discount rates for all the years.

Year 1 = 1 / 1.06 = 0.94

Year 2 = 1 / 1.124 = 0.89

Year 3 = 1 / 1.191 = 0.84

Year 4 = 1 / 1.262 = 0.79

Year 5 = 1 / 1.338 = 0.75

The table below shows you the final computed figures of the formulas above.

Years	Discount Rates
1	0.94
2	0.89
3	0.84
4	0.79
5	0.75

Yes, that was geeky stuff. Don't worry, once you've built a spreadsheet with your discount rates in, you'll be able to copy it again and again and again.

Next, simply take the cash flow figure and multiply it by the discount rate to get the NPV of cash flows for each year.

*So, year 1 = $12,365m x 0.94 = **$11,623m***

*Year 2 = $15,826m x 0.89 = **$14,086m***

*Year 3 = $20,259m x 0.84 = **$17,017m***

*Year 4 = $25,932m x 0.79 = **$20,485m***

*Year 5 = $33,191m x 0.75 = **$24,893m***

And finally, add the NPV figures together to arrive at the total value of five years of Amazon earnings of **$88,104m.**

The table below includes the discount factors for the five years, NPV of cash flows for the five years and the total NPV of cash flows computed.

	Years (in $m)				
	1	2	3	4	5
Net Income	$27,304	$34,949	$44,734	$57,260	$73,293
Depreciation	$32,321	$41,371	$52,955	$67,782	$86,761
Working Capital	$17,256	$22,088	$28,272	$36,188	$46,321
Other non-cash items	$11,786	$15,086	$19,310	$24,717	$31,638
	$88,667	$113,493	$145,271	$185,948	$238,013
Capital Expenditure	-$76,302	-$97,667	-$125,013	-$160,017	-$204,822
Disposals	$0	$0	$0	$0	$0
	-$76,302	-$97,667	-$125,013	-$160,017	-$204,822
Cash Flow	$12,365	$15,827	$20,258	$25,931	$33,191
Discount Factors	0.94	0.89	0.84	0.79	0.75
NPV of Cash Flows	$11,623	$14,086	$17,017	$20,485	$24,893
Total NPV of Cash Flows	$88,104				

As a quick check, the NPV of cash flow number you get should always be *less* than the cash flow figure because you've had to wait for the money (the present value of a future sum is always less than the future value, reflecting the time value of money - the fact that you have to wait for it.) **This is the NPV of the cash flow for that year.**

Now I have a problem. The problem is that I've only calculated what Amazon is worth if it keeps going for five years and then liquidates at nil value.

When you use DCF calculations within a business, it's often for limited-time investments, like a mine that would eventually be exhausted or a power plant with a useful life of 20 years. So, they reach the end of the period, and the plant is decommissioned.

But with Amazon, you'd expect it to keep going, maybe at a lower rate of growth. So, there are two ways that you can build that into the calculation.

- You can think about what Amazon shares will be worth on a P/E ratio basis in five years' time and then discount that back.
- Or you can assume that Amazon will grow in perpetuity by a certain amount and work out a terminal value with a formula similar to the previous one we used in the *constant dividend model*.

A terminal value is what we expect the company to be worth in x years' time when we end the DCF calculation. So basically, we're saying we will get this cash flow which we forecasted for x years, and after year 2022 + x years, we will sell the company for what it's worth at the time.

Looking forward five years, I think Amazon will still be a growth stock. Maybe, not growing quite as fast. It will probably still be dominant in e-commerce, though Walmart might be doing some catching up.

So, it will probably still trade at a premium to the market. I don't know where the market will be trading, so let's take a long term average P/E ratio for S&P 500 over the last 30-40 years. That gives us a 16 times P/E ratio, according to MacroTrends.

I would assume Amazon will get 50% more because it's fast growing and has a dominant market position with high returns. So that'll give us a P/E ratio of 24, and a terminal value of **$1,759,032m** (that is, the last cash flow forecast in year 5 of $73,293 x 24 P/E ratio).

Then, *adding* the terminal value to the NPV of years 1 to 5, which is $88,104m. And this gives us a total of **$1,847,136m** (or $ 1.847trn), which compares with the $1.5trn market capitalization today (in March 2022).

The market capitalization is one of the numbers you see anywhere on the internet that you look up stock prices - it's an absolutely basic number. Of course, you can always check it against shares in issue in the annual report if you are suspicious.

If the terminal value is higher than market capitalization, that might mean the stock is a bargain. Or it might mean our valuation is too optimistic.

So, can we assume that Amazon is trading at a bargain right now? Well, yes. But do I really believe that? No. I think the terminal value accounts for far too high a percentage of the total valuation.

I think what I'd rather do - and this might be worth doing - is actually run a 20-year full model and get the discounted value from that model instead of just doing five years. And I'd be making some assumptions about much reduced growth during the second decade. You cannot always be right. In fact, Amazon might not even look like the same business in 20 years' time, it might be a drone delivery company. But you're trying to assess the shares with the best assumptions that you can.

So, let's try the other way. How fast do I think Amazon can continue growing? A 10% growth rate would be fairly modest in the medium term, and I don't see any reason the company couldn't get that through geographical expansion and increased market penetration.

But in fact, we're looking at *perpetuity* here. We're looking maybe 20, 30, 40 years ahead. So over that period, will Amazon still be growing faster than the economy or should we assume it grows at the same level as GDP of 3% (according to major economics websites).

I think for the early part of the period, it will be growing faster than the GDP rate.

Anyway, do you remember WACC? It's the weighted average cost of the company's finance, split between equity and debt. I'm not going to go through all the calculations, but for Amazon, it's 8% (which I found through a number of quant websites and analyst reports, and that's pretty much what I'd expect for a major corporation).

The formula below is terminal value based on **cash flow (CF) in perpetuity**, rather than terminal P/E ratio which I calculated previously.

Year 5 cash flow x (1 + perpetual growth rate) / WACC - perpetual growth rate.

So, I can plug in the numbers into the formula as;

$33,191m x (1 + 3%) / (8% - 3%) or simply, $34,186m / 5% = **$683,735m.**

Then, *adding* the terminal value to the NPV of years 1 to 5, which is $88,105m. And this gives us a total of **$771,839m.**

A bit different from the other figure, and even when you add in the NPV of the first five years' cash flows, it's a lot lower than the company's current market capitalization.

The table below shows the complete cash flows, and terminal value-based estimations for Amazon for the next 5 years.

	Years (in $m)				
	1	2	3	4	5
Net Income	$27,304	$34,949	$44,734	$57,260	$73,293
Depreciation	$32,321	$41,371	$52,955	$67,782	$86,761
Working Capital	$17,256	$22,088	$28,272	$36,188	$46,321
Other non-cash items	$11,786	$15,086	$19,310	$24,717	$31,638
	$88,667	$113,493	$145,271	$185,948	$238,013
Capital Expenditure	-$76,302	-$97,667	-$125,013	-$160,017	-$204,822
Disposals	$0	$0	$0	$0	$0
	-$76,302	-$97,667	-$125,013	-$160,017	-$204,822
Cash Flow	$12,365	$15,827	$20,258	$25,931	$33,191
Discount Factors	0.94	0.89	0.84	0.79	0.75
NPV of Cash Flows	$11,623	$14,086	$17,017	$20,485	$24,893
Total NPV of Cash Flows	$88,104				
Terminal Value Based on P/E Ratio					$1,759,032
Total Value					$1,847,136
Terminal Value Based on CF in Perpetuity					$683,735
Total Value					$771,839

I was worried enough by the way my DCF analysis undervalued Amazon's current valuation so I looked Amazon DCF valuations on the internet. Alphaspread has an automatic valuation system that suggests Amazon is 31% overvalued. A couple of other commentators had similar views. However, Wall Street has Amazon down as a 'buy' with a target price 43% higher than the current share price - so according to them, it's undervalued.

Pros and cons of DCF

What I'd like you to do as an exercise is to build your own spreadsheet and then play around with it.

For instance, what happens if you assume a 4% perpetual growth rate? What happens if you think earnings growth will run at 50% in year one, then 40% in year two, then 28% year three? It could be fun to jot your different estimates of Amazon's value on a piece of paper.

And now, think about it the other way round. What do you have to do to the assumptions to justify today's market capitalization? Are you happy with those assumptions?

I hope you'll have seen by trying those ideas out that a small change in one of the assumptions can lead to a much greater change in the DCF valuation. This is one of the key disadvantages of this method - in particular, the discount rate you use, and the growth rate you use, will 'swing' the valuation one way or another.

So, it's important that you don't use the DCF as some kind of scientific method which will 'tell' you what the value is - it's better used, at least in my opinion, as a way of exploring which assumptions need to be correct to justify a given value.

For instance, you might like to use DCF analysis together with a number of scenarios to create an expected value. Or you might want to use it simply as a way of examining what underlying assumptions analysts are making when they come up with a target price.

Let's look at some of the other **disadvantages** of the DCF valuation.

- One thing I really dislike is that the terminal value often accounts for most of the valuation. If you're using a five year ahead P/E ratio as your valuation, I wouldn't think that it gives you better information than you'd get by using today's P/E ratio. And at least you can guess that this year's earnings forecasts are probably pretty close to the actual result, whereas the further out you go, the less probable it is your forecasts will be accurate.
- The model's dependence on forecast growth rates makes it particularly unsuitable for valuing the very companies where it's used the most, early-stage technology companies and start-ups.
- The model tends to use smooth growth predictions. That makes it most suitable for businesses with smooth and predictable cash flows, such as utilities, or companies with subscription or rental business models.

On the other hand, the DCF does have the advantage of producing an absolute value using a set of clear assumptions. As long as you remember the IT saying, "Garbage in, garbage out", you'll get a lot of mileage out of the DCF model without being deceived into believing it as a flawless method.

By the way, "Garbage in, garbage out" means that what you get out of a computer is only as good as the data you input. Put in faulty data and you'll get a useless answer.

Other **advantages** of using a DCF model are:

- it can help value a company that may have a couple of years of below-average earnings as you are looking at the value of earnings over a period rather than at earnings at one particular point,
- it's about cash flow, not earnings;
- and it includes medium term growth rather than just looking at the next two years.

Choosing a discount rate

There are numerous different ways to choose a discount rate. Quite often, the company's WACC is used. That may be sensible, as it relates the company's value to the amount it has to pay to fund its operations, but it means your valuation of one company may be based on a discount rate very different from your valuation of another.

You can use the 10-year Treasury rate or a corporate bond yield which you can find using FINRA's TRACE database. But the 10-year Treasury rate is a risk-free rate; the U.S government is extremely unlikely to default. On the other hand, investing in equities are riskier, so investors get a *risk premium* (that is, investors want to be paid more for the higher risk of holding them).

That's why most analysts use a blended rate (because it assesses the company's returns in terms of what it actually costs the company to fund its operations), by adding the *risk-free rate* (the rate on 10-year Treasuries) to the excess *return of the market* over *risk free returns*, multiplied by the *beta* of the stock, which you can find on most finance websites.

RFR + [(market return / RFR) x Beta].

Frankly, I don't think you need to do that. Use a standard rate representing equity market returns over the long term. If you use something like 8% you won't go too far wrong. If you use 8% then you're basing your assessment on long term actual outturns for all equities.

This has two advantages. First, you don't have to do all those calculations every time you do a DCF valuation. And secondly, you know that all your valuations use the same basis.

Forecasting

This is another thing you might not find in many books about fundamental analysis, as they tend to concentrate on analyzing historical figures. But I think it's worth having a go at making your own forecasts.

It's a great way to find out how the business works, particularly if you've built in industry -specific data like occupancy rates in a hotel business. It also makes you examine your thoughts about the future; is it consistent to think a hotel business can keep growing without spending any money opening new hotels, for instance? By attempting to forecast the cash flow, you'll find out whether your revenue expectations are incompatible with your ideas of capital spending.

Be clear about the two or three main factors that affect the business. For instance, for a retailer, things like volumes, mark-up (which gives you your gross margin), and property costs are the big three.

With a consultancy firm, hours worked and billed, and the hourly rate are the big drivers, so you'll want to work out some ratios based on employee numbers and salary costs.

With retail banks, the two big factors are interest (the interest rate they have to pay on deposits, the interest rate they get from lending money out, and the difference between the two), and the cost of running the branch network.

A good exercise for you to do right now would be to pick three or four different stocks and think about what are the key drivers for their business. If you have friends who are interested in investment this can make quite an enjoyable discussion over a few cups of coffee. (By the way, coffee is *not* one of Starbucks' 'big three' - coffee beans have historically accounted for less than 10% of Starbucks' costs. Interesting?)

It's easy to build a massively complex spreadsheet. I made one for an airline once that linked its profits to jet fuel prices, passenger numbers, the average lease cost of a Boeing 737, employee numbers, currencies, the mix of long haul versus short haul business, and a half dozen other factors. I was really proud of it until it went live. I had managed to forecast British Airways losing more than its market capitalization, and most analysts thought it was going to make a profit.

For once, the other analysts were right, and I was wrong.

The trouble with that spreadsheet was that I couldn't see the wood for the trees. That's why you should concentrate on just the most important factors - and that's why you probably shouldn't use the company's formal income statement as your basis for the spreadsheet. Simplify as much as you can. No one's ever going to ask you to explain your workings; the important thing is that you understand them yourself.

When you've done your forecast, take a look at the analyst consensus. Compare your own ideas with the analysts'. If you're wildly adrift, don't assume you've got it wrong - ask yourself what the differences in assumptions are. You might be right. Or you might have missed something - like the effect of currency movements on foreign earnings, or a lawsuit you didn't know about.

Analyst consensus is available on most finance websites like Yahoo Finance or Zacks. You'll usually see the average and the range of forecasts plus buy or sell recommendations, and the number of analysts. Obviously if there are 23 analysts predicting around 25 cents for Big Stock with a range of 24.5 cents earnings to 25.55 cents, that's very different from having just two analysts looking at Itsy Bitsy Corporation with predictions of 20 cents and 59 cents!

Also, important to check, where given, the dates of recommendations and forecasts, as sometimes a year-old forecast gets left up when an analyst hasn't bothered to update for whatever reason.

It's sometimes interesting to see how widespread the analysts are. Sometimes, they are all clustered around the same area pretty tightly. Other times, there's just a single outlier, and sometimes the forecasts are all over the place. If they can't even agree amongst themselves, your guess is as good as theirs. Alternatively, if all of them agree, and you think differently, if you're right, you've probably found a great profit-making opportunity.

Chapter 9 Quiz

1. Which of these is not a major cost for a hotel chain?
   a. Staff
   b. Property costs
   c. Raw materials
   d. Marketing and finance costs

2. Which of these is a major weakness of DCF valuations?
   a. They are not easy to calculate
   b. Changing the inputs even slightly can change the valuation a lot
   c. They don't use the same accounting treatment as the income statement
   d. No one ever talks about them on CNN

3. Discounting to get a net present value is the reverse of
   a. The compounding effect
   b. The Coriolis effect
   c. The carryover effect
   d. The catch-up effect

4. What kind of company is most suitable for DCF analysis?
   a. One with predictable cash flows
   b. One that isn't making a profit
   c. One that has a lot of debt
   d. One that begins with I

5. Which of these is crucial to building an earnings forecast?
   a. Inside information
   b. An advanced econometrics software package
   c. A good forecast for economic growth
   d. The two or three key drivers of costs

10

Chapter 10: Macro vs Micro, or Top Down vs Bottom Up

Stocks don't exist in a void, nor do the companies in which you own shares. They exist in the real world, in the larger economy, and they are subject to big economic trends and to socio - demographic trends, like the growth in single-person households and the increased proportion of older people in the population.

When you do fundamental analysis looking at individual companies, you're doing 'bottom up' analysis - starting with the details of the company itself. That lends itself to a stock-picking approach, trying to find excellent businesses to invest in at the right price.

But you can also carry out 'top down' analysis. That means looking at socio- economic trends and then focusing on the stocks that are likely to do well in that situation. For instance, with an increasingly aging population, you might decide you want to look at healthcare, pharmaceuticals, and medical and elder care REITs.

Or you might decide to look at stocks involved in renewable energy, sustainable materials to replace plastics, and other environmentally sustainable niches.

Let me say that some people will find they make really good calls here, others not. Top down can be useful, but it's a matter of style. I personally love reading *Wired* for stuff that takes modern tech almost as far as science fiction, which I find quite challenging - but that doesn't do my investing any good at all. It's just fun.

I find bottom-up analysis gives me a much better bang for my buck. Your mileage, as they say, might differ.

The same goes for fund managers. Some, like George Soros and Stanley Druckenmiller, make big top-down bets and they've made them very successfully. Others, like Warren Buffett, are very much bottom-up guys. Some sit nearer the middle - Peter Lynch is best known for his bottom-up bets, but he knew how to use economic data to spot interesting situations in cyclical stocks.

Where to find economic data

You can obviously find economic data in the media - economic stats are always well covered on TV and in the press. But to do proper analysis, you need more than the latest number. You need a full run of the relevant stats.

Look on the U.S Department of Commerce site and you can find full runs of economic, environmental and demographic data. You'll also find the release schedule for economic indicators. You should also cast an eye over the Conference Board (www.conference-board.org), where you can find global economic indicators, including other areas of the world as well as the U.S. So, for instance, if you had invested in a couple of stocks with important operations in the Far East, you can access data from Japan, China and South Korea. However, a lot of the content has to be paid for.

Particular data series to look at are:

- GDP - Gross Domestic Product. This is the total size of the economy as a whole. It's the growth (or decline) in the overall number, that is the important factor here.
- The Conference Board produces a 'Leading Economic Index' (LEI), which uses various indicators to find the peaks and troughs in the business cycle.
- Inflation has not been an important factor for most of the past 30 years, but this could change as wage rises and soaring oil and gas prices push the cost of most goods higher. Higher inflation usually leads to the Fed putting up interest rates.
- Interest rates, like inflation, are currently at historically low levels despite a recent hike. Obviously, they affect the rate at which companies can borrow. They may also depress the consumer sector if individuals find home loans too hard to pay at higher rates, or in the capital goods sector, if cash in the bank is earning a good rate of interest and business investment doesn't seem particularly attractive so that businesses don't invest. Equally, higher rates can lead to lower equity valuations (a *higher* earnings yield, remember, is equivalent to a *lower* price/earnings ratio).
- Non Farm Payrolls is an important number for gauging the U.S economy. It shows whether businesses are growing and need labor; it shows whether people are in employment and so able and willing to spend money. If there are labor shortages, that could impact labor-intensive services businesses.
- The Manufacturing PMI (Purchasing Managers' Index) shows whether the manufacturing sector is expanding (if PMI is over 50) or contracting (if PMI is under 50). There's also a Non-Manufacturing PMI which gives you data for the services sector. These indexes are made up of data on orders made, backlog, inventory changes, and they have proven to be quite useful in assessing the health of the corporate sector.

You can also find detailed data that can help with researching particular sectors. For instance, if you're investing in home builders or residential REITs, you'll want to look at building permits; if you own shares in Walmart, you'll want to follow month-by-month retail sales. Often, companies will show or refer to relevant economic data in their annual reports or (more often) in the analyst presentations, so when they do, make a note to add those series to your regular data feed.

A data series that a lot of investors used to see as a good lead indicator for global trade is the Baltic Dry Index (BDI). It measures the price of bulk shipping, which used to be a good proxy for trade flows. However, as global trade shifts from bulk commodities to container shipped manufactured goods, some observers feel the BDI isn't doing its job anymore.

Economic cycles and how they work

Knowing how economic cycles work is crucial to understanding cyclical sectors like energy and mining, chemicals and automobiles. While there's a powerful economic cycle that affects the top line of GDP, each industry sector also has its own cycle, and it works like this:

- Everyone needs a new XYZ. There's not enough XYZ to go around.
- The manufacturers of XYZ are making great profits, but they can't make enough XYZ to meet demand.
- So, they invest their profits in new XYZ capacity. All goes well for a while, until...
- Suddenly, there are too many new XYZs on the market. Prices go down and the manufacturers are making less money.
- Some of the manufacturers of XYZ go bust.
- Now, there aren't so many XYZs being made... and eventually, demand for XYZs increases again, and the price of an XYZ increases and the manufacturers who are left in the game are doing quite well.

- Which is great till they decide to invest in new XYZ capacity...
- And it all starts all over again.

Basically, the cycle works because capacity isn't scalable - you have to buy big chunks. You can't scale up a plant that will produce 250,000 cars a year by adding small increments to get another couple of percent production; you need to make a significant investment. So, the market tends to swing between periods of excess demand and periods of oversupply.

If you look at technology, semiconductors are a cyclical sector. Software, not so much - because adding new developers to the workforce isn't a chunky investment, but building a new fabrication plant is.

So, if you want to track a cyclical sector, you'll want to look at statistics for demand, supply, and pricing. For instance, Peter Lynch always looked at the price of second-hand automobiles as an indicator of the auto market - if the price went up, it was because there weren't enough vehicles available to meet demand, and this was usually the end of the cyclical trough and beginning of the upturn.

Many investors divide stocks into cyclical and defensive stocks. In this case, 'cyclical' doesn't always mean stocks that have an inherently cyclical nature, but stocks which respond very directly to economic activity.

Defensive stocks are those which tend to perform without regard to what the overall economy is doing - for instance, supermarkets, pharmaceuticals, and consumer staples such as cleaning products, tobacco, and Coca-Cola.

Generally, defensive stocks perform better during recessions, but will tend to underperform in a growth market when cyclical stocks will outperform. One thing I like to do is to look at GDP or consumer disposable income statistics compared with a company's revenues, to see if there's a relationship - it's easiest to do this visually, as you can see very easily if the two lines tend to run parallel or not.

There's also some evidence that particular sectors outperform in different stages of the economic cycle as a whole.

Expansion	**Consumer discretionary stocks i.e. Televisions, cars**
Peak	**Metals, industrials, energy**
Contraction	**Healthcare, IT**
Trough	**Consumer staples, finance, utilities**

Don't forget that the economic cycle could have a relatively small impact on revenues but a much more important impact on profits. That's particularly the case with businesses that have;

- high fixed costs (so they can't easily scale down),
- low margins (so any fall in price hurts them very hard),
- high borrowing costs (so when profits fall, the banks take much more of the profit).

You can also look at a stock's beta (the measure of its volatility, that is, how fast its price changes compared to changes in the market as a whole) as an indication of whether a stock is likely to be cyclical or defensive. Defensive stocks will have low betas (below 1).

It's quite difficult to see the exact relationship between the economic cycle in general and an individual company's profits in particular. But although it's difficult, it's well worth making the effort, as this can be an important factor in the performance of the stock over the medium term.

What's particularly interesting right now is that automotive, a cyclical industry, is also being affected by a major disruptive factor - the move to electric vehicles (EVs). All bets are off! That makes automotive higher risk than it was last time around since as well as betting on the cycle, you have to bet on which company will make the best transition to EVs.

How to 'test' economic data

Sometimes economic data doesn't tell you everything you want to know. For instance, inflation rates in 2021 appeared low - but in fact, the basket of goods typically bought by low-income households was getting much more expensive, much more quickly. Anyone trying to live on a low income could have told you about that... but the official data didn't.

In Russia in the 1990s, economic data and company figures looked good. But in 1998, Russia defaulted (failed to fulfil an obligation), and its stock market crashed. However, if you looked at a lot of companies' figures, you would have spotted that their return on capital was way lower than the bank interest rate, which meant that companies weren't earning high enough margins for it to be worth investing in.

These are two examples of the top line economic data not giving the whole picture, so I'd suggest if you want to do fundamental analysis properly, you find some other statistics that can let you 'test' the data.

In fact, in the first case, a new index called the Vimes Boots Index was created in the UK to show inflation for the lowest-cost staple foods (thanks to anti-poverty campaigner Jack Monroe and the estate of writer Terry Pratchett).

Goldman Sachs used to create an index of newspaper advertising as a check on economic growth - nowadays, you'd probably want to look at internet ads instead.

Wall Street analysts often carry out 'channel checking', for instance, ringing companies that are customers for capital goods to find out what they are buying, or checking retail stores to see which food companies are getting the most shelf space. Some have been known to pay for people to count the number of trucks visiting a factory.

You might also want to look at the spread between the interest rate on bonds and company returns on capital. Perhaps taking the largest stock in each sector in the S&P 100 to make this comparison would be a reasonable idea. Ideally, you'd want to re-run the figures every quarter to keep up with events.

Understanding economic impact on company results

Let's take a look at how the economy could affect a given company specifically.

- Interest rates - for an indebted company, a rise in interest rates could be very bad news. On the other hand, a company with strong cash generation and large cash reserves could add something to profits - though you probably wouldn't consider those earnings very high quality.

- Cost inputs - higher inflation might lead to significantly higher costs. In 2022, wind turbine manufacturers are facing a hike in their costs, and because they generally work on long term contracts (in which the delivered price has been set and is not adjustable), they're going to see their margins squeezed. On the other hand, some producers, such as those of luxury goods, are better able to pass on cost of inflation to their customers.

- Asset prices - for a real estate company, even one with a relatively well-structured balance sheet, a fall in asset prices could be a major concern. Banks often grant loans on the basis of a covenant which ensures the bank can call in the loan if it's not covered by a certain amount of assets. If the valuation of the properties in the company's portfolio falls, it may no longer be covered - and suddenly faces having to refinance or file for bankruptcy.

- Credit squeeze - a company which is burning cash may find it is unable to borrow to invest in its activities; companies with cash resources may take advantage in order to 'leapfrog' indebted rivals.

- High yield stocks may be downgraded if interest rates increase, as investors are able to get better yields from lower risk investments such as Treasuries.

Chapter 10 Quiz

1. Two major types of investing are;
    a. Bottom up and top down
    b. Forwards and backwards
    c. Straight and crooked
    d. Macroeconomic and macaroni

2. What are the phases of a cycle, in the right order?
    a. Expansion, peak, contraction, trough
    b. Contraction, peak, expansion, trough
    c. Trough, peak, expansion, contraction
    d. Invention, hype, bubble, crash

3. Which of these is not a way of testing economic data or company data?
    a. Creating your own index, for instance of food prices
    b. Relating the data to corporate results
    c. Visiting retail outlets to see what is selling
    d. Ordering the most expensive drink you can at Starbucks

4. What is a defensive stock?
    a. One with a big moat
    b. One whose results aren't much affected by economic change
    c. Boeing, General dynamics or Northrop Grumman
    d. One which has no foreign earnings

5. Why is the auto sector no longer a typical cyclical investment?
    a. There are not so many automotive manufacturers as there used to be
    b. No one buys cars anymore, they lease them
    c. It has been disrupted by the change to electric vehicles
    d. Mexico and Korea now have a big share of the market

11

Chapter 11: Defining 'buy' and 'sell'

Fundamental analysis is a tool, and it's a great tool. But it's not a commandment, and it won't answer the questions "Should I buy Tesla shares?" or "Should I sell Pfizer stock?". In that case, you might as well try asking your car where it would like to go this afternoon!

What you buy will not depend just on your analysis, either. It will also depend on your overall financial objectives. For instance, you may be driven by the desire to create a store of wealth through investing, or you may already have wealth but want to take an income from your investments. Even if you decide to invest in dividend paying stocks, you might decide to buy stocks with fast growing dividends and perhaps a lower yield or try to get the best yields you can, depending on your time horizon and need for funds.

Your decision will also depend on your particular risk appetite, whether you're more risk-averse or less. (When I was working a full-time job, I could afford to buy all-or-nothing tech stocks - now that I'm self-employed, I have to play things a bit safer.)

For instance, the 'dash for trash' as markets started recovering from the credit crunch saw some people investing in very highly indebted real estate companies. Basically, they were making a binary bet - one with only two outcomes - either that the company would go bust or that the share price would triple or quadruple. In fact, investors in many of these companies won their bet handsomely; but if you didn't like the amount of risk involved, you would have been right to stay out of the market.

However, while fundamental analysis won't tell you whether to buy or sell, it *will* tell you:

- whether the stock is vulnerable to particular external risks;
- whether the company is a good and growing business;
- the balance of risk and reward represented by the stock;
- whether the stock is trading at a cheap or expensive valuation.

That's all really useful information that you will use in making your decision.

Types of situations

As you gain experience, you'll probably find that there are particular types of situations where you do well. Let's take a look at these.

- Value, which can often involve buying the sector or company everybody hates. In 2003-4, it was technology, and in the 1990s, it was breweries. Right now, it seems to be biotech (unless the company has a COVID vaccine). If you find an out-of-favor sector selling at a significant discount to its intrinsic value, buy all the good quality stocks you can find. (It doesn't have to be *either* Pepsi *or* Coke - you can buy both if they both have the same attractions.) In simple words, an out-of-favor sector basically is a sector no one wants to buy, for whatever reason, and which is really undervalued.

- Turnaround. Sometimes you'll find a company which made a mis-step a few years ago, or where new management is expected to improve the business. If you can work out on the spreadsheet how the company can turn around within 18 months to 36 months and what it should be worth, then if it does, you may have a good investment. But remember, there is an execution risk.

- High growth. These stocks have driven the market for the last few years, and there's always an attractive story to go with the growth. The key is not to pay too much for that growth - and to have a good feeling about whether the growth forecast is realistic or way too optimistic. That's where high quality fundamental research will make all the difference to your investing.

- Dividend yielders. You could just buy the highest yielders in the index - but if you did, you'd end up with some real deadbeats. Your analysis will tell you if the company is paying a high yield because it's close to bankruptcy or because it's attractively valued (cheap as chips) with a strong cash flow.

- Misvaluations. This is where a business is valued in the wrong way. For instance, BAA, the owner of several British airports, was initially valued as a transportation stock. When it was looked at instead as a real estate stock, owning significant retail properties, it justified a price nearly three times higher. (Remember when you looked at Amazon's annual report and found out that it was a massive cloud services stock with a retailer attached? That's the kind of misunderstanding that creates this type of situation.)
- Cyclicals. If you get these stocks right, you can buy at just the right time in the cycle - before the business starts to turn around and when no one else wants the stock. Timing is crucial. You'll also need to have some way of averaging out earnings, as at the bottom of the cycle the price-earning ratio may look deceptively high on a single-year basis.
- Boring. Lots of people remember Peter Lynch buying retail and restaurant stocks like McDonald's, Home Depot, and Taco Bell. But he also loved buying stocks with really boring names and really boring businesses (though they were good quality) - because he found they were almost always overlooked by other investors.

You'll probably find out that your best deals come in two or three of these styles of investment. Concentrate on what you're good at, and keep working out what it was that tipped you off that these were the right stocks to buy. (I do well at misvaluations and turnarounds; I'm the world's worst investor in cyclicals, which somehow, I always get wrong.)

You may find that several of the stocks you like are trading very slightly above what you consider the right price. It's well worth setting an alert with your broker or on a finance website so that you are notified when the stock trades at the level you think is right to buy.

Recently, my friend built a position in French dividend payer Sanofi, a big pharmaceutical firm, buying when the dividend yield rose above 3.8%.

The first time he looked at it, he thought it was too expensive, but share price volatility had been his friend here, with the early 2020 Covid crash, then a vaccine failure story, helping him purchase it at a cheaper price.

Timing or value?

Timing an investment is difficult. If you spend your time looking at share price charts, you'll find it's never the right time to buy - either the shares have already gone up, so you feel you've 'missed' that amount of share price growth, or the shares are going down, so you worry that they'll carry on bleeding. Do you risk buying just before the results, or wait till afterwards?

Using your target price, set at a given percentage discount to the intrinsic value of the stock, spares you these uncertainties. The right time to buy a stock is whenever it's valued correctly. (Of course, if you're a growth investor, you might decide that buying the stock exactly at its intrinsic price is the right time, given that most growth stocks trade at a high valuation.)

You can build a stake gradually, buying whenever the price is right and you have money available. Unless the underlying fundamentals change, your target price remains the same. (Remember to check up on the tax treatment of gradual purchases and sales, which can differ depending on the jurisdiction within which you invest. And keep your records safe!)

Obviously, the right time to sell is when the shares are overvalued. You might decide that up to a 30% temporary overvaluation, you're not too worried - but above that level, you would want to take another look at the basics. It may be that the company has achieved growth and is now worth more - or it may be that the market has run away with enthusiasm, and the stock is trading too high. Don't decide to sell before you check which of these is the case!

If you always base your buying decisions on what you believe is the stock's real value, rather than on ideas of momentum or market timing, you'll make better decisions. And in fact, you are probably going to buy towards the bottom and sell towards the higher end of the range - even though you're not trying to 'time the market'.

Other times you might decide to sell

There are a few other times that you might decide to sell a stock. Let's run through those.

- When bad news undermines the entire basis of the valuation. For instance, if you buy a pharmaceutical stock and its main drug is found to be unsafe, or if you buy a mining exploration company and it doesn't find any mineral reserves, get out of it!
- When there is a major economic threat to the company's future, such as an interest rate hike when a company has high debts.
- One thing many brokers believe is that "profit warnings always come in threes". For the bigger, well-covered stocks, a major profit warning is unusual - analysts' expectations are usually well managed. So, a profit warning means not just that the company is underperforming, but that things worsened suddenly or that management didn't find out till it was too late. So, a hefty warning could be time to exit. However, a small underperformance wouldn't normally justify an exit.
- The resignation of the CEO or CFO is almost always time to go, particularly if it's coupled with a profit warning. When finance officers quit, it often means they have discovered something in the accounts that they didn't know was there, and it is *never* good news. If there are also other signs of poor governance (such as large related party transactions) that would confirm your decision to exit.

- Slow but steady deterioration in the growth rate, in the company's financial strength, margins, or cash flow - particularly if the company is in denial rather than actively trying to improve matters.
- A cut in the dividend may mean it's time to quit, particularly if the yield is one of the main reasons for buying a stock. However, it's not always the case - some companies decided to cut their dividend in 2020 because they wanted to retain more margin if the pandemic damaged their business and then reinstated the dividend later on. But if a dividend cut accompanies some signs of deterioration or financial stress, it is usually a sign that something is wrong.
- Increasing risk. If a company is beginning to lose its 'moat', if new and well-funded rivals have entered the market, or if the company's major foreign market sees a regime change which could imperil its earnings, those are all examples of increased risk. The valuation should reflect that higher risk - you would want to buy at a higher discount to the intrinsic value. But this wouldn't necessarily justify an immediate sale.

You might also want to sell because you've changed your investment strategy. For instance, if you decide to prioritize regular income rather than capital growth, you might want to sell the companies that are not paying a dividend. Or, of course, you may simply need to cash out some of your stock position to raise cash if you're buying a house or taking a sabbatical.

While fundamental analysts generally ignore what the share price is doing in the market, I'd like to suggest that there's one time that you shouldn't do that. This is when the share price falls very significantly for no apparent reason. I don't mean a 3% fall - I mean something of the order of 15% or 20% over just a couple of days. I have found through experience that that is often the first sign of something very bad - perhaps fraud or a series of profit warnings.

So, if I see a stock fall far and fast, the first thing I do is check out why. Sometimes I can explain it easily; an earnings miss, a change to guidance, or a competitor spreading bad news. A failed clinical trial, or a contract that the company saw go to a rival, could also explain a sudden fall in the share price.

But if there seems to be no reason, you might be best taking a loss and making your exit.

Chapter 11 Quiz

1. Which of these is not a type of stock situation you might invest in?
   a. Turnaround
   b. Value
   c. Cyclical
   d. Titanic

2. Which of these should not affect your purchase decision for a stock?
   a. Your investment objectives
   b. The stock's valuation
   c. Past share price performance
   d. The company's past performance

3. Which of these is not a possible reason for selling a stock?
   a. Steady deterioration in financial ratios
   b. Sudden resignation of the CFO
   c. A single negative earnings surprise
   d. A big cut in the dividend

4. If you are highly risk averse, and you refused to buy a stock because it had a 50% risk of going bankrupt, and it subsequently doubled in price, you made;
   a. A stupid decision
   b. A good decision
   c. A bad decision
   d. A mathematically incorrect decision

5. Traditionally, profit warnings always come in;
   a. June
   b. The last quarter
   c. Hot weather
   d. Threes

12

Chapter 12: The best of both worlds - combining FA and TA

Fundamental analysis (FA) and technical analysis (TA) would seem to be two very different, even mutually exclusive, approaches to the stock market.

Fundamental analysis says that a stock has an intrinsic value, however volatile the market price might be, and that the intrinsic value is based on the activities and profitability of the underlying business.

Technical analysis says that a stock is worth what someone is willing to pay you for it and aims to predict share price movements by analyzing supply and demand patterns (usually graphically, which is why technical analysis is also known as 'charting').

In fact, though the two approaches are based on very different theories, they are not necessarily incompatible. To use them together, you need to understand what each approach is intended to do and what sort of decision it is best used for.

- Technical analysis tends to look at short and medium term trends, while fundamental analysis looks at the long term value of a stock.
- Technical analysis considers the stock price as the outcome of market trading activity, whereas fundamental analysis considers it as a representation of the value of the company.

Every share has this dual nature - it is both a share in a real business and a financial instrument that can be traded. If you can sell a share in a business that you believe is actually worth nothing to the market at $25, what is the "right" price - zero or $25?

A share price chart is a graphical way of assessing the balance of positive and negative emotions in the market - traders who are greedy, traders who are afraid, buyers and sellers, supply and demand. It is a summary of market behavior. It doesn't say whether that behavior was sensible or stupid, it doesn't say why traders made the trades they did - it simply sums up the facts.

So technical analysis can be useful in looking at timing. And fundamental analysis can be useful for a technical trader in giving a bit more background to the share price movements. Although I'm a long term investor for a lot of my wealth, I run part of my portfolio as a trading book and use technical analysis to trade, with some success. I'm quite realistic about the two approaches: I noticed that my technical trades had a lower failure rate when I got to understand fundamentals, and I know that as a long term investor, I can use technical analysis to show me when I'm likely to get a lower in-price if I wait a bit.

Some technical analysis basics

Technical analysis got started when Charles Dow (the same Dow who invented the Dow Jones index) created the Dow Theory. His theory was that despite all the 'noise' of daily price changes, stock markets move in trends, which are relatively predictable, and continue till a definite signal ends the trend. He sees the trend as similar to an economic cycle - it begins with an accumulation phase in which traders start buying, moves into a public participation phase in which the stock becomes popular, and ends in a panic phase (speculative bubble), ending in a crash.

He also stressed the need for confirmation; in a major trend, all the relevant indices should confirm each other by moving in the same direction, and trading volumes should also confirm the trend. So, for instance, the S&P 100, S&P 500, DJIA, and Nasdaq Composite should all be moving in the same direction if the U.S market is trending upwards. If one of them isn't, something is wrong, or the trend is weak.

Since then, technical analysis has developed into a major investment discipline. It has been particularly helped by the availability of technology that made charts easily available first via services such as Reuters and Bloomberg to Wall Street firms and then through the internet to individual investors. In Dow's day, you had to draw your own charts with paper and pencil.

Technical analysis relies on pattern recognition. Certain types of market behavior recur frequently - like booms, bubbles and crashes, but on a micro scale - technical analysis aims to spot the patterns that lead to price movements and then see where current share prices are going. It's worth pointing out that these patterns are fractal (they repeat in ever small versions) - Dow might have looked at a pattern over a number of years, but you can find exactly the same pattern occurring within a single afternoon's trading.

These patterns are generated by investor behavior, which tends to follow particular habits. For instance, investors often jump into a stock when it makes the news, and so they have all bought at about the same price. And because the human brain works this way, even though the price they bought at isn't necessarily the intrinsic price (as fundamental analysis defines it), that's the price they remember. So, if the share price goes up and then comes down, they will get very fearful when it gets close to the price at which they bought it. If it goes up again, they'll stay in and maybe buy some more - if it goes down further, they may panic and sell out. That creates zones of what's called support and resistance around particular price levels.

Often, it will create a price range within which the share trades fairly reliably up and down between the support line (at the bottom) and the resistance line (at the top). Sometimes, you'll find that support and resistance relate to fundamental data - the resistance might be roughly where the share's dividend yield falls below the average yield on the S&P 500, and the stock, therefore, becomes less attractive to income investors.

Say a stock pays a $2 dividend and is priced at $50; that's a 4% yield ($2 / $50). It's not very attractive, and if there's no other great reason to buy the stock, then the price could drift down. But as it gets towards $33, it's getting towards a 6% yield ($2 / $33), and that's very attractive if we think the dividend is safe. So, about that level, buyers will emerge, and that will probably push the price up again. But with the price pushing up, the yield will fall again, and the stock will sell off again.

Chartists (technical analysts) will often draw lines across the chart, linking up all the highest highs and all the lowest lows. This might show a horizontal channel, or it might show share prices trading within a diagonal channel, in an uptrend, or in a downtrend. Most good chart websites let you draw your own lines over the charts on the computer screen by dragging and dropping with the mouse. I find that a good way of analyzing the trends.

While as a long term investor you're not going to be trading the range (that is, buying towards the bottom and selling at the top), it's useful to know if a stock has set up a trading range. If you are looking to add to your positions in a stock you hold, when the price is in the bottom decile of the range, it's obviously a good time to buy. So here, you would use technical analysis to help your timing and maybe get a 5-10% discount on your purchase.

Most traders concentrate on **breakouts** when a stock price shoots through a support or resistance line. Traders will try to buy in really quickly and ride the breakout to a profit. However, as a fundamental analyst, that's not why you should be interested in breakouts. You should be interested because a strong breakout shows you that something is happening. An upside breakout could mean the market is reacting well to results, a new product, or some other good news, or it could mean a couple of major investors are buying in. On the other hand, a downside breakout (or breakdown) could mean there is bad news on the way. Be very cautious about breakdowns - particularly if you have begun to worry about a stock's high valuation or about an area of its business performance.

Technical analysis indicators

Technical analysis indicators take the price data and perform various mathematical operations, such as creating an additional chart line that can give you extra information. For instance, moving averages aim to smooth out short term fluctuations in the share price to give you a better idea of the trend.

You don't need to know all the kinds of technical indicators - On balance volume, oscillators, aroon indicators, accumulation/distribution lines, and stochastics. However, there are a few indicators that I think you ought to be acquainted with, as they can give you useful information.

Moving averages (MA) are a good place to start. The share price movement is averaged out over a certain period. Technical analysts often like shorter term averages, but as a fundamental investor, it's probably best to look at the longer term moving averages, for instance, 50 and 200 days.

The 'golden cross' (and its opposite the 'death cross') is a particularly strong indicator that I find helpful. When the shorter term average crosses over the longer term average, it tells you that the trend is reversing. When you're using two relatively long term averages, it's not likely to be a short term blip. So, if I've already identified a stock as one I want to buy, and I see a 'golden cross', with the shorter term average crossing from below to above the longer one, then I think this is a good time to buy the stock. I'm not going to hang around!

Equally, if I've seen a few things that make me feel worried about the stock, or I have a feeling that the stock is getting overvalued, and I see a 'death cross', that might be the nudge I need to act on my concerns and sell at least part of my holding. Seeing this pattern emerge when I'm already losing money is also a potential warning to cut my losses - unless I'm a hundred percent sure of my analysis.

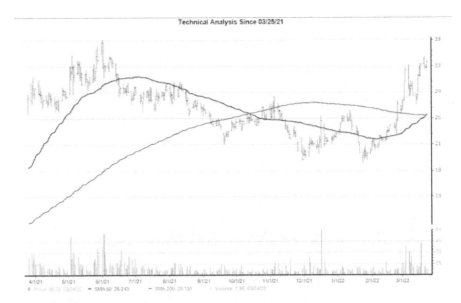

Technical Analysis Since 03/25/21

In the chart above, you see an example of the Olympic Steel stock. (Its ticker symbol is Zeus, which I found really clever!). You'll see that there was a death cross at the end of October 2021. The 50-day MA red line went below the long 200-day MA green line. But you can also see that it's forming a golden cross right about today!

Bollinger bands are another useful indicator. To explain them, I do need to get into a slightly nerdy area of statistics, though you don't need to understand stats to make use of the bands. Bollinger bands are plotted one standard deviation away from the moving average line.

What's a standard deviation? It's a measurement of how dispersed a set of data is. For instance, if you look at how big different breeds of dog are, they go from chihuahuas all the way up to English Mastiff, but probably most dogs are around the size of a labrador retriever or vizsla. The standard deviation is a measure of 'normal'. Usually, it covers nearly 70% of the relevant data.

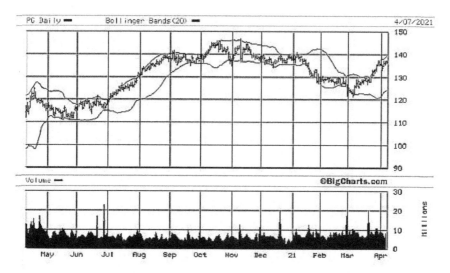

If you draw a line one standard deviation above and one standard deviation below the mean, so it makes a solid band. Then chihuahuas are below it, English Mastiff above it, and most breeds will end up somewhere within the band.

Back to Bollinger bands. They show how dispersed prices are, how much prices are going up and down - they show volatility. When they are wide, they show that the share price is moving around a lot. When they tighten, that shows share prices are tending to trade around quite a concentrated area. Now, this wouldn't normally be very useful to know, but there are a couple of times that the bands show a message;

- when the bands tighten significantly, it's likely that the price will break out in one direction or the other;
- when the price breaks out of the bands and keeps moving in the direction of the breakout, you can expect that trend to continue.

However, normally you wouldn't use the bands as your lead indicator - you'd look at the bands to confirm a signal from the other indicators (support line, resistance line, golden cross).

Volume

Share price charts intended for use by technical analysts almost always show an indicator of the volume of shares traded at the bottom. That's important because it tells you how seriously to take a share price move.

If, for instance, there's not much interest in the stock, and it falls 5% on a single trade, you wouldn't take that too seriously. But if it falls 5% *and* there's a lot of volume, that means a significant number of investors have decided to sell. You'd take that a lot more seriously.

It's also interesting to note that a crash in the market or in a single share's price is often followed by a period of very low volume. Investors who got their fingers burned are staying out of the way.

And of course, if you remember Dow Theory, trends are confirmed by volume... so this aspect of markets has been recognized for over a hundred years.

Other ways to use charts

One thing that charts show very clearly, whereas numbers on a page might not, is momentum. When a share price starts going up more quickly than before, you immediately notice that the curve becomes steeper.

As a fundamental analyst, you're not interested in share price momentum. But if you use your spreadsheet charting function to put a company's financial data in chart form, you may find you can see trends more clearly than simply looking at the numbers. I find that a quarterly revenue chart is really helpful in seeing whether a company is gaining traction or slipping behind. I also like to chart net income per share. It's really easy to see acceleration or deceleration in growth.

I also like to compare the price charts of different companies in the same sector. For instance, I want to look at Ford, GM and Stellantis together. That shows me clearly if one of the companies is out of step with the rest of its sector. I may know why - or I might want to see if I can find out. That's useful information, though, as so often, it's just a pointer to the need to do a bit more research rather than telling me whether or not the stock should be bought.

Before we end this chapter, just so you know, in my free bonus #2 — Charting Simplified Masterclass I share various technical analysis strategies which can help you determine whether it's the right time to buy a stock. I highly recommend you visit www.az-penn.com to watch the 5-part video masterclass.

Chapter 12 Quiz

1. What is resistance?
    a. When a company won't accept a takeover bid
    b. A level above which the share price does not rise
    c. A level below which the share price does not sink
    d. Resistance is useless

2. Bollinger bands are
    a. Labels on champagne bottles
    b. Drawn one standard deviation around the moving average
    c. Lines showing the support and resistance levels
    d. Always based on the 30 day moving average

3. The golden cross and death cross occurs when
    a. A short term moving average crosses a longer term moving average
    b. The moving average crosses the support line
    c. The moving average crosses the resistance line
    d. The Bollinger bands tighten around the moving average

4. What is a breakout?
    a. When a stock price breaks through a trendline
    b. When a stock price jumps suddenly
    c. When a stock price breaks through a support or resistance line
    d. When the moving average changes direction

5. The underlying premise of technical analysis is that
    a. Investor psychology creates behavior that is predictable
    b. Stock prices are a self-fulfilling prophecy
    c. The stock market is totally unpredictable
    d. Investors are all stupid

13

Chapter 13: Top tips

Five top tips for analyzing the quality of a business the MBA way

Although fundamental analysis is often put forward as just a quantitative way to analyze stocks, you'll really benefit by applying a few business school-style approaches too.

1. SWOT analysis

Draw a box and divide it into four quarters. Label the quarters: Strengths, Weaknesses, Opportunities, Threats.

Now, look at the company and fill in the factors that you see affecting its prospects.

For Amazon, strengths would include market share, brand name, IT infrastructure, and international operations.

For weaknesses, I think going into bricks and mortar stores is a big, big, big mistake. I think they have a great business model for delivered goods, and it works partly because their real estate costs are inexpensive. But also, search engines and algorithms work in e-commerce - I'm not sure they would in groceries.

Opportunities might include international expansion, backward integration, and moving into new product areas - for instance, business-to-business goods.

Threats would include significant bricks-and-mortar retailers moving into e-commerce or government regulation.

SWOT Analysis

Strengths	Weaknesses
Opportunities	Threats

2. Growth/share matrix

This is another four-box grid with two axes - low to high growth and low to high share.

You can look at companies or individual products this way, placing each company or each product on the growth and market share axes.

'Stars' are products that have high share and high growth - they're great news for you as an investor.

'Cash cows' have high share but low growth - also good news.

'Questions marks' have low share and high growth, they might be interesting but are high risk, so don't bother.

'Dogs' have low growth coupled with low market share - this is a very weak place to be so don't bother investing in them!

Where would you put Amazon?

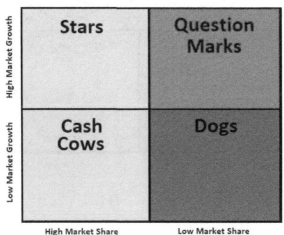

Growth/Share Matrix

3. Strategic group analysis

This is a free-form way of looking at a sector by taking particular strategies or characteristics and seeing which companies belong to which group.

For instance, you might look at which companies are taking a lowest-cost approach to the sector and which are taking a full-service (higher-cost) approach. Then you can see where the most successful companies belong.

You can look at outsourced vs own-production; direct sale to end users vs using a distributor network; market segmentation (e.g. teenager-focused products vs the market for seniors) - any way you can slice up the sector.

Strategic Group Analysis

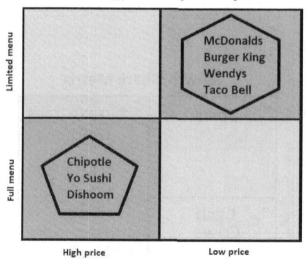

4. Porter's Five Forces

This is a way of looking at a company's power within its industry ecosystem.

The five forces are existing rivals, potential new rivals, suppliers, buyers, and substitute products or services.

So, for Amazon, you might have eBay as an existing rival, Walmart as a potential new rival, publishers and IT hardware companies as suppliers, consumers, and cloud computing users as buyers.

You then need to look at the strength of rivals, suppliers, and buyers.

Individual consumers don't have much power, nor do Amazon's suppliers.

It is rivals who are likely to do the most damage.

5. PEST (or STEP) analysis

This covers political, economic, social and technological factors affecting the company.

Amazon has plenty of political factors, from "does it pay enough tax?" to monopoly and anti-trust issues.

Economic factors would be household disposable income (going up or down?) or cost of distribution (big hike in fuel tax or prices might be an issue).

Social factors would be growing internet-aware population and emergence of influencers on Insstagram and TikTok.

Technology factors include the move to cloud computing, increased storage requirements, and Amazon's search ranking algorithms.

Pest Analysis

Political Factors	Economic Factors
Social Factors	Technological Factors

Ten top tips for becoming a successful fundamental investor

1. Do the work! Don't skimp on learning about annual reports and spreadsheets or reading up on industries. Fundamental analysis takes time, though that time will be well rewarded.

2. Diversify. If you're a doctor, the temptation might be to buy only healthcare stocks. You have an advantage there, right? But you should diversify to protect yourself from surprises. Hold stocks in different sectors, and aim to build a portfolio with between 10 and 20 stocks.

3. There is no either/or. People often ask, "which stock should I buy in this sector?" That's dumb. You can buy all the stocks in that sector that look like great businesses at a good price - though you should remember that you *will* need the time to keep up to date with all those companies.

4. Develop your instinct. Every time you say something like "I don't trust this," or "hey, this could be interesting", note it down. How did your gut feeling work out? If you regularly go back and check, you'll work out why you had that feeling, and you'll be refining your ability to pick up those tiny clues.

5. Reinvest, reinvest, reinvest. If you don't need the dividends you're paid for as income, reinvest them, whether in the company that paid them or in another company. If one of your stocks gets taken over, look for somewhere else to invest that money. If you have money left over at the end of the month, buy some more stock in one of the companies you hold. Over the long term, all these additional purchases will create a much higher return for your portfolio.

6. Read deeply rather than listening to superficial news. If you have a choice between watching CNBC and watching The Big Short or between reading a newspaper and reading an in-depth report on cloud computing or sustainable energy technologies, go for the in-depth report.

7. Don't watch stock prices too closely. Yes, you need to monitor your portfolio, but don't keep dialing up your share prices every half an hour. Spend the time on reading the company's financial statements and keeping up to date on its industry, instead.

8. Don't be in a hurry. Fear of Missing Out (FOMO) is a big driver for some investors. But if you're buying a stock for long term growth, you don't need to worry about missing a week or two - do your work properly before you make the decision.

9. Never take a stock tip. Not from the taxi driver, not from the guy at Starbucks, not from Reddit, not from someone you meet at a party, not from your best friend. Do your own research and make your own decisions.

10. Learn what you're best at. If it's not fundamental analysis, buy index funds. If it's growth stocks, buy growth stocks. If it's turnarounds, go look for turnarounds. And conversely, if your failure rate on high yield stocks is 100%, find something else for your portfolio.

Top tips for getting the best out of fundamental analysis

1. If you're a very visual person, run all your data series as charts. You'll spot trends much more quickly this way.
2. Find which ratios 'say' the most to you, and concentrate on those.
3. Always keep a written record of the reasons you bought (or sold) a stock.
4. Monitor your decisions. Take a weekend every six months when you can sit down and assess your decisions - the good ones, the bad ones, and 'the ones that got away'.
5. Read a major analyst's report at least every three months. Sector reports and IPO analyses are often the best, as they go into real detail. Take notes, and be prepared to criticize.
6. Keep a record of stocks you decided *not* to buy. Revisiting those decisions is always interesting.
7. Build your own templates and questionnaires for assessing companies, and use them every time you look at a new company.
8. Have good sources *outside* the stock market - such as trade journals, product reviews, industry bloggers, and people who buy and use the products your companies make.
9. Understand that your needs and resources will change over time. If you launch a new business, your portfolio may need to change if you don't have the time to spend on it.
10. Never invest money that you need in the short term or can't afford to lose. If you sometimes have difficulty paying the rent, the stock market is not for you - at least, not yet.

Top questions to answer before you buy a stock

1. What is the quality of the company's earnings?
2. Does the company have a defensible 'moat'?
3. Can the company manage its debt?
4. Is it generating good cash flow?
5. Does management have a track record of delivering on promises?
6. Is the industry undergoing disruptive change? If so, is the company a winner or loser?
7. Where is the saturation point for the company's service/product?
8. Who are the main competitors?
9. What are the top five risks facing the company?
10. What events would make me decide to sell the stock?

I would just like to mention before we go onto the final chapter on building your portfolio, if you are finding this book useful so far – it would mean everything to me if you could spare just a few seconds and <u>write a brief review on Amazon</u> on how this book is helping you so far.

14

Chapter 14: Build a portfolio

So far, this book has been about how to do fundamental analysis. Now, I'm going to turn to a more general investment topic - building a portfolio.

If you don't use fundamental analysis to build a portfolio of investments, it's not been worth your time unless you're actually going to put some money into the companies! (Or if you're getting paid for it as a professional analyst).

The first step on the way is identifying stocks that might be worth analyzing and also cutting out the stocks that aren't worth your time. There are a good few approaches that can help. One is simply looking up any company whose service, products or strategy you've come across and that strikes you as high quality, innovative, or interesting.

Another is to screen for stocks that fit your criteria, using sites like Finviz, Morningstar, MSN Money, Reuters or Zacks.

You might use a positive screening approach to look for companies which, for example, have a return on equity (ROE) above the S&P 500 average (currently 18%), or above the average for a particular sector.

For your information, I've shown a select few sectors in the table on the next page. You can get the lot, up to date, by pulling up the data on Aswath Damodaran's website.

Sector	ROE %
Aerospace and defense	9.1
Alcoholic beverages	4.4
Pharmaceutical	14.6
Homebuilding	27.4
Oil and gas (integrated)	1.2
Water utility	10.4
Software (system and application)	30.5
Retail (general)	20.1
Retail (online)	44.1

Source: Aswath Damodaran at:
http://pages.stern.nyu.edu/~adamodar

You might look for companies with a growth rate above 10%, companies with no net debt or companies above or below a certain size.

You can create quite a complex screening; for instance, companies with a dividend yield above 3%, excluding oils and financials, and with dividend cover of 1.5 or more, and earnings growth above 8%.

That doesn't mean every stock you find that ticks those boxes is a buy, but if you are a dividend investor who wants both security and growth, you will find stocks that are worth spending a bit more time analyzing.

You can also take a negative approach, screening out companies that don't fit certain criteria. For instance, I sometimes run a screen that works on the following exclusions:

- no loss-makers (i.e. net income >0),
- no non dividend paying stocks,
- no stocks below $50m market capitalization,
- no stocks with a price/earning more than 10% above the market (overall or by sector).

I then add a couple of extra steps that stock screeners can't help me with. I look up any bonds issued by the company, and if they don't have an investment grade rating, I chuck the company out. And I look to see if there's a Dividend Reinvestment Program (DRIP) and prioritize research on stocks that have one. It's an easy way to make sure that my money is reinvested, rather than having cash sitting in my brokerage account which I need to think about reinvesting, and there's often a discount.

I now also have a rule that says "no bargain basement stocks." I am quite good at buying undervalued stocks, and I am quite good at buying high yielders. But every so often, I get suckered into buying a deadbeat stock because it looks really, really cheap. I now screen out stocks that have a yield *more* than three times that of the market. It's possible - but not likely - that this will mean I miss a real bargain, but it stops me from wasting time on junk.

Your system might be different. This one works for me because I want income, and I want value stocks. But it doesn't always give me stocks with great growth prospects.

Sometimes, I miss a good turnaround stock because the 'no lossmakers' rule excludes the company that had a big exceptional loss last year, as well as the no-hope start-up stocks.

Before you start screening, it's worth brainstorming what you're looking for in a stock.

Diversification

You could just screen, analyze the stocks, find the stocks you think are worth buying, and buy them. But that's not building a portfolio any more than going out and buying pictures you like is 'art collecting'. To build a proper portfolio, you must consider asset allocation and diversification.

Asset allocation is a way of looking at investments in terms of what kinds of assets (bonds, real estate, stocks) or what kind of stocks (value, growth, different sectors or geographies) you own. Most brokers will show you your allocation via a pie chart according to sector and geographical split, which can help you get a feel for how you're doing in terms of diversification.

Why diversify? Because bad things happen. There are two kinds of bad things that can happen - the company can do badly, or the whole market can do badly. If the stock market crashes or the whole economy goes into recession, that's *system risk* - it's a risk you can't do anything about. If you're invested at all, you run that risk. But if a company loses a big lawsuit, loses a contract to a competitor, or launches a new product that fails, that's a *specific risk* which affects only that company.

In order to reduce the amount of specific risk that you run, you can simply buy a number of stocks with different characteristics, for instance, in different sectors. If one of them stumbles, the others should keep your portfolio on track.

Diversification doesn't just mean having 10 -20 stocks. It means you don't want to buy only consumer stocks or only banks or only REITs. You might emphasize one sector a bit more than other investors, but you should always have some backup - either in terms of other stocks or by placing a portion of your portfolio in an index fund or in mutual funds.

You also need to think about how much each stock should represent in your portfolio. To start with, you might say you'll put $500 into each stock and over a year, aim to invest in ten stocks. That's not a bad plan. But if one of your stocks really takes off, you could end up in a few years' time with one holding that's worth nearly half your entire portfolio.

That's why I suggest *rebalancing*. You do that by selling some of the best performer - not all of it because you're in this for the long term - and investing the money in the other stocks (as long as the fundamentals are still intact). I don't like any stock to get to more than 20% of my total investment. So, I sell off the top a little and rebalance. The amount I do that will vary depending on the valuation - if a stock has done well because the company has hugely improved its performance, I will sell off less, but if the company is getting highly valued, I might sell off a little more.

But never sell completely out of an investment that is doing well unless its valuation has become unsustainable. Individual investors often keep stocks that are losing them money (because no one likes to materialize a loss) and sell their best performers because they get nervous about the share price. Peter Lynch calls this "cutting down the flowers and watering the weeds". If you got your analysis right at the beginning and the company continues to grow, stay in there - just make sure you don't have your entire portfolio in one or two stocks.

Incidentally, buying more and more stocks isn't worth it for diversification. An academic study worked out that 20 stocks should be enough to diversify, and adding more stocks doesn't reduce risk by very much at all.

Many investors in tech stocks were sitting on millions in 1999 - and lost almost everything in 2000. By diversifying and rebalancing every six months or so, you should ensure that you never risk your whole portfolio. You can sleep easy at night. Isn't that what we all want?

Watch out for red flags.

The magic of compounding most of the time works for you as an investor. For instance, if you start investing in your pension fund when you're 20, you'll end up with a vast amount more in it than if you start investing when you're 40, even if at that age you have more to invest. If you stay invested in the stock market and reinvest dividends and profits, you'll end up with more than if you skip in and out of stocks.

But compounding works *against* you if you lose money. If a stock's price halves, it has to *double* before you get back the money. That's a big ask. So, the big rule of how to make money is: **don't lose money.**

That's why you need to have a list of red flags. There are more than enough investments in the world - there must be more than 20 stocks in the S&P 500 that are worth buying, right?

So, I suggest that when you come across the red flag, you don't go any further with your analysis - just walk. Better opportunities will come along.

- The company has problems getting paid. If it's making the sales, but it has 365 Days Sales Outstanding, it's junk.
- Big write-offs every year. Write-offs are like "the dog ate my homework": it might be true once, but if the same excuse gets trotted out two or three times, you know it's just an excuse.
- Cash flow is much lower than profit. This is a big red flag. It might happen one year, with a big investment, but if it happens two or three times, the company has a problem.
- Debt keeps increasing. Something is not right here if the company appears to be making money, but it keeps increasing debt every year. Unless it's making a lot of acquisitions, which would explain the debt, you should keep away.
- 'Black box' technology. If the company can't explain how it makes its money, avoid it. (Two or three major investors asked Bernie Madoff how his fund made so much money. They didn't think his answer made sense. Bernie defrauded many investors because they would invest in something they couldn't understand. However, these investors didn't fall for his line - and they kept their money out of his fund. If you try and try and just can't work out how a business makes money, then... stay away! Those investors spared themselves a lot of hassle.)
- Bubble valuations. Even if you're a growth investor, paying the price/earning multiples of 50, 60, and upwards is risky. If a highly valued share disappoints the market, its price can tumble fast. On the other hand, if a share on a low multiple has good results, sometimes the effect can be like your neighbor's no-good dumb teenager coming home with a job offer - even if it's working as a burger flipper, he's done great!
- Valuation mini-bubbles in particular sectors. In the 1970s, the Nifty Fifty were 'buy and hold forever' stocks; big, 'safe' companies. The only trouble was they were valued way too high. Result: they crashed. In 1979-80 the Hunt brothers tried to corner the market in silver; the silver price rose from $11 to $50 - and then crashed. The late 1990s saw the tech bubble - and crash; 2004-6 saw the sub-prime mortgage sector supporting high valuations for homes and home builders - and a subsequent crash.

Remember that economist JM Keynes said, "the stock market can stay irrational longer than you can stay solvent." So don't lose money, don't bet the bank, and don't risk money you need to live on or pay the rent. However sure you are of your research; you *can* be wrong. (Or you can be right about the fantastic business, but the stock market can carry on ignoring the stock for years.)

I'm also wary of IPOs (initial public offerings). Sometimes they will do well. Sometimes not. But there's often a lot of hoopla around an IPO, together with a lot of behind-the-scenes bargaining going on. They can be very disappointing, particularly when they are trying to take advantage of a valuation mini-bubble. Aircraft leasing company GPA didn't manage to raise the funds it needed - a few years later, it went bust. Uber expected $120bn for its IPO but kept cutting its target and eventually only raised $69bn. Pets.com, Etsy, and Webvan had IPOs that lost money - Etsy is actually a great business, but the shares initially fell from the $16 IPO price to $6.90 (now they're trading at $116).

As for SPACs (Special Purpose Acquisition Companies), which are formed to raise money in order to make acquisitions, you should ask yourself how you can do fundamental analysis on a company that doesn't actually have a business. SPACs are a pure gamble.

I'm also wary of stocks with no earnings. Just occasionally, a loss maker is worth buying. For instance, a company in a mature sector that has had a single disastrous year could be worth buying for a turnaround. But for the most part, if a company hasn't broken into profit, it's too early for it to be on the stock market. You need to be super sure of your analysis and very clear about how (and when) the business is going to make a profit to get involved.

Chapter 14 Quiz

1. Diversification will;
    a. Stop you ever losing money
    b. Reduce the total risk of your portfolio
    c. Reduce the risk of individual stocks
    d. Not make much difference to any of the above

2. Stock screening is useful because;
    a. You can use it to pick the right investments
    b. You can pick stocks which conform to your investment requirements
    c. It will find undervalued stocks for you
    d. It can help you avoid fraudulent companies

3. Which of these is not a red flag?
    a. 'Black box' technology
    b. Big write-offs every year
    c. Ever-increasing debt
    d. An annual report printed on pink paper

4. Warren Buffett is fond of saying, "The first rule of investment is don't lose money." What is the second rule?
    a. No one talks about Investment Club.
    b. Only invest in big-moat stocks.
    c. Remember rule one.
    d. Keep cash in the bank.

5. Why is portfolio rebalancing a good idea?
    a. Because different stock performances could leave your portfolio poorly diversified
    b. Because last year's top stock will always be next year's dog
    c. Because you should always keep exactly the same percentage in each stock
    d. Because it gives you something to do

Leave a 1-Click Review!

I would be incredible thankful if you could take just 60 seconds to write a brief review on Amazon, even if it's just a few sentences!

Customer reviews

★★★★★ 5 out of 5

4 global ratings

5 star		100%
4 star		0%
3 star		0%
2 star		0%
1 star		0%

▾ How are ratings calculated?

Amazon.com readers

http://www.amazon.com/review/
create-review?&asin=B0C1J7PB9Q

Amazon.co.uk readers

http://www.amazon.co.uk/review/
create-review?&asin=B0C1J7PB9Q

Conclusion

If you've read this far, you've got a good idea of the basics of fundamental analysis. All you need to do is go and practice with some real live companies.

You know that fundamental analysis means looking at the business underneath the shares. You've learned how to read an annual report and how to calculate the basic ratios, which will let you interpret those pages of figures to find out what's really happening in the business. You know how to look at an industry and what kinds of information can be useful in assessing a business's quality and growth prospects. You also know several ways to value a business.

That's really all you need to be able to start looking for profitable investments in the stock market. I can't promise you an immediate profit - no one can - but I *can* promise that if you get your analysis right and make sensible investment decisions to build a portfolio, over the long term, your investments should perform well for you. I can also promise that you know how to avoid the most typical mistakes that lose investors money, which is something worth knowing!

I've also introduced you to technical analysis - just enough to be able to look at a share price chart as more than a pretty picture. If you find it useful as I do, you'll find it's easy to integrate with your fundamentals -driven approach; if you don't, concentrate on the fundamentals and ignore the charts.

There are two words in this book that should now be engraved on the inside of your skull; **valuation** and **risk**. Interestingly enough, they're two words you hardly ever hear on financial TV, except in relation to the market as a whole. When was the last time you heard someone talk about the risk/reward ratio for real estate investment or the valuation of Walmart?

It's because you know about valuation and risk and because you know how to quantify them that you're now streets ahead of other rookie investors. They'll be buying a story - you are buying a business. They'll be buying hope - you'll be buying fact.

I hope you've enjoyed this book and that it's taught you some valuable lessons for your future investing success. I'm always interested to find out what my readers think, so if you can, please leave a review on Amazon! Or if you enjoyed it, I'll be really glad to find out. Just *don't* try to give me any stock tips!

HOW TO GET THE MOST OUT OF THIS BOOK

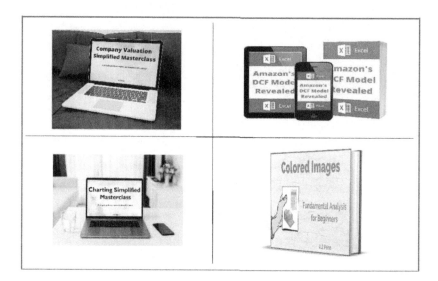

To help you along your investing journey, I've created two free bonus companion masterclasses, one which includes walking you through an investors mindset on how to find potential companies to invest in. There's also a free companion DCF model spreadsheet of Amazon which I created specifically to simplify your learning of this valuation model. I also provide an additional colored images resource that will help you get the best possible result.

I highly recommend you sign up now to get the most out of this book. You can do that by visiting the link or scanning the QR code below:

www.az-penn.com

Free bonus #1: **Company Valuation Simplified Masterclass ($97 value)**

In this video masterclass, I will be walking you through an investors mindset on how to find potential companies to invest in, which includes what to look out for and major red flags to keep in mind. This class will help you decide whether a company is worth investing in or whether you should move on.

Free bonus #2: **Charting Simplified Masterclass ($67 value)**

In this 5 part video masterclass you'll be discovering various simple and easy to use strategies on making profitable trades. By showing you real life stock examples of a few charting indicators - you will be able to determine whether a stock is worth trading or not.

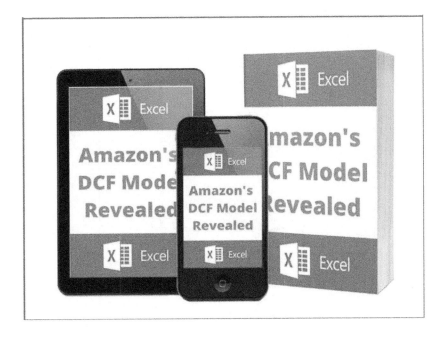

Free bonus #3: **Amazons DCF Model Revealed ($37 value)**

This Excel spreadsheet will be a great companion for you whilst reading this book. It will reveal the complete DCF model calculations I've presented in the book for Amazon. With this insightful spreadsheet, you will find it easier to duplicate my DCF model example on any company you're researching.

Free bonus #4: Colored Images – Fundamental Analysis for Beginners

To keep our books at a reasonable price for you, we print in black & white. But here are all the images in full color.

All of these bonuses are 100% free, with no strings attached. You don't need to provide any personal details except your email address.

To get your bonuses, go to the link or QR code:

www.az-penn.com

Glossary

10K - the annual report filing with the SEC.

10Q - the quarterly report filing with the SEC.

Accounts payable - amounts the company owes to its suppliers who haven't been paid at the balance sheet date.

Accounts receivable - amounts that customers owe to the company and haven't paid at the balance sheet date.

Accrual - the method of accounting which aims to 'match' costs and income with the period which they cover and which is used in the income statement. It's different from cash accounting, which shows transactions when the money is actually paid over.

Acid test - cash and accounts receivable divided by current liabilities. It's a measure of the company's ability to meet a short term cash crunch and to pay its bills as they come due.

Amortization - writing off the cost of an intangible asset such as software or goodwill over its expected useful life.

Annual report - every company has to issue an annual report giving details of its financial situation. Companies listed on a stock exchange also have to give other details.

Asset allocation - an approach to investment which looks at how an investor's portfolio should be divided between different types of assets.

Asset - something owned by a company, such as cash, plant, or real estate. It also includes amounts owed to the company by customers, which should eventually be turned into cash.

Balance sheet - the statement of what the company owns (assets) and owes (liabilities).

Beta - a quantification of a share's volatility - that is, how much its price moves compared to a given move in the market.

Bond - a security issued by a company, entitling the bondholder to a payment of interest ('coupon').

Book value - the value of a company's assets as shown on the balance sheet. This is based on the purchase cost, so it may not represent what they are actually worth if put up for sale.

CAGR - Compound Average Growth Rate: a way of measuring long term growth averages.

Capital asset - an asset employed long term in the business, such as a data server, paper-making plant, or airplane.

Capital expenditure - money spent on capital assets.

Cash flow - the cash that the company has received and paid out over the year, shown in the cash flow statement. This is different from the income statement, which shows profit on an accrual basis.

Confirmation - this is one of the rules in Dow Theory - trends must always be confirmed by another indicator or trend. As a fundamental analyst, you should also expect management's discussion of operations to be confirmed by the numbers you see in the report.

Consolidated statement - this statement consolidates (puts together) all the company's subsidiary companies to arrive at a view of the finances of the whole organization.

Constant dividend model - see Gordon Growth Model.

Contingent liability - a liability which could crystallize, but has not done so. For instance, a lawsuit *might* be lost, and if the company can estimate roughly how much that would cost, it will record this in the notes to the accounts. But since the company could still win the lawsuit, it is not fair to record the liability in the balance sheet.

Contrarian - an investor who aims to make money by taking a view that opposes the market trend.

Cost of goods sold (COGS) - the direct cost of a product or service. For a retailer, it will be the cost at which goods are bought in; for a manufacturer, the cost of the materials and components used in a product, and any other costs which can be *directly* tied to the product. It excludes marketing, sales and other overhead costs.

Current asset - an asset that is expected to be turned into cash in the short term, such as inventories or accounts receivable, and including cash and short term liquid investments such as bonds or treasury bills.

Current liability - a liability that needs to be paid in the short term, such as amounts owing to suppliers and short term debt.

Current ratio - current assets divided by current liabilities. It's a measure of the company's ability to pay its bills as they come due, but it's not as stringent as the acid test.

Debt - any money the company has borrowed, and on which it has to pay interest (or which it has to redeem at a premium).
Debt/equity ratio - debt as a percentage of equity. This shows the relationship between the two sources of funding and can indicate whether the company is running a high financial risk.
Deferred assets - a deferred asset is something that has already been paid for but hasn't been used. For instance, if a company buys its insurance in November and has a December year-end, 11 months of the annual premium will be treated as a deferred asset.
Deferred income - when a customer pays in advance, and the company hasn't yet earned the income (by providing the service or product), the amount is treated as deferred income. Companies which rent or provide subscription services will have relatively large amounts of deferred income.
Depreciation - the writing down of the cost of a tangible (physical) asset over its useful life as part of the accruals method of accounting.
Diluted net income per share - net income divided by shares in issue *plus* shares that have not yet been issued but are to be issued in the future (e.g. those relating to employee stock option schemes).
Discounted Cash Flow (DCF) - a method of valuing a company by discounting future cash flow to today's value.
Diversification - reducing risk by spreading your asset allocation between different asset classes or between different stocks and sectors.
Dividend - the amount paid by a company to its shareholders out of net income for the year. Not all companies pay a dividend.
DRIP - a dividend reinvestment scheme. Many companies offer a scheme by which shareholders can choose to receive their dividend in shares instead of cash. If the DRIP has zero brokerage fees, it may be to your advantage to choose the shares.
Dow Theory - a set of theories evolved by Charles Dow which is at the heart of technical analysis and which looks at trends in market prices and their likelihood of continuation.
Earnings announcement - stock exchange listed companies are required to announce their earnings on a regular basis. For NYSE and Nasdaq stocks, they must release quarterly figures through the SEC's EDGAR system.

Earnings per share (net income per share) - that proportion of income after tax which relates to each share; total net income divided by the number of shares in issue.

Earnings yield - the inverse of the P/E ratio: enables comparison between the company's valuation and other forms of return such as WACC or bond yields.

EBIT - operating earnings before interest and tax: a good level to judge the performance of the business operations of the company before looking at its financing.

EBITDA - earnings before interest, tax, depreciation, and amortization: EBIT with the depreciation charge shown in the cash flow statement added back to show an approximation of operating cash flow (since depreciation is not a cash item).

EDGAR - The Electronic Data Gathering Analysis and Retrieval System of the SEC, which handles company reports, including earnings announcements.

Equity - the owner's / shareholders' capital in a business. Unlike debt, it is permanent capital that does not have to be repaid.

Exchange-traded fund (ETF) - a fund, usually copying a stock exchange index and with low costs, that can be bought and sold on the stock exchange.

FINRA - the Financial Industry Regulatory Authority, which regulates brokers and exchanges in the USA.

GAAP - generally accepted accounting principles that guide auditors in compiling a company's accounts.

Gordon Growth Model - a way to find the present value of a continued stream of regular payments at a steady growth rate. Also known as the Constant Dividend Model.

Gross margin - gross profit as a percentage of sales. A key ratio for retailers.

Gross profit - sales revenue less cost of goods sold (COGS).

Income statement (or profit and loss account) - the financial statement which shows the company's revenues, costs and profit for the period, using the accruals method of accounting.

Intangible assets - assets which are not physical; for instance, intellectual property, copyrights, and goodwill in acquired businesses.

Inventory turnover (stock turnover) - cost of sales divided by the average value of inventory.

Liquidity risk - the risk of being unable to sell an asset (e.g. a stock, inventory, or real estate) in order to realize cash proceeds: the risk of being unable to pay short term debts because of the inability to realize those assets.

Long term assets (Fixed assets) - assets that are intended for use in the business over the long term.

Long term liabilities - liabilities which do not have to be repaid within the next year, including long term borrowings.

Management discussion and analysis of operations - the portion of the annual report in which management explains the industry conditions, operations of the company, and financial results. "The words to go with the numbers."

Margin - any profit figure as a percentage of sales revenues.

Market capitalization - the total value of a company's shares at the market price (the share price times the number of shares in issue).

Market risk - see system risk.

Moving average - a chart line showing the average of the stock price over a certain period, smoothing out the 'noise' of day-to-day price movements.

Multiple - see P/E ratio.

NASDAQ - one of the USA's two major stock exchanges. The other is NYSE.

Net income/profit/loss - what is left of the profits once the company has paid its debt servicing and taxes. This is the profit that 'belongs' to shareholders and out of which dividends are paid.

Net worth - the sum total of the shareholders' equity, which is equal to the company's assets less its borrowings and other non-equity liabilities.

Non-recurring items - income or expenses which are not expected to happen again, for instance, the sale of a major property, a restructuring charge, or a large legal settlement.

NYSE - the New York Stock Exchange, one of the USA's two major exchanges.

Off-balance-sheet liability - liabilities which are not shown on the balance sheet, either because they are not yet certain (e.g. a lawsuit still in progress) or because they have been put in a non-recourse special vehicle company (SPV). The latter are now much more difficult to hide.

Operating profit/loss - see EBIT.

P/E ratio - the share price divided by net income per share. A measure of valuation - how many years the company will take to 'earn' its share price.

Price to book - the share price compared to net assets per share.

Primary market - the market in which companies issue new shares for money which goes to the company itself.

POC - percentage of completion, a method of accounting for large contracts such as civil engineering works.

Pre-tax profit - profit after interest payment but before tax. It is regarded as the main figure in the UK, but in the US, analysts focus on EBIT and net income.

Provision - an entry in the balance sheet to reflect a probable, quantified risk, such as bad debts (e.g. bank customers who cannot repay their borrowings).

Ratio - a quantitative relation between two figures; a way of comparing two numbers to each other (e.g. price to sales, EBIT to sales, net income to assets).

Resistance level - in technical analysis, a share price level beyond which the share price does not rise and which 'resists' upward movement.

Retained earnings - net income once the dividend has been paid, which is kept on the balance sheet as part of shareholders' equity. It is available for investment or for paying dividends in future years.

ROA (Return on Assets) - net income as a percentage of average assets: a measure of the company's ability to use its assets to generate profit.

ROE (Return on Equity) - net income as a percentage of shareholders' equity: a measure of the efficiency of the company's capital structure as well as its use of physical assets to generate profit.

Revenues - income generated by sales of goods or services or through rentals.

Risk tolerance, risk aversion, risk appetite - are ways of describing the amount of risk an investor is prepared to run. This will depend partly on the investor's financial situation and other circumstances and partly on personal preference.

SEC - the Securities and Exchange Commission, a government agency which polices the U.S stock markets.

Secondary market - the stock market, in which existing shares are traded between investors. The money in secondary market transactions does not go to the company but to the seller of the shares.

Specific risk - the risk that is specific to an individual asset or company and that is not shared with other types of assets or other companies. This risk can be mitigated by diversification.

Spread: 1. the difference between the price at which a stock is bought and that at which it is sold by specialists; 2. the difference between a bond yield and the yield on the market or 10 year Treasuries.

Support level - in technical analysis, the opposite of a resistance level; a share price that acts as the bottom of the trading range and below which the price does not fall.

System risk - the risk of the market as a whole. You cannot diversify away from this risk.

Tangible assets - physical assets such as stock, buildings, or vehicles.

Technical analysis - looking at patterns of share price behavior to predict likely outcomes: 'charting'.

Terminal value - the expected value of a business at the end of the period used in discounted cash flow calculations.

Trading range - in technical analysis, the high and low price levels between which a share price tends to fluctuate.

Trend - the direction in which revenues, margins, and share prices tend to move.

Volatility - the likelihood of a stock price to move by more (or less) than the movement of the market as a whole.

WACC - Weighted Average Cost of Capital: the amount the company has to pay for its debt (i.e. the interest rate on each of its loans) and equity.

Working capital - inventory and accounts receivable less accounts payable.

Write-off, write-down - reducing the value of an asset which has become less viable, such as a debt that is unlikely to be paid or shares held which are worth less than their purchase price.

Yield (dividend yield) - the dividend paid as a percentage of the share price.

Endnote, for those who made it this far.

The *wrong* answer to how to check economic and company data was 'ordering the most expensive drink you can at Starbucks'. If you want to know, it cost $47.30 and is a Quadraginoctuple Frap: and if you want to watch it being ordered and made, you can look at:

www.youtube.com/watch?v=s0puNRBLH7s

Or search on YouTube: **($47.30) World's Most Expensive Starbucks Drink - "Quadriginoctuple Frap"**

Quiz Answers

Chapter 1:
1. d
2. c
3. c
4. a
5. c

Chapter 2:
1. c
2. a
3. d
4. c
5. b

Chapter 3:
1. c
2. a
3. c
4. c
5. b

Chapter 4:
1. c
2. c
3. a
4. c
5. b

Chapter 5:
1. c
2. c
3. a
4. a
5. b

Chapter 6:
1. b
2. b
3. c
4. b
5. c

Chapter 7:
1. b
2. b
3. d
4. a
5. d

Chapter 8:
1. b
2. c
3. d
4. a
5. d

Chapter 9:
1. c
2. b
3. a
4. a
5. d

Chapter 10:
1. a
2. a
3. d
4. b
5. c

Chapter 11:
1. d
2. c
3. c
4. d
5. d

Chapter 12:
1. b
2. b
3. a
4. c
5. a

Chapter 14:
1. b
2. b
3. d
4. c
5. a

Made in the USA
Columbia, SC
31 March 2024

33838467R00287